That

BOOK

about

HARVARD

SURVIVING THE WORLD'S MOST
FAMOUS *University,*
ONE EMBARRASSMENT AT A TIME

ERIC KESTER

sourcebooks

This book is a memoir. It reflects the author's present recollections of his experiences over a period of years. Some names and characteristics have been changed, some events have been compressed, and some dialogue has been re-created.

Published by Sourcebooks, Inc.
P.O. Box 4410, Naperville, Illinois 60567-4410
(630) 961-3900
Fax: (630) 961-2168
www.sourcebooks.com

Library of Congress Cataloging-in-Publication Data

Kester, Eric.
  That book about Harvard : surviving the world's most famous university, one embarrassment at a time / Eric Kester.
     p. cm.
  1. Harvard University. 2. Harvard University—Alumni and alumnae—Biography.
  3. Kester, Eric. I. Title.
  LD2151.K47 2012
  378.744'4—dc23
                                    2012003468

Printed and bound in the United States of America.
BG 10 9 8 7 6 5 4 3 2 1

For my parents.
I apologize in advance.

CONTENTS

A Note from the Author

I wrote this book to impress a girl. Might as well make that clear up front. But I also wrote it to give you a candid view of a real guy trying to survive the real Harvard with a bunch of laughs along the way. And that's my primary goal here: to entertain.

This book is based off of true events and real people. For the sake of narrative flow (and occasionally to fill in the gaps of drunken memory) I have changed details at my discretion. A few characters are composites and I've changed all names except for Mark Zuckerberg's. That dude has lost the right to privacy.

PROLOGUE

I t must have looked pretty weird to people driving by: two parents flanking their teenage son as they all made a solemn walk down the driveway. My ashen face and hesitant steps likely made it look like I was walking the plank, or being led by my parents through some bizarre driveway-based version of that punishment. But anyone who's ever opened a college admissions letter can attest that this was far more terrifying.

Mr. Lynch, our neighbor across the street, was out mowing his lawn and began to watch us. He seemed surprised to see me walk up to the mailbox. "Already time for the *Sports Illustrated* swimsuit issue?" he shouted cheerfully.

Part of me wanted to snap at him. I was checking the mail today because I was getting my admissions decision from Harvard, not because I was some sort of obsessive horndog. Besides, the next swimsuit issue was still 293 days away.

I kept quiet, though; my anxiety about the letter had me unusually irritable, and snapping at Mr. Lynch wouldn't do anything to change what was going to be in the letter when I opened it.

I was a decent college candidate (at least that's what I had been told by family members obligated to say such things). But everything I had ever heard about the prestigious university indicated that being "good enough" wasn't good enough for Harvard. So by the time my parents and I finally reached the mailbox, I had already read the letter in my mind:

Dear Eric "Failure" Kester,

After carefully reviewing your application, we have determined that we cannot offer admission to you or any of your future offspring. This was not an easy decision*, but ultimately we concluded that it reflects poorly on the Harvard brand to admit a student who would be better served attending a lesser school, perhaps as a janitor. For your benefit we've included a pamphlet to a nearby orphanage in the event that your parents abandon you in shame. We wish you the best of luck in your future, highly unsuccessful life.

   *It was.

With the utmost sincerity,
Harvard Admissions

P.S. Your ex-girlfriend was right about you.

My mom reached into the mailbox and pulled out the heap of mail. She then forced me to walk halfway up our driveway before handing over the pile. Getting into Harvard wasn't a life or death situation for me, but still my parents thought it might be best if I opened my letter a safe distance away from oncoming traffic.

Breathing, hearing, and pretty much all other bodily functions ceased to work as I hastily flipped through the mail, starting first with the thin letters at the top. The past two years of my
life were flashing before my eyes—the grueling "college process"
filled with SATs, APs, GPAs, and other miserable letters that have
left me forever terrified of the alphabet. The stakes were huge: an
acceptance letter would mean that all my hard work had actually paid off. And that my parents wouldn't have to return those
Harvard T-shirts they bought on my campus tour.

I found the envelope from Harvard near the bottom, and it
was thick. Under normal circumstances this would indicate good
news; acceptance letters include brochures and other informational material for the new admits, while rejections are normally
just a letter in a thin envelope. But I remained skeptical. I figured
that, in typical Harvard fashion, the university would make even
their rejection letters ostentatious, and I would open the fat envelope only to release a package of fireworks that would explode
above my house and spell in giant letters: YOU'RE REJECTED.

But my mind was the only thing that exploded when I tore
open the letter, scanned the first line, and saw "Congratulations!"

Holy shit, I'm going to Harvard!

In my excitement I accidently expressed this thought out
loud. But my parents didn't notice; they were too busy cheering. We collapsed into a prolonged three-way hug that made
an uncomfortable Mr. Lynch turn off his lawn mower and go
inside. My mom ran back to the house to call my grandma and
probably the local newspaper, leaving my dad and me to relish
the moment.

"I'm proud of you, son."

He looked at me with misty eyes, and we shared a long

man-hug. Now I had banned such public displays of affection back in middle school, when I learned that girls don't have "dad hugger" high on their list of turn-ons. But this was a special moment. Something miraculous had just happened. I had somehow been accepted into Harvard, and I didn't even play the violin.

While we walked back up the driveway, my dad held onto the other mail as I leafed through the Harvard brochure, excited to get a taste of my new school. It was filled with picture after picture of highly enthusiastic Harvard students engaging in various academic activities. There was one photo of a guy in a white lab coat mixing test tubes of chemicals, then another of a young woman at a blackboard writing what appeared to be Egyptian hieroglyphics. Or maybe it was calculus…I wasn't sure.

For some reason, I felt my chest begin to tighten. Next was a picture of a student relaxing with a magazine in his dorm room. It wasn't a magazine I'd qualify as "leisure reading," and it sure as hell wasn't the swimsuit issue. It was *The Economist*, and the guy was giggling with delight while reading it.

My hands felt sweaty as I quickly turned the page. Now I was faced with a picture of a student just standing there and staring intensely at me, his unnaturally wide eyes bulging like they were being squeezed out of his skull by his oversized brain. I looked at his shirt, neatly pressed and tucked in. I glanced down at my shirt, the host of an ongoing territorial war between ketchup and mustard stains.

I closed the brochure, and the iconic crimson shield stared me in the face.

Oh shit, I thought, *I'm going to Harvard…*

Chapter One

THE LAST PACKAGE

*S*he giggled when she saw the underwear I had on. I could feel her eyes probing my body and I sucked in my stomach, desperately trying to conjure the six-pack that had expired many Hostess cupcakes ago. I didn't even know her name, but at this point I didn't really care. While there was no chance she and I would ever speak again, I would remember this moment for the rest of my life.

I kept replaying the day's events in my head, wishing there was some way I could just start over. Normally I would consider myself lucky to be naked in the presence of such an impossibly hot girl. But not like this. Not on our first day at Harvard. Not with her mother watching.

———◆———

ENTER TO GROW IN WISDOM.

I read the inscription carved above the iron gate of Harvard Yard as I lugged my belongings to my freshman dorm. I paused a moment to contemplate these imposing words looming over my head, intimidated to join the world's brightest scholars in this exceptional academic setting. I thought of the many great minds that had preceded me through this gate: visionaries like Henry David Thoreau, John F. Kennedy, John Adams, and Bill Gates. Would I be the next Harvard scholar to make a profound impact on the world? Only time would tell. I took a deep breath, picked up my industrial-sized case of animal crackers, and walked through the gate.

My first disappointment came soon after, when I discovered that my dorm room was on the first floor. I feared that a passerby could peek through my window and see me changing—or worse, catch a glimpse of my Google search bar. Now I would have to take preventative measures when I wanted to explore the exotic wonders of high-speed Internet, and eventually people would question why my shades were down two or three times a day. On the bright side, I figured that in a few weeks when Harvard inevitably noticed that they had admitted me by mistake, I wouldn't have to haul my big-ass futon down a flight of stairs.

Upon entering my suite, I noticed that one of my roommates had arrived before me. He wasn't there, but a pile of his unpacked belongings was stacked in the corner of our spacious common room. I assumed he dropped off his bags before heading to the library to get a head start on studying for the classes he hadn't even signed up for yet.

Spotting a folded Irish flag in one of the boxes, I realized that this stuff must belong to Dermot. A few weeks earlier I had received a letter from Harvard that provided me with a short background on my two freshman roommates. I was shocked when I first read their names—I figured there would be at least one Chin, Wang, or Chang, but there was no one of the sort. This was coming from Harvard, right? Who's going to help with my math homework now? Dermot was international at least, hailing from Ireland, and I was confident that any cultural differences would be minimal. I had never actually met a true Irishman, though a girl once puked on me after drinking too much Guinness, so I figured that was close enough.

After exercising my right as an American to search through Dermot's stuff, I discovered a bungee cord, a broken Ping-Pong paddle, and a bag of powdered breast milk. Apparently the gap in our cultures was much wider than I had anticipated.

This intensified a deep anxiety I had been having about Harvard in the days between my acceptance and arrival: that I wouldn't fit in with the students. I am not a genius, but I was about to be surrounded by students who had already accomplished a great deal at a young age. I mean, there were some students in my class who already had a "net worth" and who managed their own investments. My net worth was reflected only in my baseball card collection. A few others had won gold medals in the Olympics; all I had was a "#1 Grandson" sweatshirt. For all I knew the strange materials in Dermot's bag were components of some bizarre experiment he was conducting on time-travel.

I didn't know exactly how smart my classmates would be, but I expected that most, if not at all, were past winners of the national spelling bee, making me especially nervous. I imagined a class full of home-schooled geeks with gigantic heads walking around campus saying "penultimate" and other big words that scare the shit out of me. These were students who used their lunch breaks during their summer internships at the White House to read thick novels by dead Russian authors whose names I'm not even going to bother trying to spell out. I, on the other hand, had spent my summer coaching youth soccer while having prolonged arguments about *Harry Potter* with fourth-graders. "Prevention of insect consumption" was literally part of my job description, and even at that I was mediocre.

How could I possibly compare to these freakishly talented and accomplished students? Would my intellectual shortcomings be painfully transparent at Harvard? I felt like an undercover agent who was a single moronic move away from having his cover blown. One look at me pulling on a door that reads PUSH, and these kids would know that I just didn't belong.

At least I foresaw the unique academic environment of my new school and had prepared accordingly. While a typical incoming freshman might get ready for college by building a kickass beer-pong table or learning how to identify various forms of STDs, I had spent the previous four weeks memorizing the first ten digits of pi. (I also committed to memory the first five digits of e, just in case it was the preferred mathematical constant on campus.) I even found a website that could translate words into binary notation, which I figured would come in handy sooner or later. A few geeky jokes packed into my arsenal and my preparations for the nerd herd were complete.

After rooting through Dermot's bags, I continued moving the rest of my stuff in. When I finally hauled in the last of my boxes, I was completely soaked in sweat. Fearful of reclaiming my high school nickname of "Splash Mountain," I decided to hop in the shower before anyone could see me drowning in my own perspiration. On a day of critical first impressions, I wanted to avoid dripping bodily fluids on people.

Like many of the suites in Harvard's ancient dorms, my room was equipped with its own private bathroom—a feature I was very pleased about until I saw its layout. The toilet was right next to a window that opened onto a busy street in Harvard Square, allowing for some seriously awkward moments with people strolling by on the sidewalk. There's just something deeply unsettling about making eye contact with a seventy-year-old man as you take a dump. Even worse, the toilet-paper dispenser was about five feet away from the toilet itself.

The shower made about as much sense as the toilet, with the showerhead placed about four feet off the ground. I knew Harvard's dorms were centuries old, but you'd think the architects would've been smart enough to account for human evolution. I guess that's what you get for attending a school that predates Darwin.

I was especially bummed because I had been looking forward to showering in college. You see, I was totally fired up to try out several new soaps and shampoos I had brought with me. While living at home I resigned to use whatever shampoo I found in the shower, leaving my hair at the mercy of my mother's taste. I was sick of smelling like Passion Fruit Explosion, Mango Tango, Fresh Mountain Waterlily, or other scents advertised to give you an orgasm in the shower. Girls generally don't fall for guys who smell like a midsummer sunset, so entering college I made sure to load up on masculine-sounding bath products that were scientifically designed to help guys like me get laid. I couldn't help but imagine hearing this exchange as I walked into my first college party:

Wicked hot girl #1: Do you smell that? It smells like an arctic fireball.
Wicked hot girl #2: I think my nostrils just came.

Despite the cruel placement of the showerhead, I did actually leave the shower feeling refreshed and smelling like midnight thunder. I began to unpack the multitude of boxes that sat in the middle of my room, starting with the ones I valued the most. I soon discovered, however, that I had accidently left the third box of video games out in the hallway.

I was wearing only my boxers, which presented me with a minor dilemma. Harvard's dorms are coed, so I figured that venturing out in the halls in your underwear is generally frowned upon. But this was an urgent task; leaving a box of fantasy video games in a Harvard hallway, I figured, is like abandoning a baby in a lion's den. I couldn't easily get clean clothes, as my wardrobe was still zipped up in a suitcase, and I certainly wasn't about to compromise the power of midnight thunder by putting my sweaty T-shirt back on. The box was only a few feet outside my room though, so I determined that this rescue operation was relatively low-risk.

I poked my head out the door, made sure the coast was clear, and quickly darted to grab the box labeled "Video Games III (H thru K)." Just as I grabbed my treasure, I heard someone call my name. I looked up and saw a guy my age wearing a pair of Reef sandals, his sky blue polo shirt half-tucked into khaki shorts.

I know this son of a bitch, I thought to myself.

I had met this guy before, though I had never caught his full name. We played hockey against each other in high school, and after many intense games we developed a bit of a rivalry. Back then he rocked a mullet, which made me kind of hate his guts, but also oddly made me want to throw back a few beers with him. Because you know anyone with a mullet is bound to be a good drinking buddy.

I stood in silence as I contemplated my next move. Should I do something badass, like narrow my eyes and whisper "So, we meet again…" before challenging him to an old-fashioned duel of fists? Or do I just drop him with a swift kick to the nuts and be done with it? Before I had the chance to act, he extended his hand and introduced himself as Josh, my new roommate.

Josh no longer had the mullet. This was Harvard, after all, where neatly cut hair is an unwritten rule. The only students who would dare have a mullet were the members of the Star Trek club, and I silently thanked god that my roommate wasn't one of those loser Trekkie geeks. I'm more of a Star Wars guy myself.

Josh and I established that yes, in fact, we had played each other in hockey, and that yes, in fact, I had once slashed him with my stick and threatened to rip off his mullet and use it to wipe my ass. We agreed to put the past behind us and came to an understanding that what we said to each other in the heat of competition was not to be taken personally. Josh acknowledged that he no longer considered me "Captain Dipshit," and I admitted that I had never actually met his mother, let alone had relations with her.

With our past rivalry settled, Josh then explained that he wasn't moving in for a few more days, as he was staying with his older brother who lived nearby. He just wanted to stop by to introduce himself and make sure that his roommate wasn't the type who wandered around the hall in his underwear.

Josh then said he was late for lunch with his brother, which was a nice way of saying that he didn't want to be seen having an extended conversation with a guy in his boxers. He said goodbye, took two steps toward the exit, then stopped.

"Dude, what the hell is that?" Josh turned around and pointed at the nametag that was taped to our door. My name had been crossed out and replaced with a series of zeroes and ones.

I played it cool. "Oh, you know, it's my name in binary

notation. Like I always say, there are 10 types of people in the world: those who understand binary, and those who don't!"

"Oh…okay." A brief, awkward silence. "Alright man, I'll see you in a couple of days."

Josh walked out of the dorm's entryway, leaving me stunned at how badly my binary joke bombed. It was okay, I assured myself; there would be other non-hockey players who would appreciate its subtle hilarity.

Once Josh was out the door, I picked up my stash of video games. Awkwardly balancing the box between my arm and hip, I reached with my free hand and twisted the doorknob to my room. It didn't budge. I tried again. Nothing.

Panic swelled inside of me as I thought of my key resting on my desk inside the locked room. What genius invented doors that automatically locked when they closed?

As I looked down at my boxers and then back at the locked door, I felt a rush of impending doom and embarrassment—the kind you get when you're at a party, flush the toilet, and see the water rising *up*.

I dropped my box and frantically rattled the knob with both hands, as if the door would magically unlock itself after fifteen failed attempts. No such luck. My cell phone was also locked in the room, but it wouldn't have been of use anyway. I didn't know anyone at Harvard yet, and I was determined not to call my parents to bail me out of yet another situation involving my underwear.

I racked my brain trying to come up with a solution to this disaster, but my desperate thoughts reached the same horrifying conclusion every time: *You're totally fucked.*

There was only one choice—to walk to the superintendent's office.

But this was an even bigger problem than it may seem. For the office was across the sprawling green lawn of Harvard Yard. Harvard Yard bustles with activity year-round, but move-in day takes it to another level. The Yard is lined with dorms, and on this day nearly all of the sixteen hundred incoming freshmen were moving in.

Before beginning my trek, I peeked out my dorm's front door to scout out the terrain, like I was some sort of mountaineer planning my route to the top of Mt. Humiliation. What I saw wasn't pretty: between the superintendent's office and me was a five-hundred-foot gap of lawn occupied by an army of students and their families. I sucked in my stomach, put my head down, and stepped outside, instantly lowering the community's pants-to-people ratio.

I decided that the best approach to my journey across the Yard was to walk as if nothing was wrong, like I was some foreign student who hadn't quite learned the proper outdoor etiquette of America. It's difficult to act casual, though, when a micro-thin piece of 85 percent cotton is the only material left standing between your privacy and dozens of mental measuring tapes. The absence of a shirt didn't help my confidence either—I was so pale I could've gotten a sunburn from a full moon. While I tried to maintain a façade of self-assurance, internally I was drowning from embarrassment. I was also starting to regret buying these Incredible Hulk boxers.

Students and parents alike stopped what they were doing to gawk at me as I weaved through an endless maze of suitcases, boxes, and furniture. I could feel hundreds of eyes fixed on me, and suddenly my insecurities about my body became overwhelming. I was keenly aware that I have enough hair on my chest to intimidate a virgin or frighten a small child, and I'm pretty sure I heard one smartass mumble something about *Teen Wolf*.

Most people I passed tried their best to contain their laughter, though I'm not sure whether their restraint was due to politeness or fear of provoking the hairy beast. I cringed when I saw one mother cover the eyes of her crying toddler, and quickened my pace a moment later when her husband winked at me. I even saw a group stop and put down a couch they were carrying as they silently wondered, "Who's this asshole in his underwear, and does he know his fly is wide open?" You know you've become a total loser when even the guy unpacking a replica Gandalf staff laughs at you.

I always feared that when I entered Harvard I would never be able to stand out among the hordes of brilliant students. I had no idea it would be this easy.

On my walk, I tried to steer clear of the bronze statue of John Harvard, but its radius is impossible to escape. The statue of the school's founder resides smack in the middle of the Yard where all can see him and he can see all. Sitting confidently in a large throne atop a stone pedestal, the founder silently observed his new crop of disciples as they took residence in his dominion: a world-class musician unpacking her elegantly carved cello; an award-winning poet absorbing the inspirations of a beautiful day; a half-naked troglodyte slogging across the pristine lawn. One of these things didn't quite fit John Harvard's grand vision when he founded the school nearly four centuries ago. I am convinced it was this moment when Mr. Harvard decided he was going to spend the rest of the year kicking my ass.

When I finally reached Weld, the dorm that housed the superintendent's office, the soles of my feet were covered in dirt, and my hair was soaked in sweat. The old guy working the counter was pretty nice about my situation, or at least he was once I convinced him there was no need to call for backup. "HANK" was etched in block letters on the nametag pinned above his left breast pocket, and his wispy grey hair and tired sunken eyes revealed a man who had dealt with far too many drunk kids in his life.

"It's alright, this sort of thing happens all the time," he said in a this-sort-of-thing-never-happens tone of voice. "But I'm sorry to say I can't give you another key. We don't keep 'em here."

"You gotta be shitting me." I don't usually swear in front of adults, but after hearing this news I couldn't help myself.

"Son, the only thing I'm shitting today is my wife's tuna salad. Now what dorm are you in?"

I hesitated a moment and allowed myself to recover from the disturbing image of Hank sitting on the john, his clenched fist shaking in the air as he cursed his wife.

"Uh, my dorm is Lionel," I muttered weakly.

Hank took the toothpick he had been chewing on and casually flicked it into a trashcan under the counter, then grabbed the walkie-talkie hanging from his belt and spoke into it. "Marty? You still by Lionel?" The raspy voice on the other end confirmed that yes, he was. "Well, I've got a kid here who's been locked out of his room. Can you let him back in?"

"Yeah, no problem," the voice responded. "Just tell me what he looks like so I know who to look for."

Hank looked at me and grinned. "You'll know."

"Hold on—there's a security guard with a master key already at my dorm?" I stammered.

"It's move-in day, for chrissakes. We have at least one stationed at the entrance of every dorm. You probably walked right past him." Hank paused, as if he was watching a replay of my expedition in his mind, and a smile emerged on his creased face. "Oh boy, that's good! Your pale ass walked all the way here for no reason at all! Ha! Typical Harvard genius!"

Hank broke into a cackle of laughter so fierce that it evolved into a sharp wheezing. I legitimately thought the old dude was going to die right in front of me. He finally settled down after he pulled an inhaler out of his pocket and took a couple of puffs. Thank god; having already murdered my dignity, the last thing I needed was another death on my conscience.

Humiliated to a degree I previously thought unattainable, I turned around and started to walk out of the office.

"Hey," Hank called out in between heavy breaths. "What I *can* give you is a towel. You look like your own personal water park!"

I shook my head and began the parade of misery back to my dorm.

On the way, I found that my embarrassment had dissipated and been replaced with a blend of disappointment and self-loathing. I had set only one goal for my first semester at Harvard: DO NOT EMBARRASS YOURSELF. Somehow I managed to fail this one, simple objective in the first hour of the first day.

I strolled back lost in the thought. I imagined my first day at Harvard was nothing like Franklin Roosevelt's, and probably more similar to that of noted Harvard alumnus Ted Kaczynski (better known to future generations as The Unabomber). And it occurred to me that it was only lunchtime, the day couldn't possibly have gotten off to a worse start, and still ahead of me was a jammed schedule of unpacking, registration, and freshman orientation. And now I had to find time to jump off a bridge.

And that's when I first saw her. I was about one hundred feet away from my dorm when I spotted her leaning against a red Jeep, taking a break from unloading her car as she sipped water from a Nalgene bottle. A gorgeous brunette with Heineken-green eyes and a body so perfect that it looked photoshopped, she was the type of girl that makes you want to stop what you're doing and make a playlist dedicated to her on your iPod. I could make out the outline of her lacy bra under her tight, light blue tank top, which hugged her stomach and stopped an inch above the waistband of her shorts. There was something written in script across the chest of her shirt, but who knows what it said. You don't bother reading the card when unwrapping an incredible present. Her bronzed legs accentuated her bleach-white shorts, and my eyes instinctively scanned the sky in eager search of rain clouds.

I couldn't believe my eyes. I pictured Harvard girls as retainer-wearing geeks with multiple frizzy ponytails sprouting from random spots on their head. I had no idea they could be complete smokeshows. This girl was so hot that it would be an honor to lower my shades and poke around her Facebook page later.

It just sucked that the girl of my dreams made an appearance in the middle of my worst nightmare.

I had plenty of experience embarrassing myself in front of pretty girls, but nothing quite like this. As if being in my underwear wasn't bad enough, now my boxers were completely drenched in sweat, making it looked like I had just pissed myself. There was absolutely no way of getting back to my room without walking directly past her, so I prayed that I could channel my sixth-grade magical power of being invisible to girls.

Her parents were engaged in an animated discussion a few feet away from her, marveling at the fact that they had actually just "pahked the cah in Hahvahd Yahd," and I hoped that might distract her but I wasn't confident it would. My pulse quickened as I drew closer to the girl. If only there was a way that I could make light of the situation, I thought. My brain scrambled to come up with a good quip I could use to relieve the awkward tension. But recalling the outcome of the joke I used on Josh earlier, I decided it would be best to just keep my mouth shut.

As I strolled by her, I made sure to flex as many muscles as possible, as if somehow she would look at this hairy guy walking in his underwear in broad daylight and think "nice body!" And then I heard her release a faint giggle.

In a state of panic, I actually opened my big, dumb mouth and said something to her. The combination of her beauty and my humiliation overwhelmed my brain with conflicting emotions, causing it to malfunction. As I passed her I glanced down at my crotch then back at her, smiled, and said, "Just carrying in my last package!"

I'm not sure what freaked her out more: my crude joke or the way I delivered it. When trying to impress girls I tend to speak in a voice that's about two octaves lower than my normal pitch. Women might find it kind of sexy if I could mimic the deep, masculine voice of one those narrators of a movie trailer, but instead I just sound like a creeper who shouldn't be allowed within three hundred feet of an elementary school.

The girl didn't laugh or even crack a smile. Her father must have heard me too because he stepped close and put his arm around her shoulders, watching every step I took with fierce, challenging eyes. Her mother crossed her arms, shook her head, and muttered, "Fifty thousand dollars for a ticket to the zoo."

I slunk away, trying to escape the joke that achieved the

seemingly impossible task of vaulting the seminude stranger to an even higher level of creepiness. I was so upset with my idiotic remark that I could've punched myself in the face. And believe me, I would have, but I was still in public and didn't want to give people the impression that I was some sort of demented lunatic. Still, I wouldn't soon forgive myself for the swift assassination of my eligibility with such a stunning girl. Walking past her in my underwear certainly wasn't a good first impression, but any slim chance of the girl mistaking my doltish nudity for charming individuality was ruined by the wisecrack. Bad jokes are one thing, but bad jokes about one's genitals can end social careers.

Once I was a safe distance from the family, I gave in to temptation and looked back at my goddess one last time. Our eyes met briefly, and though I had not done it since my Xbox broke a few months earlier, I felt like crying. She looked like a model out of a magazine, with eyes that matched the ivy cascading down the stately brick building behind her. And at that moment I was crushed by a wave of inadequacy. What started as a day of excitement and cautious optimism quickly deteriorated into a nightmare that confirmed my deep suspicion that I was, in fact, a complete moron who had no business at this institution. I had been exposed in every sense of the word, and suddenly the next four years seemed like a burden that not even the Hulk could bear. I had been here for only a couple of hours and already I wanted nothing more than to get away from these perfect people and their judgmental eyes. I wished I could just go home to the accepting embrace of my mom, a woman who is still supremely impressed when I remember which side of the plate the fork goes on. Home, where being in my underwear was not only acceptable, but expected.

Thinking of home helped a little, though. I was reminded that there's life beyond these venerable brick walls. I was able to lever-age this comforting perspective into further positive thoughts. Not *that* many people took pictures, I told myself. Also, that crying toddler was, to be honest, being a bit of a pussy. Things could have been worse. At least I wasn't wearing my homemade Chewbacca underwear, or as I liked to call them, my Chewboxers. And, for most of the walk, I was able to keep my lightsaber in its holster. Not bad.

Of course, had I known that today was merely a single snow-flake in the avalanche of disasters rumbling toward my freshman year, I probably would've walked to the nearest airport and asked for a one-way ticket to the moon. I had no idea that this would actually be a high point of my year.

But at this point I was a naïve freshman who still believed my life was headed in the right direction because I was going to Harvard, which, I was assured, guaranteed a life of abundant success, happi-ness, and pants. My doubts about whether I belonged at Harvard were amplified today, but at least I maintained some hope for a better future. I walked the rest of the way feeling just a bit reassured.

I was only a few yards from my dorm when I noticed an ornate sundial settled in a small clearing of shrubs and flowers. It would've been nice if Harvard provided an outdoor clock that didn't require advanced knowledge of trigonometry, but it was an aesthetic piece of masonry nonetheless. Before stepping inside the dorm, the engraving on the sundial's stone base caught my eye. I felt a foreboding slap of reality, as I read:

ON THIS MOMENT HANGS ETERNITY.

Chapter Two

.38 CALIBER SHOCK

S o, in concussion, de 'Couchy-Shorts inequality' plays a crootchial role in de 'Hilbert space treory,' where de left zide of de equation is, umm, interpereted as de inner produce of two square-intergable functions over de, ahh, interbul."

My professor paused a moment to allow this information to fully sink in. I glanced up from my crossword puzzle to check the clock hanging at the back of the lecture hall. Class would be over in just a minute or two, but I honestly didn't think I could survive that long. I have no idea why I even bothered showing up to these lectures—I cared about the Cauchy-Schwarz inequality even less than I understood it. The only equation I truly grasped was Kester's Law of Endless Misery, which states: (integral calculus) + (a professor who can barely speak English) = an agonizing pain in the ass.

Harvard has a habit of hiring foreign professors, particularly in the math and science departments. The university covets faculty who boast impressive résumés filled with accolades and honors, while other details, like whether or not the professors can even pronounce the name of the course they are teaching, are of secondary importance. My calculus professor was a typical example of this trend: a distinguished scholar in his field, he left his homeland to continue his personal research at Harvard. Only on arrival did he receive the bad news that he actually had to teach a course or two. If you were to review his accomplishments in mathematics, he technically lived up to Harvard's claims that they have the very best professors in the world. Unfortunately, Harvard doesn't seem to care that there is a difference between the best professors and the best *teachers*.

As a "favor" to his students he went by Professor Phlymstrochstrzy, short for Phlymstrochsklyphymn. (Don't bother trying to pronounce it; just make a sound like you have a popcorn kernel stuck in the back of your throat and you'll be close enough.) I gave up after the first syllable, and have referred to him as "Professor Phlegm" ever since. I forget the name of his country of origin, but I recall hearing that they are actively seeking vowel donations.

I suppose I should cut him some slack, considering English is his fourth language and he probably taught it to himself during the transcontinental flight from Consonantia to Cambridge, but half the time I had no clue what the hell he was saying. I don't need a math professor with pristine English, but at least give me someone who doesn't say things like "whore times nine equals dirty-sex." While the language barrier was annoying, at least mispronunciations occasionally spiced up a dull class with unintentional comedy. I would eagerly await the end of calculus for a chance to hear Professor Phlegm remind us to visit him during his open office-hours, which he held in the Pusey Library.

Phlegm's calculus class, along with most math courses at Harvard, met in the Science Center. A cement monstrosity built just outside the northern edge of the Yard, the Science

Center is, to be realistic about it, the most hideous building ever constructed. It was erected in 1973, or about two and a half millennia after most Harvard buildings, and was funded by a $12.5 million check from Edwin Land, class of 1930 and the founder of the Polaroid Corporation. Land reportedly wanted the exterior of the Science Center to resemble a massive Polaroid camera, and Harvard happily obliged, figuring that a technology as awesome as Polaroid instant cameras would *never* become outdated. Unbelievably, the building's Polaroid design quickly lost its appeal, leaving Harvard's beautiful, red-bricked campus with a massive hunk of grey cement that resembles a giant metal robot turd.

The interior of the Science Center, unfortunately, also embraces 1970s design. There are four main lecture halls, all of which feature a few hundred creaky desk-chairs arranged in rows of stadium seating. Today I was sitting in the second-to-last row (the last row, reserved only for slackers, was empty), and I slouched uncomfortably on my seat's coarse, snot-green cushions. This faraway vantage point may not have had the best view of the blackboard, but I found the view of my crossword puzzle to be just fine.

Tap tap tap tap. The girl sitting next to me began anxiously drumming the end of her pen against her desk, a common tick among high-strung Harvard students that I found to be profoundly irritating. I tried to ignore it for a couple of minutes, but I had very little patience today. Unable to contain myself, I finally turned to the girl.

"You know, I play air guitar," I whispered. "We should join forces and start the most annoying band of all time."

The girl snapped out of her trance and abruptly stopped her

beat. Clearly she was not used to being called out or, judging from her purple scrunchie and jeans that came up to her midsection, being spoken to at all. I sat and stared at her with irrational hostility for a couple of minutes, wondering what her "specialty" was.

I learned early on that everyone at Harvard could be labeled by their "specialty," their unique trait that, when combined with exceptional grades, landed them admission to Harvard. There was the nationally ranked baton twirler. The prince of Yemen. The human calculator. And me? I was a football player who could read and write pretty good.

I probably should have given the little drummer girl a break, as today's class was particularly tense. We were getting back the grades of our first tests, the midterm exams, at the end of lecture, and the room harbored a type of restless angst that I imagined could only be found in a bomb shelter.

I had received a few graded assignments in the class before, though nothing as serious as a midterm exam. Professor Phlegm had given us a few short quizzes, or as he affectionately called them, "quizicles." (It was incredibly tempting to ask him what he called a short test, but that would have required me to raise my hand and that's almost never worth the energy.) I had performed reasonably well in the quizicles, though I had a sneaking suspicion that their purpose was to ease us into the class and build up our confidence before devastating us with a soul-crushing test, like fattening the pigs before the slaughter.

And apparently I had not been the only one living in fear of the midterm exam, as made evident by the bomb threat that was called in on the day of the test.

The day of the test, I had arrived early for some last-minute cramming, though the only thing I ended up reviewing was my life's greatest regrets, as one tends to do before his execution. I was slumped in my chair and thinking about how I really should have bought the textbook for this class when a frazzled teaching assistant busted through the doors of the auditorium. He announced that Professor Phlegm wanted to meet everyone outside, preferably sooner rather than later.

I wasted no mental energy trying to figure out the reason behind this request; the news of a potentially delayed test was enough for me to happily collect my things and start proceeding on my vacant way. But my inquisitive classmates buzzed with concern. Apparently there was a precedent for this at Harvard, and soon the whispers began to spread through the aisles: *bomb threat.*

I thought of the barks I heard echoing from the hallway earlier, which I had assumed belonged to the seeing-eye dog of Anika, the blind girl in my class who was majoring in (no joke) art history. Did those woofs actually come from a bomb-sniffing dog? I wasn't sticking around to find out. Neither were any of my classmates, who began to rush toward the exit in a panic.

Even though I suspected this was most likely a false alarm, I wasn't taking any chances. Sprinting through the mass of students bottlenecked at the doors, I tossed aside several weaklings on my way to freedom. I even body-checked one slowpoke into a trash bin. It wasn't my finest moment.

Once safely outside, I stood in a crowd of people and winced at the Science Center with a sense of foreboding. My classmates huddled in small groups and shared stories of their harrowing escape ("It was such a struggle to make it out…I nearly gave up, but then I thought, 'How am I going to make it to my afternoon classes if I'm dead?'"). The whispers of the rumored bomb threat turned into shouts, and soon there was a minor hysteria. *Jesus*, I thought to myself, *when it comes to tests, Harvard kids don't fuck around.*

Students everywhere know if you want to get out of a test, there are several easy excuses that work every time: food poisoning, family emergency, or for female students, "girl issues." Any of these simple tactics would have worked, but instead this person really went above and beyond what was required. I guarantee the culprit is the type of person who turns in fifteen pages for an eight-page English essay. Of course, that constitutes about 90 percent of the Harvard student body, so this theory didn't help narrow my personal suspect list.

Professor Phlegm gathered my class under a nearby maple tree and announced that, due to an "unexpectorated circoomstance," our test would be postponed for two or three days, whichever came first. Fears of imploding buildings were immediately forgotten; the news of our delayed midterm was received with a boisterous celebration filled with hugs, fist-pumps, and a few girly screams from both sexes. I gave an enthusiastic high-five to the neurotic pen-tapper, though she didn't seem to appreciate the gesture. Granted it was less a high-five than a slap on the ass, but come on, no test!

It was hard not to notice the one stone-faced guy standing in the back of the pack, nodding silently before zooming off on his Segway, the personal transporter that made him a minor celebrity on campus. My personal suspect list was reduced dramatically. Nothing happened to the Science Center, of course, and the class gradually dispersed with our spirits lifted by the idea of two more precious days of studying.

You know you're in an intense academic environment when a bomb threat actually relieves stress.

———◆◆———

The test wasn't easy, but at least I got through it without crying, which is more than the girl sitting next to me could say. I actually thought I had performed pretty well, so on the day we got the grades back, I was feeling confident.

When Phlegm wrapped up his lecture, he handed out the stacks of graded tests for his teaching assistants to distribute. A hush fell over the entire lecture hall, the only audible noise coming from a couple of students quietly hyperventilating in the rows below me. All eyes were locked on the stack of tests as they made their way around the room. For most of us this was our first major grade at Harvard—our first indication of whether we would graduate and grow up to have stable jobs, good health, and a spouse who wouldn't cheat on us. A lot was riding on these midterms.

"Overalls, I vas quit happy vith de class preformanence on de, ahh, teasts." Professor Phlegm dimmed the lights and flipped on the overhead projector, revealing a scatter-plot graph on the large pull-down screen behind him. Like many Harvard professors, Phlegm liked to make the data of the test scores public knowledge. "Azz you can zee by de, umm, chart, dare vas an even distrubation of grades between zevendy-tree and ninedy-sex."

Groans.

Clearly the graph didn't unclench many stomachs in the room, as there were a number of scores in the seventies—unacceptable grades that would carry a lifetime of shame for most of these students. I looked at it slightly differently and silently congratulated myself. *I passed my first Harvard midterm!* In an absolutely worst-case scenario I would have a 73, but there were a bunch of grades in the 90s on that graph. Who knows, maybe one of those was mine! I was legitimately excited when the teaching assistant reached my row and handed me my exam.

My jaw dropped when I saw the red "38" on the top of my test.

Then I realized this number must denote my score on the first page alone, which was out of a possible forty points. I eagerly flipped to the last page of my test to see my final grade. At the same time, Professor Phlegm spoke up.

"Oops! I must adjust dis ting. Very zorry!" I glanced up from my test to see him tinkering with the overhead projector. "Dis zilly ting is never vorking right!"

I briefly returned my eyes to my test, but was quickly interrupted by a snickering that now echoed throughout the room. It took me a few seconds to realize the class wasn't laughing at Phlegm, but at the image on the projection screen. The proportions of the scatter-plot graph had been reduced dramatically, and I had to squint to make out the resized chart. Professor Phlegm had zoomed out on the graph, revealing a second half of the x-axis that covered an interval from 0–50. One lonely point labeled "38" was floating helplessly in that vast sea of incompetence.

"Mother. Fucker." I blurted in disbelief.

Phlegm raised his voice to speak over the room's restrained giggles. "Ass I zed, most did very vell on de teast. But anyone who scort below zevendy, please zee me after glass."

This request barely registered with me, as I was busy staring at the chart of scores and the accompanying sidebar with a detailed breakdown of the test data. In addition to the mean, median, and mode of all the grades, Phlegm included the standard deviation, correlation coefficient, chi-squared test, and Gaussian distribution. Shit, I would have to take an advanced statistics course just to fully comprehend the true depth of my ineptitude.

I felt dizzy and the room began to spin. My stomach felt like the last time I had a few too many adult beverages, only in this case I didn't quite feel like putting an empty beer box on my head and declaring myself as "the fucking man." I swallowed hard to prevent spewing my humiliation on the row in front of me. *How the hell did this happen?* Not only did I have the lowest grade in a class of 148 students, but the next closest person scored almost twice as many points as I did.

Searching for answers, I frantically looked over the red markings that were spattered on my test, the crime-scene of a double-murder where calculus and logic were brutally hacked to death by my stupidity. Professor Phlegm's comments were not especially helpful, as he decorated my test with plenty of question marks, a few crudely drawn frowny faces, and, on the last page, a frowny face with tears coming out its eyes.

———◆———

As the class ended, I thought about just skipping the meeting with Professor Phlegm and leaving with the rest of the class. But considering I was the only person to score below a 70, my absence would likely have been noticed.

My classmates slowly filed out the back of the auditorium, their heads on a swivel as they searched for the one failure who would be walking against the current as he made his way toward the professor. This is Harvard's version of "The Walk of Shame." Clutching my test, I put my head down and trudged to the front of the lecture hall.

Professor Phlegm was snapping shut his briefcase when I reached him. "Ah, you must be Meester Keester." He put on his reading glasses and squinted his eyes, examining me like I was some disfigured creature in a laboratory jar. "You had zome troobull with de teast."

No shit. Your graph made that quite clear to the entire goddamn class.

"Vee are going to need to meet for zome von-on-von tutorialing. Can you meet me on Turds-day night in de Pussy Library?"

I had heard Professor Phlegm mispronounce the Pusey Library several times before, but having him say it directly to me was unbearable. I quickly faked a scratch on my nose to cover my smirk. "Yeah, sure. That works for me."

"Good. Do you know vhere de Pussy is? I know zome freshmens have not yet visited de Pussy."

I bit my lip and forced the corners of my mouth to stay down. "Sure, it's right near Hurlbut Hall, right?"

Professor Phlegm nodded. "Yes, yes. De Pussy is right around de corner from Her-but."

Now I couldn't help myself. Sure, I had just gotten a 38 on my test and my life was ruined, but this was just too damn funny. A snicker exploded out of my pursed lips, launching a fleck of spittle that landed on Professor Phlegm's left cheek.

His cavernous nostrils flaring, Professor Phlegm pulled out a monogrammed handkerchief and wiped his face. "Is zometing funny?" He snatched the test out of my hand and aggressively pointed at the red "38" in the top right corner. "You tink getting dirty-aids is funny?"

"Absolutely not," I managed to choke out.

"Den vhy do you laugh? You a joker? No vonder you get dirty-aids!" He snapped my test back at me.

Sensing his anger reaching a potentially dangerous level, I forced myself to calm down by thinking of something sobering. The image of that scatter-plot graph quickly came to mind, and I was able to collect myself. "Professor Phlymstrochstzy—"

"It's *Phlymstrochstrzy*," he snapped, "vith an *r*."

"Right, sorry. Listen, I don't mean to be rude," I explained. "I'm just really embarrassed about my grade."

"Ass you should be." The tone of Professor Phlegm's voice was challenging, but noticeably more relaxed now. "Vucky for you, I am de von person who can teach interegable calculus to anyvon, even apes. I didn't get nominated for de No-ball Prize in Matamatics for nothing."

I thanked Phlegm for his patience with me and said I looked forward to our rendezvous in the Pusey.

Before leaving the building I folded up my test and tucked it securely into my jeans pocket. I couldn't risk anyone at Harvard seeing my name attached to the failed exam, which might as well have been an official government document certifying my authenticity as a genuine imbecile. Clearly this Scarlet Letter had to be destroyed as soon as possible. I could "accidentally" leave it in my pocket and toss my jeans in the laundry, but that would require me to actually learn how to operate the washing machine, and that could take weeks. Burning it would be simple enough, but I feared its smoke would reach perceptive nostrils and give me away—I swear some of these Harvard kids could *smell* stupidity. I couldn't even cut it up into a million pieces because of the risk that its weakened soul would somehow survive, only to come back in the future stronger than ever before, like Lord Voldemort. No, it had to be completely obliterated. Which is why I ultimately settled on flushing it down the toilet, figuring it would be an appropriate sendoff for this piece of shit.

———◆◆———

Once outside I began to hustle back to my dorm, looking forward to celebrating my failure with my buddy Jack Daniels. With one hand firmly grasping the folded-up test in my pocket, I smiled and waved hello to friends who I passed along the way. It felt horribly awkward cheerfully greeting people and acting as if nothing was wrong, all while harboring a secret shame in my pants. I had newfound sympathy for those coping with herpes.

I was almost home-free when I heard a high-pitched voice call my name. I looked down to see one of my classmates, Vikas Gupta.

"Oh hey, Vikas," I said softly, patting the top of his head. "What's up?"

"Not much," he replied casually, "just waiting for my mom to pick me up."

Vikas was only fourteen years old, a boy genius who was forced to enroll in a couple of Harvard's math courses in order to challenge his freakish brain. There were a few of these adolescent prodigies at Harvard, and if you kept your eyes peeled you could occasionally spot one of them wandering around campus. These little geniuses were mythical creatures, like gnomes or Oompa Loompas. I had heard the rumors of their existence and had noticed the short urinals installed in all the men's rooms, but I had never been lucky enough to see one in person until I met Vikas in calculus.

Vikas was hunched forward due to the oppressive size of his backpack, a bright red Northface with his initials embroidered on the back and a Pokemon keychain dangling from the zipper.

His bag must have weighed almost as much as he did, and his bent posture caused his oversized glasses to keep slipping down the bridge of his nose. He wore a white button-up shirt, pleated khaki pants, and a pair of black Air Jordan sneakers, the only part of his outfit his mom clearly didn't pick out for him.

Vikas and I developed a unique friendship in our calculus lecture, probably because we were the only two people in the entire class who still ate Lunchables.

"How'd you do on the test?" I asked, knowing that he probably crushed it.

Vikas scrunched his nose, contorting his face like he just smelled something vile. "I got a 91. My parents are gonna freaking kill me! What about you?"

"Vikas, you already know what I got. The whole class does."

"Yeah…I know. I saw you talking to the prof after class. That shit is whack, bro."

I had been teaching Vikas how to talk more like a regular college guy, but clearly we still had some more practice to do. His goal was to ask out Beth, a nice girl in our class who had short, tapered hair and played on the women's rugby team. Vikas had been in love with her ever since she flawlessly explained the Heine-Cantor theorem in front of the entire class. I didn't have the heart to tell Vikas that Beth probably wasn't interested in dating him. His brain may be advanced for his age, but at fourteen years old, his gaydar had not yet been fully developed.

"Yeah, I don't think Professor Phlegm was too happy with my performance," I said. "My 38 must've brought down the class average a lot."

"Well your grade fell 2.5 standard deviations away from the mean, so, technically speaking, it's an outlier," Vikas explained.

"Outliers aren't even calculated in the class average, so don't worry about it."

I should have chastised Vikas for his nerd-speak, but I wasn't in the mood. The term "technically speaking" was on the ever-expanding list of words and phrases I instructed Vikas to stop using in conversation, along with "yet I digress" and "aforementioned." Most people who use those aforementioned terms are, technically speaking, douchebags. Yet I digress.

"I'm an outlier, that's for damn sure." I said. "But nice job with that 91, man. That's like…umm…three times my score."

"2.4," Vikas mumbled.

"Right, that's what I meant. Anyway, I just don't understand how I bombed that test so badly. I wish I could use Professor Phlegm's unintelligible accent as an excuse, but that doesn't explain how every single other student passed."

"Maybe you need to study more?" Vikas suggested, a hint of criticism in his voice.

My defenses were up. "I'm sorry if I'm not like everyone else here, prioritizing study-time ahead of all of life's other necessities," I spat back. "Sure, I could've used that strategy, but life is too short to be studying all night, especially when you have to do important things like eat and sleep and watch *American Idol*. And it's not like I slacked off. I studied extra hard during the commercial breaks."

"Not good enough, bro. You need to make sacrifices. Also, you gotta start taking better notes in class. Like, for the love of god, get a freaking notebook or binder or something."

Vikas had a point here. It wasn't easy writing on the back of Starbucks receipts.

"And you haven't had perfect attendance in lecture. I don't get how you can oversleep a class that meets at two in the afternoon!

And remember how you missed the first two lectures because you were showing up to the wrong classroom? Maybe if you actually paid attention in class, you would've realized sooner that calculus professors don't typically lecture about freaking Japanese literature! And don't get me started on your calculator!"

"Alright, enough!" I snapped. Vikas was on a roll and I was not about to let him lambaste my beloved calculator, a solar-powered machine with buttons the size of quarters designed for arthritic old people. Having recently been compared to an ape by Professor Phlegm, I was in no mood to get harangued by someone who still purposely walks through puddles. "Don't be mad at me because I don't kill myself over school," I snapped. "Not everyone has to get good grades in order for their parents to love them!"

I regretted my comment as soon as it left my mouth, and I looked down at my shoes. Vikas's wide eyes revealed that my snarky remark held some truth to it. Vikas's parents had migrated from India to America shortly before he was born, and they were absolutely terrifying. Mr. Gupta was an expert engineer who worked for the government building rockets out of subatomic particles, while Mrs. Gupta was a professional psycho devoted solely to Vikas's academic development.

Parental pressure is a sensitive subject for many Harvard students, and it shocked me to discover how many of them felt compelled to dutifully report every grade they received to their mom and dad. Luckily my parents didn't hound me about my grades. They had tempered their expectations of me after I was expelled from my first preschool, so any academic achievement after that was a pleasant surprise. Hell, they still got excited if I lasted an entire year without biting anyone. But in all seriousness, I always got respectable grades in high school and there was no reason to believe that would change once I got to college. My parents never flipped out over a bad grade, but to be safe I decided to keep my calculus test to myself. They were so unconditionally proud of me, but I wondered if that would change if they knew their son was getting dirty-aids.

But for Vikas it was different. As an eight-year-old simply tying my shoe was an arduous task; at the same age, Vikas had built a robot that could do it for him. Like his moustache, Vikas's brain blossomed at a young age and his parents were going to make sure he got the most out of his gift, even if it was at the expense of a normal childhood.

This upbringing was not uncommon for Harvard students, many of whom had their entire lives structured with the goal of getting accepted into the prestigious university. For some it started as early as infancy when their parents took the rattle from their tiny hand and replaced it with a violin. Wearing a "Future Harvard Freshman" bib, they sat in their highchairs and stared at their periodic-table placemat, spit dribbling down their chin as daddy informed them that, if they were good and ate their broccoli, then maybe after dinner they could play with their Rubik's cube. Then came the years of accelerated learning programs, a time in which the child lived by the family motto, "Why go to sleep-away camp when you can take summer classes in organic chemistry instead?" By the time they reached high school, almost all hope for recovering a normal, teenage lifestyle was lost. The only sex they cared about occurred in a Petri dish during biology class.

Vikas may have been only fourteen, but he had already missed his teenage years. Instead of playing soccer after school with his buddies, laughing and scraping his knee like a normal kid his age, Vikas was scraping microorganisms off a test tube with his phytopathology tutor because, as his parents once told me, it was critical for every young boy to have a solid foundation in the study of plant diseases. Now that he attended classes at Harvard, every test was a family event.

"Not just any family event," Vikas later confided in me, "but a life-altering event. Like, the stress on test days is as intense as the morning my baby sister was born. The only difference is my mother screams more on test days."

I wish I had thought of that before I made my insensitive comment. Now I felt like both a failure and a dick. "Hey, man, I'm sorry. I didn't mean that. I'm just so rattled about my grade. I can't shake the feeling that I don't belong at this goddamn school."

Vikas lurched forward and readjusted the position of the cumbersome bag on his back. "You're talking to a kid who gets picked up after class in a purple minivan."

We began to crack up, our laughs heartier than usual. Still smiling, Vikas changed the subject. "So you got mad plans for tonight? Gonna hang with any hot bitches?"

As a Harvard student uninitiated in the school's social scene, Vikas was fascinated with my life on campus. His adolescent mind was particularly interested in my experience with girls, and he was somehow convinced that my nights were filled with unbridled debauchery and wild sex parties.

I'd be lying if I said I didn't do my best to perpetuate Vikas's image of me as a smooth-talking Casanova whose sexual misadventures were both frequent and epic. Every Monday before calculus class, Vikas would eagerly await a juicy update on my love life, and I would never let him down. His naïveté enabled me to make up ridiculous stories, intentionally leaving them vague to allow his imagination to fill in the blanks.

"Vikas," I'd say gravely, placing my hand on his shoulder, "if a girl ever asks you to come to her room with an empty Pringles can, a bag full of popsicle sticks, and a fake moustache, take my advice: DON'T DO IT." His wide eyes bulging, Vikas would giggle uncontrollably.

It didn't matter how absurd my story was, he would believe it. "I was with this one girl and…wow. You're still a little young to hear the details of what she did to me, but let's just say that now I'm lactose-intolerant."

Vikas just couldn't get enough, and neither could I. Recounting these stories to such a captive audience made my life feel important, like I was some sort of big shot, even though I was bragging to someone who was four foot eleven about stories that weren't even remotely true. I suppose your life is truly pathetic when you start living vicariously through yourself, but that's exactly what I was doing.

This afternoon, though, I didn't have the energy to continue the charade. But feeling bad about my earlier remark, I decided to humor the kid a little. "Yeah, I've got some real big plans for tonight," I lied. I didn't want to disappoint him and say what I was actually going to end up doing, which was switch on my emo playlist and play *Mario Kart* with a bottle of brown liquor until I passed out on my futon.

"Yeah, shit is going to get real crazy with the bitches later," I continued. "I've got to release some stress tonight, if you know what I mean." Vikas grinned and nodded vigorously. He had no idea what I meant. "In fact, this one chick told me she wanted to show me something later tonight." This was actually true, though slightly embellished. The "chick" was Rosie, a sixty-two-year-old cafeteria worker who I was friendly with, and the thing she wanted to show me was a mole on her right shoulder, which she routinely asked me to inspect to make sure it didn't have "the cancer."

Vikas beamed. "And which one of your babes is this?" he asked eagerly.

"You'll just have to wait and see, my man," I said.

"You're totally gonna eff tonight, aren't you?" he asked. Poor, naïve Vikas. If only he knew that the only thing I "effed" lately was my calculus test. "You're such a libertine. I freaking love it!" he exclaimed.

I smiled and nodded, taking a mental note to look up that word later. "Yeah, well, I should probably spend more studying and less time doing the no-pants-dance. Seriously, dude, I don't know how I'm going to pass the final exam."

Vikas shook his head and sighed. "Calculus: the agony and dx/dt." He giggled at his ridiculously geeky joke. "It won't be easy, but you can definitely do it," he assured me. "And I suppose if you get really desperate, you could always just cheat like the other meatheads."

Vikas had been kidding. But even if I didn't realize it in the moment, the seed had been planted. Cheating is not in my nature, but it would be a matter of virtue versus survival instinct.

Because it wasn't just about the grades themselves. I was having a difficult time making friends. Fitting in supersedes all other goals for a first-semester freshman, and flunking a class was *not* the way to blend in with Harvard kids. I had made the painful discovery that social circles work differently at Harvard. I wouldn't go so far as to say that getting good grades automatically makes you popular at Harvard, but bad grades can damage your reputation because it makes you look like a fraudulent asshole who somehow snuck into the Genius Club. The grade-obsessed culture of Harvard was contagious; most students desperately wanted to prove that they were the "best of the best." I just wanted to prove that I belonged here, and I was failing miserably.

"Vikaaaaaaas!"

The shrill cry came from across the street, where Mrs. Gupta was pulled over in her Toyota minivan. Vikas wasn't kidding—it was purple, and offensively so. It resembled a giant eggplant, and both bumpers were completely plastered with "Oak Hill Middle School Student of the Month" bumper stickers.

"Crap, I gotta go," Vikas said hurriedly as he extended his fist for a pound. "Slay some babes for me tonight. No excuses. And jeez, if you see Natalie Portman at the bar again, try not to lose her number this time! Oh, and don't forget to use protection. We don't want any little Eric's running around, do we?"

I jammed my test deeper into my pocket. "Don't worry," I said as he ran away toward the van. "I wouldn't want anyone to be subjected to what's in my genes."

Chapter Three

MAC ATTACK

I'm sure anyone who saw me as I stumbled through my first months of college, whether I was failing my midterm or burning my toast in the dining hall, had one question on their mind: how the hell did *he* get into Harvard?

I have to admit that my journey to Harvard was probably not a typical one. I wasn't a child prodigy in anything. I must have displayed some level of acumen when I was a kid though, because I remember often hearing my parents anxiously mumble something about "potential" as I played *Super Mario*. Of course at the time I thought they were discussing my "potential" to beat the game. And when they said I was "going places," I would respond, "Yeah, I'm going to Bowser's castle to save the princess!"

I guess I did exhibit some nerdy behavior from time to time—I recall being ecstatic at my eleventh birthday because I was a prime number *and* a palindrome. But for the most part I wasn't overly concerned with my education. My two sisters would love visiting local museums while I enjoyed spending time in places a little less academic, like the mud.

When it came time to apply to colleges my senior year of high school, it was difficult for me to be confident about my chances at the top schools, when two of my top five accomplishments in life were related to eating contests. Sure, I had been named "Most Likely to Succeed" in a poll from the student newspaper, but that probably had less to do with any of my achievements and more to do with the fact that I was the one who counted the votes. I worked hard and had good grades, but they alone weren't strong enough to get me accepted to a place like Harvard, which has close to thirty thousand elite students applying for a class of sixteen hundred. Like many high school students I endured hours of SAT prep (it seemed every day I would arrive home and there would be a new SAT workbook sitting on my desk, with my parents swearing they had no idea how it got there), though ultimately my scores were merely passable for a university that annually rejects hundreds of applicants with perfect scores.

I did manage to find success on the football field, though. And at six foot two and 225 pounds, I possessed enough size and athleticism to be recruited as a linebacker at some Division I schools, including those in the Ivy League.

In the spring of my junior year, I began to receive letters from Harvard's football coaches expressing their interest in me. During my senior season these letters became more frequent and encouraging, and they even started to spell my name correctly. After reviewing my transcript and the game films of my senior season, Harvard's director of recruiting visited me to make sure I wasn't lying about my height and weight, sizing me up the way a farmer might inspect a mule he was about to purchase. Apparently satisfied with what he saw, the coach assured me that I would have the football team's full support in admissions.

Like every red-blooded American boy, I had dreamed of cracking heads at a Division I level. And now Harvard was extending me the opportunity, while getting an elite education at the same time.

I was blown away the first time I stepped into Harvard Stadium. *I can't believe I get to play here!* Built in 1903, the nation's oldest stadium has endured for over a century to become an iconic symbol of the university's most cherished values: power, prestige, and, most importantly, tradition. Hundreds of pillars form a colonnade that lines the horseshoe structure, emulating the architectural design of a Greek stadium or Roman circus. Evergreen ivy crawls up the exterior walls of the immense concrete edifice, which is crowned at its apex by a massive Harvard flag that continuously flaps in the wind swirling off the banks of the neighboring Charles River. I closed my eyes and imagined myself running onto the field to the cheers of thousands of fans, proudly donning the crimson jersey that had been worn by generations of exceptional alumni before me. I couldn't wait to be part of the storied tradition of Harvard football and make my contribution to the great university through the glory of manly contest.

It turned out my expectations of Harvard football, though, couldn't have been further off.

———◆◆———

"Get your ass over here, you motherfuckin' motherfucker!"

This was a bad turn for a day that had started off well. It was unseasonably warm on this late-October morning, and I recall appreciating the extra splash of sunlight. Typically, rolling out of bed at 6:00 a.m. for football workouts was a painful exercise, but the additional light streaming through my window that morning helped lift my spirits from a piercing agony to a dull misery.

Still, the reality of just how early it was came into focus when I stumbled into my common room to find my roommates just getting ready for bed, Josh having just completed a marathon of Internet poker and Dermot, my eccentric and mystifying roommate from Ireland, having finished his project of removing all the marshmallows from a box of Lucky Charms.

They could only stare and shake their heads at me, and how I had been turned into a zombie by my relentless daily schedule. My days began with a mandatory 6:30 a.m. workout, followed by a full day of classes, then an hour-long football meeting and two-hour practice. After football I would have time to grab a quick bite to eat before starting my calculus problem set, which would usually conclude with my head on my desk as I slept in a puddle of drool and incorrect answers.

That morning, though, I found a note pinned to the door of the weight room. I had no clue what it said. The note, written by Coach Mac, one of our strength and conditioning trainers, looked as if it had been scribbled by a spastic five-year-old. As if the illegible writing weren't bad enough, Coach Mac had written it in yellow highlighter on a white piece of paper. I stood at the door for a few minutes trying to decipher the mess of symbols like I was in the goddamn *Da Vinci Code*. Finally I gave up. Looking around the empty weight room, I figured it was safe to assume that our workout had been canceled.

I couldn't believe my luck. Coach Mac *never* canceled lift. According to a few of my older teammates, this was a guy who once slept in the locker room so a blizzard forecasted for the next morning wouldn't prevent him from coming to the scheduled 6:00 a.m. workout session. Ignoring the disconcerting notion that Coach Mac would only call off a workout in the event of an impending nuclear holocaust, I happily made my way back to my dorm, invigorated by the idea of a much needed nap.

I had been walking for less than a minute when I ran into Coach Mac and the rest of my teammates huddled on the side of the street.

"Get your ass over here, you motherfuckin' motherfucker!"

I quickly realized what was going on. The practice had been moved, and I was now late. Well, technically I was still five minutes early, but in Coach Mac's universe, being only five minutes early means you are actually five minutes late.

"Sorry, coach. I didn't know we were meeting here. I was in the weight room."

"Are you blind? Did you not read my fucking sign?"

Coach Mac was a man of limited patience and vocabulary. He was also a massive human being, a physical specimen who stood out even among a crowd of burly college football players. At six foot four, he was a self-described "260 pounds of twisted steel and sex appeal." His jet-black hair, prominent eyebrows, and oblong head gave him an almost cartoonish appearance, as if Fred Flintstone had taken an obscene amount of steroids. A tape measure once proved that his neck was literally twice the girth of his head. His demeanor was as prickly as his chin stubble, and my stomach churned as I joined my teammates gathered around him.

As I stood with my teammates around Coach Mac on the sidewalk, I took a moment to get my bearings and make sure I wasn't dreaming. My teammates were dressed in our standard workout gear: crimson mesh shorts and grey T-shirts with "Harvard Football" stamped on the left breast. Thinking the workout had been canceled, I had already changed back into my street clothes—a pair of jeans and a grey Gap hoodie. Looking around at my teammates in their workout uniforms, I couldn't help but feel like that one creepy guy you always see at a public gym running on a treadmill with khaki pants and a flannel shirt. I was in the right place, at least, but I couldn't figure out why we were huddled outside on the sidewalk instead of in the weight room. Judging from the confused expressions of my teammates, neither could they.

"Men, I think you know why we're out here!" Coach Mac barked in his deep, raspy voice that always sounded like he just gargled glass shards.

My teammates and I looked at each other anxiously. We had no idea why we were out there, but judging from the crazed look in Coach Mac's eye and the dumbbells lined up on the sidewalk, we knew things were about to get pretty damn weird.

"It's time for Arm Farm, baby!" Coach Mac yelled. "Everyone grab a pair of dumbbells and find some open sidewalk!"

Arm Farm, Coach Mac explained, was a workout he designed to "grow" our arm muscles through an ungodly amount of biceps curls and triceps presses.

"During Arm Farm, *this*"—he picked up a dumbbell with his left hand—"is your rake, and *this*"—he picked up another in his right—"is your hoe. I'm Old MacDonald, and for the next hour, you're my bitches."

"We're doing Arm Farm out *here*?" a teammate asked, watching the traffic whiz by on the street a few feet in front of us.

"Hell yes!" Mac declared. "The entire city—no, the entire *world*—is going to know that the Harvard football team is the strongest, meanest, most baddest motherfuckers on the goddamn planet!"

Shane, the only player on our team with a neck-to-head ratio larger than Coach Mac, pumped his fist in the air and cheered. The rest of us stood in silence.

Coach Mac's plan to showcase our strength in public was a manifestation of a severe inferiority complex that plagues Harvard football. Despite our status as a Division I football program that annually contended for the Ivy League Championship, we just weren't taken seriously on campus. Concerts by our student symphony orchestra would routinely draw a greater crowd than our football games, and I'd say most students would require some sort of GPS device just to locate Harvard's athletic facilities. Honestly, Harvard might be the only school in the nation where a member of the marching band in the stands actually has a better chance of getting laid than any of the players on the field. Unlike the athletes at most colleges, who are viewed as campus celebrities, football players at Harvard are somewhat despised. To many Harvard students we were nothing more than useless meatheads who traveled in packs across campus like a herd of buffalo, stopping frequently to graze at the cafeteria and fill our bellies with ice cream sandwiches and chocolate milk. Others openly loathed the football players (and athletes in general), feeling that we had taken the back door into Harvard.

The players, coaching staff, and especially Coach Mac were deeply offended by our lack of legitimacy on campus. We desperately wanted to revel in the glory inherent in the rugged culture of football, but achieving this ambition was almost impossible at a school like Harvard, which forced our program to hover between the worlds of badass football and tight-ass academia. We had an intimidating fight song, but its lyrics were in Latin. We had an exceptional stadium, but we shared it with the intramural kickball teams. Some of our players were destined to play in the NFL after college, but others (me) were destined to move back in with our parents and sleep in a room with rocking horse wallpaper. We had won twelve national championships— the eighth most in college football history—but they came between 1874 and 1920, a period in which there were only six teams in existence, with Harvard's primary competition coming from Yale, Princeton, and the since defunct Applewood School for the Blind.

The university would put restrictions on Coach Mac's strength and conditioning program, an interference he frequently ignored. Trying to explain to Coach Mac that we weren't allowed to work out on major holidays was like telling a six-year-old that Santa doesn't exist—his brain could hardly fathom such a reality. "Well, the pilgrims didn't miss weights on Thanksgiving, so neither are you!" he said. The Harvard weight room was locked that day, so he invited a few key players to his house for Thanksgiving dinner, where, in between courses, he ordered them into his garage for a few sets of power squats on his makeshift weight rack.

It was Coach Mac's personal quest to make Harvard football legit, to prove to the university and the country that we were every bit as tough and hardcore as the college football teams that were revered on other campuses. I suspect he was hired specifically for this purpose, as he was the antithesis of the typical Harvard authority figures who wore tweed blazers with elbow patches and referred to football as "the pigskin pastime." Coach Mac was always plotting stunts to bring recognition to the football team, but today, as he lined us up along North Harvard Street for Arm Farm, he might've been taking things a bit too far.

"Alright, men! Shirts off! Let's go! Sun's out, guns out!"

Oh god, is this really happening? I looked down the line to make sure other people were following orders before removing my sweatshirt and undershirt. Given my move-in debut at Harvard, there was absolutely no way I was going to be semi-nude in public without at least blending in with a crowd.

The next thing I knew, I was among fifty shirtless Harvard men standing in a horizontal line facing the street, dumbbells in hand. Despite being just one of dozens participating in this exhibition of epic embarrassment, I felt like every motorist or pedestrian passing by had their eyes on me. *Hey! Isn't that the kid with the Hulk underwear from a couple of months ago? I'd recognize that hairy chest anywhere!*

———◆———

North Harvard Street is a bustling road that lies, predictably, just south of Harvard's main campus. Running parallel to Harvard stadium and the rest of the undergraduate athletic facilities, it begins in the nearby metropolitan neighborhood of Allston, crosses the Charles River, and ends directly in the heart of Harvard Square. The stretch of sidewalk that we currently occupied was technically in Allston, an area where the brick buildings of Harvard suddenly give way to the concrete of low-income housing—an abrupt shift from urbane to urban. It was not an area you'd want to walk through alone at night, let alone put on a borderline homoerotic performance with fifty shirtless dudes lifting weights in their spandex shorts.

Although my teammates and I were only in danger of suffering emotional injury on this sunny morning, every year several Harvard students wandering through this area after dark become the unfortunate victims of a mugging. One kid I knew, Neal, got held up by a couple of shady characters one night after he strayed too far from Harvard Square (apparently, the city lights were impeding his view of a good meteor shower). The criminals left Neal unharmed, but took his wallet, cell phone, iPod—all his possessions except for his graphing calculator.

"The joke's on them, really," Neal boasted, showing his calculator to a throng of captivated students after he returned to his dorm. "The street value of this baby is close to four Benjamins, but if you count all the equations I have saved in it, the thing's essentially priceless." Neal recounted his heroic encounter with the "gangsters" to a thoroughly impressed audience, who couldn't seem to decide which was cooler: that Neal had survived an encounter with bona fide "riffraff" or that he had "Schrödinger's equation" saved in his calculator. I'm pretty sure he got laid later that night, but judging from the sweatshirt he had wrapped frontward around his waist to cover up the crotch of his pants, I doubt he was the picture of courage during the confrontation.

Local Allston residents, for the most part, disdain Harvard and everything it stands for. I suppose they have a fairly legitimate gripe with Harvard, as the university had plans to expand deeper into their neighborhood, purchasing land to build a $1.2 billion science complex. It didn't sit well with the locals that land once used to house Allston residents would now be used by Harvard to house the things the faculty actually cared about, like microorganisms.

The turf war between Allston residents and Harvard was fought on a smaller scale on North Harvard Street as well, where the locals and students would fight over the world's rarest and most precious natural resource: free parking spots. Harvard students who left their cars overnight on North Harvard Street would often find them vandalized the next day with deep scratches carved into the doors or gashes slashed into the tires. I always wondered how the local nighttime vigilantes were able to distinguish which cars belonged to Harvard students, but I suppose it's pretty easy to pick out the target when among a line of beat-up, rusty sedans there stands a lone turquoise Subaru with a bumper sticker that reads "AM I LIBERAL OR JUST WELL-EDUCATED?" I once left my Volvo sedan on North Harvard Street only to find a brick through its window the next morning with a note attached to it that said: "Harvard Douche…Your an asshole." I couldn't understand why the locals hated Harvard students so much, and why they chose to ignore such simple grammatical rules.

———◆———

North Harvard Street may be desolate late at night, but during morning rush hour the traffic is relentless. Coach Mac had us lined up close to a major intersection where North Harvard Street is crosscut by Storrow Drive, one of the major traffic arteries that leads into downtown Boston. Hundreds of distracted commuters gawked at us as they drove to their workplaces, and I could already picture the headline in tomorrow's *Boston Globe*:

CRASH COURSE: HARVARD STUDENTS CAUSE 12-CAR PILE-UP
   Three football players crushed after being forced by coach to bench-press the wreckage

This situation was going to get ugly, that was for sure, but Coach Mac had undisputed authority over us, so everyone stood obediently with his shirt off. With one exception.

Jason Thorndike, our backup left guard, was a pretty good football player. He was normally obedient to a fault, but at 315 pounds, I couldn't blame him for keeping his shirt on. I mean, the kid had boobs that housewives of Orange County would pay good money for.

"Thorny-Dick!" Coach Mac yelled as he sprinted over to Jason, "You better take off that fucking shirt!"

Jason didn't move. He stared straight ahead.

Coach Mac stuck his beet-red face within inches of Jason's. "Lose the fucking shirt!" He motioned toward the rest of us, standing tall and shirtless like a bunch of assholes. "Look at everyone else. You're embarrassing us right now!"

Jason didn't budge.

I may have been imagining it, but I'm pretty sure I saw a bit of white foam bubbling from the corner of Coach Mac's mouth. *For the love of god, Jason, take off your shirt.*

Coach Mac gave Jason a hard stare for five seconds, then, surprisingly, turned away. "Alright, buddy. I understand. You have the right to say…" Suddenly, Coach Mac lunged forward and grabbed the collar of Jason's T-shirt with both of his hands, then pulled violently downward, ripping it in two. Jason stood stunned as Coach Mac pulled off the shredded shirt, rolled it up into a ball, and threw it into the busy street.

"How do you like that?" Coach Mac screamed, again getting up in Jason's face. "How do you like it?" Then, with an open palm, Coach Mac slapped him right across the face.

Now I had seen Coach Mac hit players before—like one time before a game when he got so fired up that he head-butted me. It hurt way more than I thought, considering I was wearing a helmet at the time, but judging from the blood trickling down

Coach Mac's forehead, I'm proud to say it damaged him more. Jason wasn't fortunate enough to be wearing a helmet when Coach Mac's hand collided with his face, but somehow he only recoiled a few inches. Jason paused a moment, as if trying to determine how to react to the assault, then responded with his fist—a quick right hook that caught Coach Mac under the chin.

One of my teammates gasped. I dropped both of my dumbbells, and someone else dropped an F-bomb. The world stood still as Coach Mac stumbled backward toward the traffic, catching his balance just in time. He then charged toward Jason, extended both of his arms, and reached for his neck. I took a step toward the two of them, ready to pounce on Coach Mac, when I realized that he hadn't actually grabbed Jason's neck, but his shoulders.

"Woooooh baby! That's what I'm talking about!" he screamed, vigorously shaking Jason by the shoulders. "That's what the fuck I'm talking about!"

He slapped Jason again, who immediately returned the favor. Coach Mac proceeded to move down the line, smacking players and then accepting a retaliatory crack, cheering with every blow. "You crazy motherfuckers, I love it!" he yelled. "Now let's do this!"

In unison, my suddenly inspired team bellowed a vicious war cry and began pumping our dumbbells in a whirlwind of biceps curls.

As ridiculous as the situation sounds, our enthusiasm had developed organically, yielding an intensely rousing Arm Farm session. I do wonder about the commuters who witnessed this event out of context, though. I can imagine a businessman, a Bach violin concerto echoing through his BMW as he drives to the Financial District, looking out his window to see a mob of shirtless brutes punching each other in the face then jumping around like a bunch of Neanderthals celebrating a successful hunt. Our coaches always preached good behavior off the field, reminding us that we were representing the world's top university. I think we were doing a pretty good job of that this morning.

Coach Mac always found unique ways to inspire us during our workout sessions. Easily the most unforgettable example of Coach Mac's motivational tactics occurred a few weeks earlier in the weight room. We had a professional cameraman recording our lift for a recruiting video that day.

Coach Mac was even more insane than usual when he was in front of the camera, and I was prepared for something absurd as the team gathered around him for a quick motivational speech before we began our back squat max-outs.

"It's time to decide what kind of man you want to be," he started. "Do you want to be a man who's weaker than a fart in an astronaut suit? Or do you want to be a man who stares adversity in the face, and tells it to fuck off?" I thought about it for a moment, and decided I didn't really want to be either of those things.

"Do you want to be a man who can't give his own son a piggyback ride because you have chopsticks for legs? Or do you want to be a man who squats four hundred pounds five times with enough testosterone leftover to impregnate a woman just by looking at her?" Coach Mac continued, the intensity in his coarse voice growing. "Now when you get in that squat rack, you've got to be a *real* man. Not some boy who worries about his arithmetic test or whatever you guys study at this goddamn place."

He then pointed at the cameraman. "Turn that thing off."

Oh god, here we go…

"If you want to be a beast at lifting, at football, at *anything* in life, you need to have big balls! Look at me! I may have a small dick"—Coach Mac pulled his shorts down to his knees, completely exposing himself—"but I have big fucking balls!" He cupped his package with both his hands, proudly presenting it to his audience like a magician who had just pulled a rabbit out of a hat. A round of gasps escaped from the players, but the loudest screams came from members of the women's volleyball team, who were stretching a few yards away. Coach Mac pulled up his shorts and nonchalantly tucked his motivator back inside. "Now follow me; I've got a surprise for you guys!" he said, as if whipping out his dick in public *wasn't* a surprise.

As we followed Coach Mac to the opposite end of the weight room, I turned to my buddy Ryan for a quick review, to make sure what I just saw actually happened in real life. "Holy shit! Could you believe that?"

"I know!" Ryan said excitedly. "His balls really *are* huge!"

Coach Mac led us to a squat rack wedged in the corner of the weight room, facing the mirrored wall a few feet away. The weight room was a beautiful facility, a large, well-lit room with high ceilings above rows of brand-new bench presses, squat racks, and Olympic lifting platforms. Decals of the Harvard shield were stamped on the platforms' glossy wood and "HARVARD CRIMSON" was imprinted in enormous block letters across the far right wall, in case you ever forgot which team you were on. (That was one thing I learned quickly about the university: they used every opportunity to remind you that you weren't at any old college—you were at *fucking Harvard*. Even our waffle irons at breakfast were molded in the shape of the Harvard shield.) The weight room was located within steps of Harvard Stadium and only varsity athletes were allowed to use it. "Regular" students were granted access to their own weight room in the basement of the Malkin Athletic Center ("the MAC"), located across the Charles River and closer to the Yard. So while the athletes enjoyed the expansive, asbestos-free environment of the varsity facility, the remaining 95 percent of the student body was given access to a weight room with the ventilation and spacious quality of a utility closet. Judging from the number of Harvard students who actually used the weight room, it could have been smaller.

Coach Mac's big "surprise" was that he was going to squat four hundred pounds five times to help inspire us. But I suspect this was more for the camera, which was rolling again. A couple of us began sliding forty-five-pound plates onto the bar that was suspended five feet in the air while he ran over to the stereo and turned on "Hells Bells" by AC/DC, the song he claims was playing on the radio when he lost his virginity. Before stepping up to the bar, Coach Mac performed a couple of neck rolls and then took a deep breath.

The first two repetitions went smoothly, as Coach Mac gripped the four-hundred-pound bar that rested on his upper back, and steadily squatted down and then back up to a standing position. The third rep, however, was a major struggle for him, as his quivering knees barely produced enough force to power the weight up from his crouching position. It was clear that Coach Mac was not going to be able to complete the final two reps, so the entire team cheered for his effort as a couple of the guys rushed to help him get the bar off his back and onto the rack.

"No!" he barked. "Don't you fuckin' touch me!"

A few of the seniors on the team quickly tried to talk him out of it, explaining that he could really be injured—maybe even killed—if he didn't put the weight down. But Coach Mac's mind had been transported into some alternate universe. He stood in a trance as the bar applied relentless pressure on his back and knees. Sweat poured down his face, which now matched the crimson color of his shirt, and a vein popped in his forehead. He stared at his reflection in the mirror for a moment with pure hatred in his eyes. Then he spoke to himself.

"You...fucking...PUSSY!"

Coach Mac then spat in the reflection of his own face. As his loogie slowly trickled down the mirror, he performed two perfect squats in rapid succession, threw the weight back on the rack, turned around, took one step toward us, and collapsed flat on his face.

We had heard from other varsity teams that Coach Mac had pulled this motivational stunt before, so we let his massive body lie motionless on the ground for about a minute. It wasn't until his body began to spontaneously twitch that we decided to act. I made a movement to the telephone to call for help, but someone told me to stop. Coach Mac was waking up.

"Coach, are you okay?"

Coach Mac groaned and slowly rolled over onto his back. His eyes were looking in two different directions.

"Did I make it?" he mumbled. "Did I make five reps?"

Since that day I arrived to all our workouts expecting the unexpected. It was actually pretty exciting dealing with a coach who was clearly more unstable than plutonium and Britney Spears combined. Our lifting sessions were always dynamic, though today

I would have definitely preferred a dull workout in the weight room over Arm Farm, which was quickly proving to be the worst experience of my life. My arm muscles burned fiercely and I had to muster every ounce of my strength just to keep going, grunting with each rep like I was some disgusting orc from Mordor. I didn't know how much longer I could last. Good thing we had Coach Mac, pacing up and down North Harvard Street like a general, inspiring us with words of motivation mixed with threats of death.

"Come on, men! Keep pumping that iron! Pretend those dumbbells are Yale players and make them your bitches!" Our game against Yale, Harvard's lifelong rival, was five weeks away. "Yale thinks you guys are a bunch of soft-cocks," Mac bellowed. "They think Harvard football is unlegit. But deep down they're terrified of you because they know you guys are a bunch of tough-ass, blue-collar animals who can destroy anyone!" He said this as a group of teenage girls waiting for a bus across the street caught sight of us and broke out into a giggle-fest.

"Yale thinks they're so tough," he continued, "but let me tell you something: they have tiny fucking balls. Tiniest balls I've ever seen!"

So far I'd give Coach Mac's speech a 7.2 on the inspiration scale, deducting a couple of points for the implication that he had studied the Yale players' balls.

"The 'Yale Bulldogs,'" he mocked their name with a high-pitched voice. "What a bunch of frauds! We're going to neuter those sons of bitches!"

I had to give Coach Mac credit for the clever use of canine nomenclature, though the wordplay was likely unintentional. Harvard coaches and students were always ripping on Yale's mascot, the bulldog, but I didn't think we could really talk. I mean, we were the "Harvard Crimson," which is a measly color. At least Yale has a mascot with teeth—we're just a shade of lipstick. I guess if you really wanted to stretch it you could say we are a type of crayon, but even then the worst we could do to a bulldog is give it colorful poop.

"We're going to crush Yale because we're going to outwork them, starting right now, on this goddamn street! Those Yalies are doing nothing but sitting in their armchairs and sipping their tea and talking about the queen." I had the sneaking suspicion Coach Mac had no idea where Yale was even located, but the sheer emotional conviction of his speech coupled with my exhaustion had me drinking the anti-Yale Kool-Aid.

Yeah, fuck those crumpet-eating bastards! A surge of energy coursed through me as I cranked out several more curls.

I maintained my furious pace for a couple of minutes, but soon my adrenaline faded and was overtaken by an alarming reality: *I can't lift anymore. My arms are going to fall off.* I wasn't sure what Coach Mac would do to me if I dropped my weights, but considering he had neutering on his mind, I didn't want to find out. I glanced over at Mac, who was standing near Jason and poking his man-boobs for motivational purposes. *Please don't come this way*, I thought as I slowed my curling pace considerably. Panic overwhelmed me as I struggled to keep lifting the dumbbells with my burning biceps, and I could feel my grip loosening on the cold metal bars. I had to think of some new motivation—and quick.

If you want to be a beast at lifting…you need to have big balls.

The image of Coach Mac's ginormous testicles popped into my head, and I immediately dropped the weights. They crashed to the pavement with piercing clangs.

"KESTER!" Before I could even process what had just happened, Coach Mac was standing in front of me. "Why am I not surprised? Sometimes I think you *want* to be small the rest of your life." He put his hand on my left bicep and laughed. "This is Arm Farm, not Ant Farm!"

"I—I'm sorry, I didn't mean to…"

"Kester, did you know that ninety-nine percent of small businesses fail? If you want to be small, that's your fucking business!"

I felt like explaining to Coach Mac that the reason most small businesses fail is because they expand too quickly, but I didn't want to short-circuit the wiring in his brain. I understood that size and strength were essential ingredients to a successful football team, but Coach Mac was under the delusion that large muscles would give us the mental edge in any matchup because of their ability to intimidate the opposition. Like the opposing quarterback would see me rushing toward him with my bulging biceps then curl into the fetal position while I grabbed the ball from his trembling hands and ran into the end zone, claiming a touchdown and *ius primae noctis* on his girlfriend.

Size was everything to Coach Mac, and he had made my life a living hell ever since my very first day on the team, when I fell short of my weight goal by ten pounds.

Coach Mac had several different techniques to help me gain weight—all slightly insane, all damaging to my self-worth. Sometimes he would use a subtle approach, using passive-aggressive comments to hint at ways in which I could get bigger.

"Kester, do you know why I eat so many bananas?" he once asked, stuffing a piece of the fruit down his throat.

"I don't know. Because they're delicious?"

"Have you ever seen a small fucking gorilla?"

Other times Coach Mac would try to be discreet, like when he would sneak up to me while I was bench-pressing and stuff powdered donuts in my mouth. He would also sit with me after almost every practice, tossing handfuls of protein bars at me the way a kid might throw peanuts at a depressed animal in the zoo. It was at one of these feeding sessions that Coach Mac first suggested I try a supplement called creatine, a performance-enhancer that was gaining popularity with athletes seeking to gain muscle.

"It will help you pack on weight, and it isn't even illegal yet," Coach Mac explained, handing me a giant bottle of the white powder. "Just mix it with water and drink it before and after every workout. Personally, I like to add a couple of scoops to my coffee every morning. Nothing like caffeine and creatine to get your day going. It's like killing two birds with one sledgehammer!"

"Isn't this kind of dangerous?" I asked. "What are the side effects?"

Coach Mac snatched the container back from me and inspected the label on the back. His eyes grew wide. "Oh dear," he said gravely. "It says here that 'side effects may include getting fucking huge, with occasional bouts of manliness.'" He shoved the can of creatine back in my arms. "Stop being such a Sally and take out your tampon. Get with the goddamn program."

"Getting huge" became an obsession of mine, as it seemed like the only way I could impress the coaching staff and start making an impact on the football team. The season was coming to a close, and at that point I hadn't even stepped on the field in our games. The lack of playing time didn't bother me so much, as this wasn't uncommon for a freshman, but it was a little humiliating during practice when I was repeatedly asked to stand in for the new tackling dummies because they were expensive and the coaches wanted to reduce their wear and tear. The physical abuse I endured during practice, coupled with Coach Mac constantly haranguing me to get bigger, made it easy for me to gulp down my creatine twice a day. I have to admit that taking the supplement made me feel like a superhero, not because it made me super-strong, but because my acidic pee could burn through titanium steel.

Even with the creatine, I just couldn't put on the amount of weight the coaching staff wanted to see. The pressure of getting bigger developed into a serious complex of mine, and I developed what could best be described as a state of "reverse anorexia." I soon found myself standing in front of a mirror every day, judging my body like a sixteen-year-old girl living in upside-down world: *Oh hey, slim. Have a good dinner tonight? Yeah, you would turn down that extra dessert. Look at you with your tiny size 38 waist. Want another celery stick, skinny? I hate you.*

The stress of getting bigger and stronger was only intensifying my growing sense of isolation at Harvard. Every student seemed to have a defined purpose there, using his or her remarkable talents to enhance the prestige of the university. In turn, the university provided the students with exceptional resources to help them cultivate their talents, creating a mutually beneficial environment where both the students and the school would prosper from the other's excellence. Upon entering college, I assumed that I too would benefit from Harvard's seemingly magical ability to turn awkward teenagers into well-adjusted, high-achieving adults. I figured I would take my seed of potential, sprinkle a little Harvard on it, and then watch it blossom into a spectacular flower that would make my parents proud and my friends jealous.

I had considered myself an intelligent guy and talented football player, but it didn't take long for Harvard to teach me that I simply wasn't as good as I thought. It seemed like every guy on my team was bigger, faster, and more talented. The same could be said about the brains of my classmates. It was truly depressing to discover that my self-worth was built on what now seemed like a fraudulent foundation. I realized that back in high school I crushed my football opponents not because I was insanely talented, but because half of them had asthma. And those bubbles I filled out so expertly during the SATs? They were just that: empty bubbles. The only thing I had actually accomplished to this point in my life was getting accepted into Harvard, and now I was stripping that feat of its merit.

As a "student-athlete," I wasn't living up to either aspect of my identity. If I couldn't excel in the classroom or on the football field, then what was my purpose at Harvard? How was I contributing? How did I matter? With so many daily reminders that I sucked, it became very difficult for me to justify my place at such an accomplished university. I was failing calculus and struggling at football, and the only person in the entire school who thought I was cool was a fourteen-year-old who tucked his T-shirt into his underwear.

It felt like I was coming up short in every facet of life at Harvard, and my confidence began to wilt. Succeeding at this school no longer seemed like a goal I could achieve on my own, causing me to slip into a mind-set of desperation that was rapidly weakening my values. I didn't like who I was becoming, but I couldn't stop the transformation.

And now I had a coach who was upset that I wasn't more like a gorilla. But if you asked my crush, who had seen my hairy chest, and Professor Phlegm, who had seen my grades, they would say I was pretty damn close.

Chapter Four

INTO THE DEPTHS OF THE PUSEY

I had heard it so many times I finally accepted it as fact: "Getting into Harvard is the hardest part. Once you're there everyone gets straight A's." It was all anybody said about my future college, so I entered my freshman year keenly aware of Harvard's infamous grade inflation.

I imagined myself returning home after my first semester to a hero's welcome as I triumphantly waved my report card above my head for all to see. With a tear of joy forming in the corner of his eye, my dad would sit me down and say, "Son, remember the time we discovered that you recorded over one of our home videos with an adult movie, and your mother vomited and I looked you in the eye and said in a painfully somber voice that I was very disappointed in you?" "Yes, dad, I think of that moment every day of my life." "Well," he'd say, pointing at the column of A's on my report card, "this little masterpiece has made me forget all about that."

My mom would then give me a big hug. "And I'm sorry for all the times I made you get a haircut," she'd say. "Now let's get that report card in a frame and set it on the mantel. There's a spot right in front of that picture of your sister."

As it turned out, I spent my entire freshman year standing on

the corner alone and cold, waiting for the Harvard grade inflation bus to pick me up. Apparently I was not on its route. Was I
the only person who wasn't getting good grades? It was difficult
to tell, as most Harvard students would rather admit to getting
a C on their hepatitis test than on their history test. All I knew
was that if there was a war between vowels and consonants on
my report card, the vowels wouldn't stand a chance. And now
my dad would have that shocking scene of *Indiana Bones and the
Temple of Poon* forever seared in his memory.

Perhaps the most humiliating part of getting poor grades at a
school known for its grade inflation is that I had made a serious
effort to sign up for the easiest classes I could find. This strategy
required several hours of perusing Harvard's imposing three-
hundred-page course catalog, which, I learned, conveniently
doubles as a blunt weapon for smashing against your head.

The vast majority of the classes seemed way over my head. I read
over every course title, each one seemingly more terrifying than the
last: *Neurobiology 135: Current Topics in Cognitive Neuroscience
Research; Literature 137: Postcolonial Bildungsroman; Biophysics
360: Enzymatic Mechanisms and Antibiotic Biosynthesis.* Holy
shit, are these for real? Does Harvard *actually* have 360 biophysics classes? As I read further, I learned the curriculum does little to
debunk the university's reputation of being pretentious, a perception only strengthened by the fact that Harvard offers not one but
two history classes *about itself.* I found the offering of these two
courses to be almost as offensively vain as those cocky assholes
who write books about themselves.

The language used in the catalog seemed ostentatious and

superfluous, and I needed a dictionary by my side just to get through the intensely verbose course descriptions. Here's an example of an actual course description pulled straight from Harvard's catalog:

Physics 289: Functional Integration and Renormalization
The course will revolve around Euclidean expectations, functional integrals, and real-time quantum theory for bosons, fermions, and gauge interactions, with properties of symmetry, supersymmetry, and renormalization.

Um...what? I know literally five words in that entire description. "Bosons?" "Gauge interactions?" "Revolve?" What is this crap? And what the hell is "supersymmetry"? Symmetry is an all-or-nothing type of thing, isn't it? How can something be MORE than symmetrical? What am I getting myself into? I wish I were dead. No, I wish I were superdead.

Harvard's academic reputation spoke for itself, but I had a hard time envisioning how these types of courses would serve me in my adult life. I tried to imagine a situation on a plane where a woman collapses in the aisle. "Help!" her daughter would cry, "my mom has collapsed! I think her Euclid has closed up!"

"Everybody stand back!" I'd shout, flashing my enormous Harvard class ring like a badge as I rushed to the woman's side. "I once took a course on Euclidean expectations. Now, does anyone have any spare fermions? We need to renormalize this woman, ASAP!"

By the time I finished scanning the catalog, I seriously questioned whether this whole college thing was really meant for me. Frustrated, I tossed the catalog under the radiator in my room, out of sight. Later that night, after the firemen arrived, I reconsidered my stance and decided that maybe I should continue my education after all.

While I'm sure the majority of Harvard's classes were interesting, I was looking for something more along the lines of *Science: An Introduction.* I wasn't fortunate enough to come across any courses quite so rudimentary, but I did manage to discover a handful of classes in Harvard's expansive directory that met my strict requirements of (a) not containing any words in the course description longer than four syllables, and (b) not meeting before 10:00 a.m. After much deliberation, I narrowed down my final schedule to a history class about gladiators, an English course on fairy tales, a science lecture about dinosaurs, and an anthropology seminar about space aliens. On paper, my schedule of "GLADIATORS— FAIRY TALES—DINOSAURS—ALIENS" looked strikingly similar to a list I had written as a five-year-old entitled "MY FaVoRiTE ThINgs!!!!!" It wasn't exactly the type of rigorous curriculum you'd expect from The World's Greatest University. Nor was it something you'd pay fifty thousand dollars for.

"This has to be some sort of joke, right?" my dad said when he first heard my proposed class schedule over the phone.

"No, Dad, these classes are legit," I answered. "They have syllabuses and everything!"

"But fairy tales? Son, we talked about this last year. You have to move on to more sophisticated books."

"According to the class description,"—I paused a moment to open the course catalog—"fairy tales are anything but, uhh, 'platitudinous.' So…yeah." I wasn't going down without a fight.

"And the class on aliens? That's about immigration policy, I hope."

"Well, not exactly. But I'm sure we will have to come up with some sort of immigration standard once they actually arrive."

"Where did your mother and I go wrong with you?" my father groaned.

"Come on, Dad. You've always told me to follow my passion. Remember how I wanted to be a dinosaur when I grew up?"

"Of course. It was kind of cute, until you hit puberty." He sighed, and I could hear faint whispers as he began to mutter to himself like he always does when I stress him out. Finally, he reached a decision. "If you really feel strongly about this, I'm not going to stop you. But gee whiz, at least take one math class or something."

I wasn't crazy about the suggestion, but I figured one math course wouldn't kill me, and it might even be useful. Ever since I was accepted into Harvard it was a common occurrence at restaurants for the table to expect me to calculate the gratuity on our check, like it was *so hard* to know that to compute a 20 percent tip you simply move the decimal one spot to the left, then multiply that number by twenty. Still, maybe the knowledge I gained in a math class would save me the trouble of discretely fumbling with my cell phone under the table as I tried to use its calculator feature.

So one of my carefully selected courses had to be replaced and, like every major decision at that time, I made my choice based on how I thought girls would perceive me. "Fairy Tales" was the least masculine sounding class of the bunch, so it had to go. I replaced it with the integral calculus course taught by Professor Phlegm, a decision that, according to my therapist, I need to forgive myself for.

If calculus was the big bully who beat me up and stole my

lunch money, then my three other classes were my supposed "friends" who secretly talked shit about me behind my back. My dinosaurs professor was a super-enthusiastic, friendly guy with a cheerful Australian accent that made it sound like he was lecturing about golden retrievers rather than vicious reptiles. His obsession with dinosaurs was borderline insane, but as an avid dino lover myself, I had to respect anyone who reportedly named his two sons Ty and Rex. When it was time for our first test, though, he made us memorize the names of about two hundred different dinosaur bones, none of which, I learned the hard way, were called "legs," "tail," or "head."

I was ecstatic when I first learned my gladiators professor was the historical consultant for the blockbuster movie *Gladiator*, a film I had seen maybe, like, five hundred times. But instead of writing essays about the proper techniques of decapitation, I found myself laboring over a paper discussing how the architectural design of amphitheaters in the southwest region of Gaul reflected the changing socioeconomic structure of the Roman Empire. As for my class about aliens, let's just say I grossly underestimated how seriously Harvard students take their science fiction. I simply couldn't compete with kids who spent their free time producing podcasts touting Captain Picard over Captain Kirk.

I certainly struggled with these supposed "cupcake" classes, but at least I was performing well enough to pass them. The same could not be said about calculus. My 38 on the first test was a cruel reminder that grade inflation at Harvard is largely an urban myth perpetuated by the media and jealous Yalies. Logically, I should have realized that the idea of grade inflation was too good to be true. Many of Harvard's classes are graded on a scale, meaning that your success in the class is relative to the performance of other students. Only a predetermined percent-age of the class could receive A's, so you are competing with your classmates for a ration of high grades. *Someone* had to fail, and in the case of this calculus midterm, that someone was me.

I tried to look at the bright side by thinking of myself as a kind of humanitarian, a noble citizen who sacrificed himself for the greater good by bringing down the scale for everyone else. It was like a form of community service, I convinced myself. Sure, it may have been community service against my will, but so was the social work I did after my brief infatuation with firecrackers and mailboxes; and let me tell you, those smiling old folks didn't give a damn that my visits to the retirement home were actually ordered by the state.

Despite my attempt to focus on the positive aspects of my struggles, I finally realized that, if I wanted to make it past fresh-man year, I would have to pursue extra help in calculus. At first my pride prevented me from signing up for a tutor, as I hated the idea of actually paying a fellow student to feel superior to me. But I was willing to endure anything if it meant I didn't have to hang out in the Pusey with Professor Phlegm, so I reluctantly signed up for a calculus tutor.

On the day of our first session, my tutor introduced himself as "Marc, with a *c*" as if I gave two shits about how he spelled his name.

"Hey, I'm Eric," I said, slamming my calculus textbook down on the table, "with an F."

Marc was tall, about six feet, and very overweight. His ample cheeks hogged the majority of his face, forcing his eyes to be crunched into a permanent squinting position.

I wasn't surprised by Marc's appearance because I had thoroughly researched him on Facebook prior to meeting him. "TheFacebook," as it was called at the time, was a new phenomenon my freshman year, a little side project launched a few months prior by this Harvard kid who was a couple of years ahead of me. Harvard students are constantly inventing random shit in their dorm rooms, turning brilliant ideas into reality. Personally, I wasn't really into the whole "entrepreneurship" craze at Harvard. It didn't bother me too much—different people are into different things. Mark Zuckerberg spent his time making Facebook in his Harvard dorm room, and I spent my time making cups of ramen noodles. Both are special in their own way.

Anyway, Facebook proved quite useful for shy students like me who wanted to get to know their classmates without going through the pesky trouble of actually talking to anyone. My first extended session on Facebook was a few weeks back when I spent nearly two hours clicking through the pictures of all sixteen hundred of my classmates in an effort to find the smokeshow that I walked by on move-in day. I couldn't get the girl out of my head and, despite my epically bad first impression, I was determined to get to know her. As much as I liked Vikas, I *had* to expand my social circle beyond pubescent nerds. This quest for the girl, for reasons I didn't understand at the time, seemed as critically important as passing calculus.

My obsessively diligent search through Facebook, though, came up empty. Maybe she hadn't signed up yet, or maybe she had set her profile to "private," as pretty girls tend to do when they suspect guys are visiting their page for less than honorable purposes. Her absence was certainly a discouraging setback, but, as the coming days would prove, it wouldn't be enough for me to give up on her. Unfortunately, an idiotic eighteen-year-old with a serious crush is not easily deterred.

Marc the tutor had a Facebook page, at least, and his profile revealed quite a bit about him. You could tell that he was self-conscious about his weight just by looking at his profile picture, which was a blurry image of him standing about fifty yards away from the camera. I'm guessing Marc chose this particular picture because he actually looked fairly trim in it, at least compared to the Rocky Mountains sitting in the background. Any fat-kid sympathy I felt for him quickly dissolved, however, when I saw that under "Favorite Quote" he wrote "Stock." I grew even more skeptical of the kid when I saw his "About Me" section, which read: "Meddle not in the affairs of dragons, for you are crunchy and good with ketchup!" When I finished reviewing Marc's Facebook page, I opened the door to my bedroom and called out to my roommates: "Guys, you gotta check out this fucking loser!" My voice echoed through the empty room. It was Saturday night and they had already left for a party a few hours earlier.

It turned out Marc wasn't such a bad tutor, though. So I felt especially bad for firing him halfway through our first session. But, to put it nicely, the guy smelled like ass. When he reached out to shake my hand, a waft of invisible nastiness shot out from under his arm and punched me in the face. Marc's odor was so pungent that I could literally taste him, resulting in a level of intimacy that no student should be forced to share with his math tutor. During my time at Harvard I found the stereo-type about nerds smelling bad to be mostly exaggerated, but Marc had an impenetrable force field of B.O. that extended a good five feet from his soft, pudgy body. If you look like the

Pillsbury Doughboy, I think it's your obligation to society to at least smell delicious.

Not wanting to risk another nauseating session with a new tutor, I asked Vikas if he would help me with calculus. He was ecstatic about the idea, but his parents quickly shot it down. Apparently they felt I was a bad influence over the impressionable youngster. "We got in a fight the other day," he explained, "and I told them I thought my physics class was some gay-ass shit."

Out of options and with the final exam fast approaching, I reluctantly made my way over to the Pusey Library to meet with Professor Phlegm. If I knew how short our meeting was going to be, I wouldn't have even bothered.

———◆◆◆———

Harvard possesses so many libraries that the university has literally lost count of them. Recent estimates place the number somewhere between seventy and ninety, though the most popular approximation seems to be "a shitload."

The Pusey is one of only three libraries situated within the Yard. A small structure that is built mostly underground, the Pusey rests in the shadow of the stately Widener Library, Harvard's most monumental erection. It was ceremoniously named after Nathan Pusey, the president of the university from 1953–1971. Like President Leonard Hoar before him, Nathan Pusey had a difficult time commanding the full respect of the students.

The Pusey Library boasts the oldest map and atlas collection in America. It seems pointless to me to save a collection of outdated and inaccurate maps, but Harvard loves to own anything they can tag with "oldest" or "largest," even if it's something as useless as the world's largest collection of VHS tapes. The school's admissions catalog shows no restraint when boasting about all of Harvard's superlatives: "Oldest institution of higher learning!" "Largest academic library in the world!" "Most varsity sports in the NCAA!" I wouldn't even put it past Harvard to advertise "Most Virgins!" but until they come up with statistical proof, they'll have to settle for the next closest thing: "Largest glee club!"

Professor Phlegm didn't have an office of his own, so he spent most of his time at a tiny desk in the basement of the Pusey. He had been conducting serious research on a topic that required dusty old books, so having an isolated spot inside the library stacks was ideal for him. He stood up when he saw me approaching his table in the corner of the basement.

"Ah, Meester Keester, you hov arrived for tutorialing," he announced, like I needed assistance figuring out where I was and what I was doing there. "Please, zit down." I had already taken my seat when he said this, so I acknowledged his request by crossing my legs. "Deed you hov troobul finding dis place?" Phlegm asked pleasantly.

"Nope. It was pretty easy, actually," I replied.

"Good, good. Dis libury eez my favorite." He surveyed the room, smiling. "Vhen you zee it outside you tink de Pussy eez small, but den you come inside and realize dare eez much room. Still, it eez alvays stuffed vith great schoolers."

Prepared for such a moment, I immediately pulled a clump of tissues out of my pocket and pretended to blow my nose, effectively concealing my smile. Just like on dates, you only make the mistake of showing up without protection once.

"Ah, you hov de allergies I zee." Phlegm said. "I used to hov terrible allergies right here." He demonstrated by pinching the bridge of his nose between his index finger and thumb.

"Vhenever I entered de Pussy, de pressure vas so great I felt like I vas going to explode!"

I blew my nose again. *Is he fucking with me?* He seemed completely oblivious, but part of me suspected I was the unwitting subject of a hidden camera show.

"I am allergeek to doost," Phlegm continued, "so you can imageen my exit-ment last year vhen dey removed de carpet from de Pussy."

Completely out of tissues and restraint, I made a sprint for the bathroom and, once safely inside, burst out in laughter. A guy using one of the urinals quickly zipped up his fly and hurried out, blushing. I took a moment to collect myself, then returned to Professor Phlegm and explained that I had a severe medical condition that would prevent me from completing our meeting.

As I recounted my conversation word for word to my roommates later that night, I couldn't manage to shake the unnerving implications the failed meeting would have on my calculus grade. Tutoring wasn't effective. Studying didn't seem to help either. And there was no way I could go back to Professor Phlegm, especially now that he believed I had an acute diarrhea disorder.

I could have dropped the class, but that would have resulted in a nasty "INCOMPLETE" on my transcript—a designation even worse than an F. I pictured a future employer, like Goldman Sachs maybe, calling up Professor Phlegm to receive a reasonable explanation of my "INCOMPLETE" before presenting me a lucrative job offer.

"Vhy yes, I taught Meester Keester," he'd say. "I did not tink he vas de type who vas innerested in Gold Man-Sachs. But I do not know vhy he quit my class." He'd pause a moment in thought. "It vas probully because of his loose stools."

Surely it was better to suffer an F then drop out of the class at this point, but Harvard forces you to retake any course in which if you receive a D+ or below. Just the thought of another semester of integral calculus made me feel physically ill, and the stress induced by the class would probably trigger the very ailment I had lied to Professor Phlegm about.

An even bigger consequence was at stake. Between my utter incompetence in calculus and my considerable struggles in my other three classes, failing out of Harvard was now a frightening reality. How would I explain to people back home that I flunked out of a school where grade inflation supposedly kept everyone afloat? My friends and family were so incredibly proud of me, their Harvard boy. Maybe it was my imagination, but it seemed like they held me in higher esteem ever since I got into the prestigious university. And I knew that if I failed out, I would feel as irrelevant at home as I did at Harvard. I wouldn't matter anywhere.

It was startling to see how far my ambitions had fallen since the summer when I was an enthusiastic prefrosh. Sure, I had been nervous going in, but I held on to a small hope that maybe I wasn't an admissions mistake; maybe Harvard had actually seen something special in me that I had yet to discover myself. My perspective had changed now that I knew I was even further behind the students than I originally anticipated. Now my goal was no longer to thrive at Harvard, but to survive Harvard.

My entire life I had heard the endless praise heaped upon the university, and I was well aware that I had been given a truly special opportunity to go to school here. There were thousands of people who would do anything to trade places with me, and here I was on the verge of wasting my privilege. I mean, this was *HARVARD*, the world-renowned pinnacle of education. I couldn't just let it slip through my fingers. Failure was not an option. I decided right then and there that I was going to survive it at all costs.

As the crisp days of late October became shorter and the winter final exams drew nearer, it was clear that drastic measures were needed. There was only one person left at Harvard who could help me, and I really, really didn't want to visit him.

Chapter Five

TRIPPING ON A-BOMBS

After the second knock, Tripp opened the door to his room. He was buck-ass naked and holding a roll of duct tape. He looked at me and frowned.

"You don't look anything like the girl I ordered."

I was not in the mood for Tripp's shenanigans. "Quit the act, Tripp. I just texted you, like, two minutes ago. You knew I was coming over." This was not a leisure visit. I was here on business.

"Just fucking with you, man." Tripp laughed and revealed bleach-white teeth, which popped against the shade of his dark tan. This was genuine laughter from Tripp, a rare occurrence reserved only for his own jokes and people who fall down stairs.

He invited me inside, and as I passed by him he offered his fist for a pound at the exact moment I went for a high-five, creating an awkward situation where I sort of clasped my hand around the nub of his clenched fist. This is an uncomfortable situation under any circumstance, but it felt infinitely weirder doing it with a guy whose peacock was on full display.

There are three types of students at Harvard: nerds, athletes, and legacies. These categories will overlap occasionally, but if you go to Harvard, you undoubtedly fit into at least one of these three classifications.

Now every university has these sorts of students, but at Harvard the stereotypes are amplified. We have the dorkiest nerds, the wealthiest legacies, and the most athletic...umm, well, I hear our squash team is outstanding.

Legacies—wealthy kids who got in because their rich families had always gone to Harvard and likely donated a bunch of money there—were the minority group on campus, but easily the most despised. A sizable fraction of the student body had spent their entire lives honing a unique talent to improve their chances of getting into Harvard—baton-twirling, tuba-playing, Guatemalan basket-weaving—anything that may distinguish them from other applicants and enhance their candidacy. So you can't really blame these students for loathing the legacies who got accepted into Harvard just because they put their last name on the application.

Despite the widespread acrimony toward them, male legacies always had the easiest time picking up girls, a trend that I found puzzling. I suppose a pickup line like "Want to come back to my dorm? It's named after me," is a bit more persuasive than what I had to use: "Want to come back to my dorm? I just vacuumed my futon." In the competition for girls, there was a clear hierarchy among the three categories of students: legacies beat athletes, athletes beat nerds, and nerds beat off.

Now in his third year at Harvard, Tripp was exclusively a legacy. Since its founding in 1636, thirty-three of Tripp's relatives had attended Harvard. "Thirty-five, if you count Gramp's illegitimate kids," he would brag. Contrary to popular belief, an applicant is not necessarily guaranteed admission to Harvard if one of their relatives attended the university. (I imagine the children of former Enron president Jeffrey Skilling, for instance, would have a hard time even making the waitlist.) But there are a number of powerful families whose lineage is so entrenched in Harvard that even an offspring with the approximate IQ of a beach ball would be embraced by the school. Tripp was a member of one of these influential families, which is lucky for him considering he's more than a few fries short of a Happy Meal.

I should point out that Harvard admissions does make some effort to avert the unqualified legacies away from the school (without losing the family's generous donations, of course). While regular applicants who don't quite meet admissions standards get placed on the waitlist, powerful legacies who don't measure up are placed on what's known as the "Z-list." This means the legacy is officially admitted into Harvard (saving the family from shame and embarrassment), though he or she must take one or two years off before coming to school. The hope is that the Z-listed legacy would rather attend another college than wait two years to start his or her education at Harvard. It's the most desirable outcome for the admission's office, as the school can maintain a positive relationship with a powerful family while keeping the unqualified student from diluting Harvard's renowned excellence.

The Z-list doesn't work quite so well in reality, though, because most of these legacies are perfectly happy to wait to attend Harvard. When the choice is either to attend a third-rate school now or take two years to ski in Europe then enter Harvard as a twenty-one-year-old freshman, it's a no-brainer. It was for Tripp, anyway.

To be honest, I barely remember the first time I met Tripp. It was a Saturday in late September, and the football team had just pulled off an exciting one-point victory over Brown. A junior wide receiver held a victory party in his room that night, and of course I was there, since I was never invited to any non-football parties and this seemed to be the only perk I got for being on the team. In addition to my teammates there were a bunch of girls and a few other upperclassmen, including Tripp, who was always at the center of the popular scene.

Unfortunately, being at a cool party and being cool at a party are two different things, so I spent most of my evening leaning against a wall with my lips locked to various cans of light beer. Without much conversation to distract me, I soon exhausted my supply of alcohol—a situation that had to be rectified ASAP. I began to stagger around looking for some more beer like a desert wanderer searching for water. I would have done anything for an oasis, or in this case a beer funnel or similar apparatus designed to simultaneously destroy my liver and make me cooler.

As I searched, I recall concentrating my impaired vision just long enough to make out the blurry image of Tripp standing on a table, a cigar in one hand and a funnel in the other. We were a match made in heaven. The ensuing drunken moment served as the foundation for a bond between us, though our friendship was about as watered down as the Keystone Light he poured down my throat that night.

———◆———

"It took you long enough to visit me, Kes. It's already November." Tripp walked over to his door and turned the bolt lock.

"Yeah, I can't believe I haven't been here yet," I said with forced incredulity as I took a seat on the leather L-shaped couch that wrapped around a corner of Tripp's common room.

My inherent social awkwardness prevents me from looking people in the eye when I talk to them, but sensing that Tripp had little intention of putting on clothes anytime soon, I locked my stare above his neck. His dirty blond hair was a perfect mess of organized chaos, giving off the "I'm too chill to give a shit about my appearance" look, even though it was painfully evident that he spent an hour positioning each strand of his tussled hair. It was difficult to tell if the light blond streaks developed from extended periods of lying out in the sun on his family's yacht or from one of his hair products that cost more than any liquid indigenous to earth ought to. Combine his boy-band haircut with a symmetrical face and a cleft chin that punctuated his prominent jawline, and Tripp looked like a male avatar a middle school girl might create in The Sims.

"Don't say I haven't invited you up here," Tripp said as he stooped down to grab a Newcastle beer out of his mini-fridge. "It's a privilege I don't bestow on many people."

Tripp didn't know it, but I had actually been avoiding him for most of the semester. He was a genuine douchehole: equal parts douchebag and asshole. The funny thing is that my animosity toward Tripp wasn't focused so much on his reprehensible qualities (of which there were many), but more on myself for feeling an irrepressible compulsion to impress the douchehole whenever I was around him. I also wasn't a fan of the nickname he gave me after he saw me sitting next to Vikas in calculus lecture. It was kind of funny on a normal day, I guess, but he definitely didn't have to refer to me as "Kester the Molester" when he met my mom and dad at parents' weekend.

Looking around Tripp's room, I was glad I hadn't spent much time there. It looked exactly like you'd expect from a rich kid who's never had to clean up after himself. A half dozen empty beer bottles rested on top of the big screen TV in the corner of the room, and his floor was littered with wrinkled sports coats, cummerbunds, and PlayStation games, most of which were still in their plastic shrink-wrap. A framed five-by-seven photograph of Tripp's family at a sailing regatta sat on the mantel above the fireplace, and a crooked poster of two girls making out on a keg hung from the wall directly above it. His large, leather couch was ridiculously comfortable, which was a good thing considering that old spilled beer was causing its surface to stick to my legs.

Tripp wasn't happy that I had ignored his repeated requests to hang out with him, and he wasn't going to let me off easy. "I mean, Christ, it's not like you have a thriving social life that's keeping you busy," he said. "I thought at least after you failed our first test you would sprint over here as soon as the class was over and beg me for help."

Tripp had received a 95 on the calculus test that had so ruth-lessly violated me. I think he had attended maybe three classes all semester, but it wasn't difficult to get that grade when you possess the specialized skill set that Tripp had perfected. His cheating prowess was renowned on campus, and his room developed into a home base for desperate students seeking "special academic help." Tripp's expertise in cheating evolved out of necessity, as his intellectual capacity was too limited to survive Harvard's aca-demic rigors. Of course, failing out of Harvard was simply not an option in his family, so Tripp found one needy student to write his essays for him, paying $750 *per paper*.

His dishonesty only escalated from there, expanding into a

cheating empire involving not just himself but every student who wanted to cheat (or get paid by those to cheat off them). His legend peaked in a legendary performance in his sophomore year after he skipped a final exam he didn't feel like taking. When he was brought in front of the college's disciplinary board, Tripp wiped away fake tears as he explained to the Harvard elders that he did not take his exam because he wasn't even in the state. He had to make a midnight trip to New Jersey so he could hold his girlfriend's hand during the abortion. Tripp received a pardon and, the next day, a bouquet of flowers from the board.

Tripp's special ability was the reason I finally visited his room. It was early November and winter exams were still a ways off, but I had to start preparing for the hurricane. "Well, I wanted to talk you about calculus, actually." I said to him. "I hate this… but the way things are going, it looks like cheating might be my only option."

"Jesus, will you keep your fucking voice down?" Tripp grabbed a towel hanging on the corner of his closet door, got on his knees, and stuffed it in the crack under his door. For a naked dude, he was really bending over way too often. I focused my eyes on the family crest that was tattooed to the upper left shoulder blade of Tripp's back. Maybe it was a mistake by the tattoo artist or maybe our symbols of prestige have changed vastly since sixteenth century England, but the crest looked kind of like a cross-eyed lion humping an irritated phoenix.

"And stop acting so high and mighty," Tripp continued in a hushed voice. "Think of it like steroids in baseball: if you're not doing it, then you don't want to be the best. And *everyone* at this school wants to be the best."

Tripp was right. Cheating is as much a tradition at Harvard

as academic excellence. Lying, cheating, and double-crossing are frequent at the university, which should come as no surprise from a school that produces so many successful politicians. Senator Ted Kennedy, for instance, dabbled in the cheating culture while he was an undergraduate in the spring of 1951. Concerned about maintaining his eligibility for his upcoming football season, Kennedy was flagged for crossing the line of academic honesty. Some supporters claim Kennedy didn't do anything, and they're technically correct, because it was his friend who took his Spanish exam for him. Like so many other elaborate, seemingly fail-proof cheating schemes at Harvard, this subterfuge was quickly foiled and both parties were expelled from the university. A year later Kennedy reapplied to the school and was admitted, as is often the case at Harvard when a student demonstrates exemplary behavior and a good last name. I don't know what happened to his partner in crime, though it's been rumored that he was "expunged"—Harvard's most severe form of punishment where the student is stricken from all university records and, for all intents and purposes, might as well not exist.

It really isn't difficult to cheat at Harvard, though the school does make some efforts to suppress its ubiquity. Some courses, for instance, force you to sign an honor code before each test. Students still cheat—they just feel a little guiltier about it. If you fall ill during an exam and need medical assistance, you are escorted to the "Isolation Chamber" in the university hospital, where you are held incommunicado until you are well enough to complete the test. My buddy Ryan experienced this prisoner-of-war treatment one time after he fainted in the middle of an exam. He woke up in the hospital, where he stayed for the next four days. I wasn't worried about his absence, as Ryan is a pretty intense dude and it wasn't unusual for him to disappear for a few days if a test didn't go well, but his parents became concerned when he wasn't on his flight home for winter vacation. When they called Harvard inquiring into Ryan's whereabouts, the university informed them that their son was recuperating from a case of meningitis, and—good news!—the doctors were now confident he would recover enough to live a full and active life, after he regained his vision and completed his exam, of course. Ryan's parents asked to speak with him, but their request was denied in case they happened to know a thing or two about quantum algorithms.

Until I reached Harvard, I never once considered cheating in school. I wish I could attribute my cheating abstinence to a highly refined moral compass, but in reality I never cheated because I was too big of a wuss. I'm not positive when my fear of cheating began, but it probably has to do with the time I entered a cheat code for *Mortal Kombat* and my father threatened to throw my Sega Genesis out the goddamn window. That was easily the most scarring experience of my childhood (at least until my dad gathered the family around to watch a home video, and instead of watching my sister's first steps we saw Indiana Bones "searching for fortune and glory" inside a busty woman's Temple of Poon).

Sensing my hesitation, Tripp offered an alternative solution. "If you don't want to cheat, I've got a few other things that can help you get ready for the exam," he said casually as he made his way over to his desk. "Are you an Adderall guy or a Ritalin guy?"

I had never tried either of these drugs, so I didn't know. "Uh, whatever you have the most of," I said. As Tripp rifled through a drawer full of small plastic bags filled with tiny pills, I took a moment to consider what I was getting myself into. Adderall abuse was prevalent on campus, but I wasn't sure I wanted to end up like the students who exploited the "A-bombs," as they were called.

When I first settled in at Harvard, I was shocked at how focused and efficient many of the students were with their schoolwork. It wasn't at all weird for a student to come back from an all-nighter in the library having completed two essays, three reading assignments, and a ranked match in his online chess league. A girl once told me that she woke up at 5:00 a.m. most mornings to sneak into a secluded room of Memorial Chapel where she would study for four straight hours so she could "you know, get ahead of the competition." How were they pulling off this insanity, I wondered. I couldn't type up one page of an essay without refreshing my email forty-five times, even though I knew the only messages I received at one in the morning were the ones that (erroneously) implied that I could use an "enhancement" in my pants.

I soon discovered that Adderall at Harvard was like M&M's at a candy store or painkillers in a football locker room. Many students were prescribed Adderall by university doctors, but there was also a thriving black market for the pills. I was just months into my freshman year and I had already heard stories about people exchanging money, sexual favors, and other un-savory business just to score some Addies. They were like our campus blood diamonds. Most students ingested their A-bombs orally, though some of the more intense abusers would snort the drug for a quicker hit.

Strange things happen when Harvard students, who are already hyperintense and overly focused, take a drug designed to amplify their concentration. It's like injecting the Incredible Hulk with anabolic steroids to create some sort of super jacked-up Incredibler Hulk. Blinking, a wasted millisecond in which their eyeballs could be reading something, is eliminated, resulting in bloodshot eyes that would startle a heroin addict. Twitches also develop, and incessant leg bouncing literally shakes the ground in the library during exam periods. Their bodies begin to sweat profusely in an effort to cool down their overheated brains, and their mouths dry up and develop a thin, white crust around the corners of their lips. One look at a 110-pound girl dripping in sweat and chugging from a Big Gulp as she stares at a computer screen positioned three inches from her face, and you would just know she was riding the A-train.

It was frustrating as hell, because if anyone needed an extra boost, it was me, not them. I was way behind in the race to begin with, and suddenly my opponents strapped on freaking jetpacks.

But of course, some students legitimately needed drugs like Adderall to help combat their attention deficit disorder. Tripp was one of these students.

"Did you find them yet?" I asked him, looking up from the *Penthouse* magazine I found wedged in the corner of his couch. Tripp had stopped his search and was now peering out the window. He waved to a squirrel scampering up the trunk of a nearby tree.

"What? Oh right, the Adderall." Tripp grabbed a plastic bag of pills, hopped over a tray of old dining-hall food that was on his floor, and joined me on his couch. He told me he needed a hit now, and asked if I wanted to join. I declined, handing him back the straw he had given me.

"If that's what you want," Tripp said in a defeated tone of

voice, like he was my mom and I had just rejected my vegetables. He used the convex side of a spoon to grind the pale orange tablet on his coffee table, and I watched with concealed fascination as he used the straw to suck up the powder into his nose like a vacuum cleaner. When the last speck disappeared, he triumphantly threw down the straw and paced around the room, sniffling in short, hard bursts while mumbling something about "good shit."

"Why don't you just take it orally? Seems like it would be easier," I said.

Tripp looked at me like I was retarded. "You're retarded. Just think about it. What does Adderall affect? Your brain. So why the hell would you swallow it and send it in the exact opposite direction? Makes no fucking sense. So you use the nose. God created a shortcut to the brain for a reason, bro. I mean, if you were driving to Canada you wouldn't hop on 495 South, right?" I didn't respond, frightened that this whacked logic from a high, naked dude actually made some sense to me.

"Have you done anything like that?" he asked as he picked up a pair of silk boxers off the floor and mercifully slid them on. "Snort, I mean."

"Once," I said, referring to the time in sixth grade I snorted a grape Pixie Stick to impress a girl I had a crush on. I think my stunt may have won her over, but then I sneezed purple snot all over her. "I prefer swallowing, though."

"Yeah, I bet you've had plenty of practice with that," Tripp said as he rummaged through his closet. "Anyway, I'll give you the rest of the Addies in that bag for $150."

My jaw dropped. "That seems like a lot."

"Come on, man, I'm not running a charity here." Tripp held

up two pairs of baby-blue seersucker pants. "Now, which of these is going to score me some ass? I'm going to a garden party at the Hasty Pudding in a few minutes and I have to look fan-fuckin-tastic." One pair was embroidered with tiny whales while the other was dotted with little crabs and lobsters. I told him that either was fine, especially if he was looking to hook up with a mermaid.

"You have a seriously twisted mind, you know that?" Tripp said.

I wanted to retort, but there was no point in arguing with Tripp, so I changed the subject instead. "You know, I doubt those pills could really save my grade at this point, anyway." I let out a heavy sigh, disappointed with what I was about to say. "I still haven't said no to…you know…cheating."

Tripp dropped the pants and clapped his hands together once. "Now we're talking!"

Of course, Tripp already had concocted a plan for our final exam. I had missed the informational meeting Tripp had previously held for all those interested in participating in the scheme, so he filled me in on the details, speaking about his master plan with the same misguided pride a mother possesses when bragging about her "adorable" toddler. The plan was surprisingly intricate, causing me to wonder if Tripp would have been better off just using all that time studying instead of devising such a comprehensive scheme. Specifics aside, Tripp's plot relied entirely on another student in the class, who would feed us answers as we took the exam.

It sounded expensive, and I said so.

"I'm not paying him a dime," Tripp said with a sinister half-smile. "I'm offering him something way, way more valuable."

I didn't want to know what that was.

Our conversation was interrupted by a faint knock at the door. Tripp looked at me and indicated silence by putting his finger to his lips, then walked over the door and put his eye to the peephole. He unlocked the door and swung it open violently. It was Brady, a sophomore legacy whose family owns one third of the land in Kennebunkport, wherever that is. Sporting a pair of leather Sperry Top-Siders, beige corduroy pants, and two layers of Polo shirts with both collars popped, Brady looked like a New England prep school just puked all over him. His outer shirt was basketball orange and featured a supersized Polo logo on the left breast. I folded my arms across my chest and discreetly positioned my right thumb to cover up my regular-sized pony. I began to wonder if I had saved any of those penis enhancement emails when my train of thought was interrupted by Brady asking Tripp if he had "the goods."

"Yeah, I got the goods alright. Check out this beauty." Tripp grabbed a stapled stack of notebook paper from his desk and handed it to Brady, who then sat down next to me on the couch and flipped through the packet. The solutions to that week's calculus problem set were written on the pages in neat, distinctively feminine handwriting.

Easily the most frequent act of cheating at Harvard was the copying of problem sets. These weekly homework assignments were common in most math and science classes, and every Harvard student viewed them as insignificant busywork that just impeded them on their quest for world domination. The primary issue with the problem sets is that they were usually pretty damn hard, and you could forget about sleep if you got stuck on even one question the night before it was due. Now a typical student would gladly give up on one question and sacrifice a miniscule percentage of his or her grade in exchange for a decent night's sleep, but asking a Harvard kid to skip a problem is like asking someone with OCD to skip a hand-washing after using a public restroom. But if one generous friend allows you to copy his or her problem set, then suddenly you have more time for fun things, like your online chess league.

And from there it would spread. For if *you*, being the munificent person that you are, show it to the girl you want to sleep with, she shares it with her roommate, who passes it on to the guy across the hall in exchange for a cup of Easy Mac, and so on and so forth until that slutty problem set has made it across the entire campus in less than four hours. I recall one particularly difficult problem set that was passed around the football team faster than Lizzie Benson, a girl with the lethal combination of a face ugly enough to cripple her self-confidence but a body nice enough to attract guys who prey on the emotionally unstable. Of course, mass copying of homework had one major drawback: if the master problem set was contaminated then everyone who used it would suffer the same negative results. (Come to think of it, that exact scenario occurred with the sharing of Lizzie Benson too.)

"So, is this a good one?" Brady asked while he examined the assignment. "The last problem set you gave me by that little Indian kid—Viscous or whoever—almost fucked me. I got an email from my teacher congratulating me on discovering a feasible solution to the national deficit or some shit. He asked me to present my findings to the entire department, so I had to disappear to the Vineyard for a few days."

Tripp shook his head. "You wouldn't believe what I had to do to get this problem set. Or should I say, *who* I had to do to get this problem set." Tripp's Adderall had clearly arrived in Canada, because now he was talking a mile a minute. "I don't remember the broad's name, but holy shit, she was the most inexperienced girl I've ever nailed. Seriously, I think I was her first kiss."

Like pretty much everything about Tripp, I was simultaneously disgusted and fascinated. "Please tell me you hooked up with that blind girl, Anika," I said.

"Fuck no! Why would I waste these good looks on a girl who can't even appreciate them? Plus, she's got a dog and a pointy stick. Way too many weapons." Tripp used his index finger to scratch off a bit of powder encrusted on the rim of his nostril. "But the girl I hooked up with was a major fucking geek, that's for sure. All I had to do was get two drinks in her and listen to her rant about how we need to switch to wind energy or whatever. After that she was practically begging me to bring her back to my place and play a game of 'Pork-a-Dork.' She was so grateful afterward I almost wanted to give her this couch as a memento for her accomplishment."

I leapt from the couch, suddenly concerned about the cause of its stickiness. Brady failed to connect the dots and remained seated. "And you did all this just so she would give you her problem set?" he asked.

"You should be more grateful, dude. This girl was like a grandma trapped in a twenty-year-old's body. She smelled like mothballs or something. I actually had to spray her with Febreze as I was doing her. Stop laughing! I'm being 100 percent serious. I convinced her it was a natural lubricant that everyone used for sex." Unbelievably, the empty bottle of fabric freshener on the corner of the couch corroborated Tripp's story. The poor girl might have been totally used, but at least she left the place free of allergens.

"Man, this girl was brutal," Tripp continued. "She was wearing a scrunchie and jeans that practically came up to her nipples. No joke. I undid her bra and pants in one motion."

As he said this, I immediately pinpointed Tripp's hookup as the neurotic pen-tapping girl. "I actually know who you're talking about," I bragged. "I touched her ass once." God, I hated myself when I was around Tripp.

"Well, don't start thinking you can steal her away from me," Tripp said sarcastically. "I marked her."

Like every good villain, Tripp would always leave his calling card on his victims. He would take advantage of the awkward "goodbye" hug after a drunken hookup to reach around the girl and tape a sheet of paper to her back, the way a fourth-grader might prank an unsuspecting friend. Instead of "Kick Me," the sign was labeled with his trademark phrase: "Road Trip." It seemed like every Sunday morning I would see some girl in heels stumbling out of Tripp's dorm with mascara smudged about her eyes and a sign fastened to her back broadcasting to the world exactly what she did last night. I guess it was Tripp's way of asserting some dominance over a student body that made him feel stupid and inferior for the first time in his life. Brady found this routine hilarious, at least until the day I managed to slap a copy of Tripp's sign on his back, leading to a new campus nickname for the couple: "The Trust-Fund Gaybies."

In addition to the problem set, Tripp also managed to procure an entire binder of notes from the girl he slept with. I leafed through the pages of exhaustive notes, not sure whether to be impressed or saddened that another human being would actually make this sort of effort. Many of the female students at Harvard take their note-taking a bit too seriously, but the level of detail in this binder was unprecedented. The girl had highlighted all her notes and equations in about twelve different colors of fluorescent pen, resulting in images that probably should've had an epilepsy warning attached. Each color corresponded to a legend in the front of the binder with categories like "Key concept!" "Ask professor after class," and "JUST PLAIN COOL!!" The lamination of all the pages, while completely unnecessary, was a nice touch. I felt like I was observing the work of a great artist, and I genuinely appreciated the mastery of a virtuoso who had perfected her craft. It was like seeing the *Mona Lisa* in person, only without the sense of mild disappointment.

"Okay, serious question," Tripp said, breaking me from my trance. "If you were a chick, would you like this cologne?" He held up a glass Lacoste bottle to my nose.

"Yeah, I guess."

"Homo." Tripp stretched out the waistband of his boxers and gave two quick sprays to his crotch. "Brady, which pants do I go with? Kester was too kinky to give me a straight answer before."

Brady voted for the pair with the embroidered whales.

"Yeah, good call," Tripp said as he stepped into the pants. "Girls don't want to see crabs in your groinal region. Plus, the whales will go perfectly with my Moby Dick."

Brady thanked Tripp for the problem set and took off, saying he needed to meet someone who was going to help him with his history paper about the Ottoman Empire.

Tripp was about ready to go himself, so we reviewed our plan for the exam one last time as he tied his salmon-colored bowtie. Just before leaving, he turned to me and offered one last nugget of wisdom. "I can tell you're nervous about this. Don't be. They say cheaters never prosper, but just take a look at me!" Tripp grinned and held out his arms to provide me a full view of his splendor.

I smiled and nodded, declining to tell him about the crimson blood that had dripped from his nose and onto his seersucker blazer.

Chapter Six

DIVERSITY UNIVERSITY

I had been monitoring the bag of powdered breast milk for more than two months. It had taken residence on Dermot's cluttered desk, sitting idly alongside the broken Ping-Pong paddle, bungee cord, and other knickknacks my roommate had brought with him from Ireland. What purpose did these seemingly random objects serve? I hadn't once spotted Dermot using any of them, yet there they were, placed prominently on his desk. I started to wonder if he waited for me to go to bed before using them to do some seriously kinky shit. It was a petrifying thought, so I began to take note of their exact position on the desk, checking every morning to see if they had been even slightly altered overnight. As far as I could tell, these items hadn't budged since Dermot unpacked them several weeks ago.

I would have asked Dermot about these mysterious trinkets, but it wasn't really an easy topic to bring up casually in conversation. What was I supposed to say? "Hey Derm, a couple of things. First, we're running low on toilet paper, so we should probably pick some up soon. Also, do you snort powdered breast milk with a bungee cord tied around your wrists as you sit on a Ping-Pong paddle with the handle facing up?" Nothing good would come from that conversation. Either Dermot would confirm my worst fear, or he would deny the allegation and wonder what kind of person spends his time thinking up such scenarios. No matter what, someone would be exposed as a total freak.

It didn't help that Dermot and I were having some trouble communicating. His thick accent and persistent usage of Irish slang made it almost impossible for me to understand him, so we were forced to rely mostly on a primitive form of body language. For instance, if Dermot wanted me to turn down the TV because he was going to bed, he'd hold his finger up to his mouth and purse his lips for a "shhh." If he began to snore, I'd use my arm to throw a shoe at him. There was no need for words—body language was the easiest way for us to express our feelings. He'd enter the bathroom, come out ten minutes later and give me a "thumbs up" while I would pinch my nose and give him the finger. It was a passable form of correspondence, I suppose, but it left me uncomfortably unfamiliar with a guy who had a key to my bedroom.

And still, the strange collection of objects sat on Dermot's desk, relentlessly taunting me like an obnoxious riddle. I became borderline obsessed with these perplexing items and examined them from a safe distance approximately several dozen times a day, determined to figure out what they said about the Irishman who cohabited my dwelling. I treated them like my calculus homework, harboring the misguided belief that if I simply stared at the problem long enough the answer would magically come to me. It never did, of course, and I was left with this puzzle occupying an embarrassingly large percentage of my finite brainpower.

Then one Saturday afternoon in November, sometime during my football game against Columbia, they vanished.

When I walked into our common room and noticed that the items were missing, my initial thought was that we had been robbed. Strange as they were, these objects had become such a staple in our room that their sudden absence felt suspicious. But who could possibly want a bag of powdered breast milk, a bungee cord, and a Ping-Pong paddle? A Chinese baby who mountain climbs? No, these baffling trinkets could only belong to a truly mystifying person, and that was unquestionably Dermot.

I scoured our room, fearing that he might've been some type of druid shaman and had slipped the items under my pillow to curse me with their devious magical properties. After confirming that my bed and desk were both safe, I checked all the spots Dermot might keep his personal belongings. I opened his sock-drawer, which was empty except for a comb, toothbrush, a can of Axe body spray, and a half-empty bottle of fish-oil pills. I found nothing under his bed except for his toiletry bag, which was stuffed full of socks. Finally, I discovered the items buried in the overflowing trash bin in our common room. There was the bungee-cord, the broken Ping-Pong paddle…wait, where was the—

"Oye! Eric! I didn't hear you come in." Dermot startled me as he walked out of the bathroom. He then muttered some incomprehensible gibberish in his deep Irish brogue, so I studied his face to try to get a sense of what he was trying to communicate. His blue eyes were relaxed under the shade of his bushy unibrow, which matched the light brown hue of his short, cropped hair. His cheeks were a little flushed and his mouth—whoa, hold on, was that a milk mustache?

At a complete loss, all I could do was utter the American male's most versatile word. "Dude…"

Dermot's face reflected confusion, so I felt compelled to elaborate on my succinct expression of revulsion. The Irish Enigma had some explaining to do, starting with the evidence I just pulled out of the trash. Dermot had kept these items on his desk for over a month, yet the only time he touched them was to toss them in the trash. Why?

"Argh, that shite was gammy," he declared. "A load of ballsch. As useless as a chocolate teapot."

"See, that's what confuses me," I explained. "Clearly this stuff was important enough for you to bring all the way from Ireland, but then you just threw it all away without ever using them. It doesn't make any sense."

"Came from Ireland to America, only to be put in the dumpster," he repeated. "Sounds like what you did to my ancestors in the 1920s!"

Damn you, Dermot! I may have had a point, but I was an American asshole, which was a trump card in any disagreement with foreign students at Harvard. There was a substantial international population on campus, and as a result I had become hyper-aware of America's defects. It's like when an unexpected guest visits your house and all you can do is apologize about the mess. I like my country, I really do, but with the endless global warming protests, the anticapitalist club, and the campus-wide vitriol toward George Bush, it was difficult not to become a little self-conscious about being American. I had become so afraid of living up to negative American stereotypes that I often found myself apologizing unnecessarily to international students. If I accidently took a Middle-Eastern girl's seat at lunch, I had to assure her that it wouldn't take me four to five years to withdraw.

Dermot had played his international trump card perfectly, and managed to turn the prosecutor into the defendant. So I quickly tried to steer the argument back to its original thesis: that Dermot was a weirdo who would benefit from adopting my views.

"And what's up with the breast milk?" I asked. "Did you just drink it?"

"Of course I did!" Dermot reported proudly. "And it was a real bag o' schwag, let me tell you. I was worried because the powder was a bit benjy at first, but then I mixed it with water and it tasted better than a caramelized pickle on St. Stephen's Day!"

I stared at him with wide eyes and a gaping mouth, body language for "I think you're a fucking lunatic." Dermot kicked off his sheepskin moccasins and sprawled out on our futon while he explained that human breast milk is rich with vitamins and minerals and can provide a great boost to the immune system before the upcoming flu season. "Think about it," he said. "Have you ever heard of a baby missing school because of the flu? I haven't."

In retrospect, Dermot's affinity for breast milk didn't surprise me all that much, as the kid was a health nut (with extreme emphasis on the word "nut"). He was obsessed with keeping healthy and treating his body well, and he even enrolled in Harvard's premed track, aspiring to someday work in a hospital where, presumably, he could help all those sick babies get back to school. His reputation as a health aficionado had been established back in his hometown in Ireland, and soon our room began receiving late-night phone calls from residents seeking free advice from Dermot, who they thought was an astute Harvard medical doctor. Many nights I would lay awake in horror as I overheard phone conversations through the paper-thin walls of Dermot's bedroom that went like this:

"Seamus, you old plonker! How can I help ya?

"…I see. And how long has it been itching you?

"…And now Sophie has it on her flange, too?

"…Okay, I think I know your problem. Both of you are allergic to latex. From now on whenever you scattle with other girls, don't wear a Johnny. Should clear things right up!"

Seeing the breast milk question as a losing battle, I questioned him further about the broken Ping-Pong paddle and the bungee cord. To my relief he admitted that they had no real purpose, and he only brought them to college "in case they came in handy." I looked at the three-foot bungee cord and cracked Ping-Pong paddle and chuckled. *In case they came in handy*. I explained slowly that, in America, we call this stuff "junk" and people who save useless things are called "hoarders" who need "psychiatric help." Dermot winced at my pronouncement, clearly unnerved by the implication.

"Junk, eh?" he said in an aggressively defensive tone. "Kind of like that book that's been sitting on *your* desk since the beginning of the term?" He pointed to my paleontology textbook, still encased in its plastic shrink-wrap.

For a kid who routinely looked in the wrong direction before crossing the street, Dermot could be pretty perceptive. He knew he landed a decent punch and he continued his offensive. "And you think the stuff on my desk is warped? How about the coddle on *your* desk? You've got a doll with a giant, wiggly head, ferchrissakes! I've seen you worship that thing like a god!"

I smiled and shook my head. Dermot was proving just how big of an idiot he really was. "That's not a doll, moron," I explained. "It's a bobblehead—big difference. Also, don't compare Tom Brady to god. Last time I checked, god hasn't won two Super Bowl MVPs. And I don't worship it. I simply tap his head with my left index finger seven times for good luck on Patriots game days."

Dermot raised his eyebrow and frowned, like now *he* couldn't understand *me*. "You're one strange langer," he said as he wiped the milk mustache off his face.

———— ◆ ————

Foreign students made up a sizable chunk of the student body at Harvard, and my small dorm alone had a number of them. In addition to Dermot, there was Petar, a self-proclaimed "prince" from Serbia, Lucina from Brazil, Kiyoshi from Japan, and my favorite of the bunch, a twenty-five-year-old Finn named Turvo. While many schools would only accept a twenty-five-year-old if they needed a new quarterback, Harvard happily made an exception for Turvo, a hand-to-hand combat specialist who had spent the previous three years working for the Finnish government on a special ops mission in the Swiss Alps. At first it was annoying keeping my music turned down out of fear of the trained assassin that lived directly above me, but soon Turvo became an example of one of my favorite aspects of Harvard.

My exposure to such a diverse and unique group of students was perhaps the most invaluable aspect of my Harvard education. The students were as compelling as they were brilliant, and I honestly believe I learned more from my classmates than I did from any of my professors. Turvo, for example, taught me some badass Finnish curse words and even showed me how to put someone in a proper sleeper-hold, which really came in handy whenever Dermot was acting like a *kusipää*.

With most of the international students, it was easy to see how they ended up at Harvard. Petar was an expert computer programmer, Lucina was an award-winning Portuguese poet, Kiyoshi learned English the previous summer and already wrote better essays than I could, and Turvo, well, let's just say the row of six skulls tattooed on his inner forearm didn't stand for each abandoned puppy he's adopted.

Dermot, on the other hand, remained a complete enigma to me. He was distinctive, that was for damn sure, but I couldn't identify a noteworthy skill or accomplishment that distinguished a typical Harvard student. There had to be *something* special about Dermot, but at this point I had no clue what it could be. As far as I could tell he was the only kid in my entire class getting worse grades than I was. And that was another thing that perplexed me: it seemed like more than a coincidence, in a class of sixteen hundred freshmen, that the two of us were assigned to the same room. It was like Harvard administration got bored and put two deformed bugs in a jar and shook it to see if they would fight.

It's never comforting to discover that your roommate thinks breast milk is part of a complete breakfast, but it's especially troubling when you're planning on having company over that night. A few days earlier I had told Dermot and Josh that I was throwing a party because it was already mid-November and I felt like I hadn't gotten to know any of the other students living around us.

Now I had been hibernating in my bedroom since my underwear incident in the Yard, so the rationale behind my party seemed plausible to them. The truth is I had very little interest in acquainting myself with more Harvard kids who would undoubtedly make me feel worse about my life. The sole purpose of this party was for me to meet, and hopefully impress, the smokeshow I had shamefully walked by in my underwear on move-in day.

There were several reasons why it became absolutely necessary for me to meet this girl. First, a day had not gone by that I didn't think about her, and I was beginning to feel like a bit of a sketchball obsessing about a girl whose name I still didn't know. I believed that with an introduction I could move her out of the "stranger" category, which in turn would slide my recurring dreams out of the "creepy" category.

I hadn't seen the smokeshow in the first few weeks following my move-in day disaster, an interval that both relieved and disappointed me. Her absence on campus and on Facebook was starting to make me believe I had hallucinated her in a state of public-nudity-induced panic, until one Tuesday evening when I spotted her eating dinner in Annenberg, the freshman dining hall.

Annenberg is a cavernous nine-thousand-square-foot dining hall, the centerpiece of Harvard's most impressive building, Memorial Hall. Located next to the Science Center just north of the Yard, this cathedral-like edifice was erected in 1866 in a High Victorian Gothic style that surely cost the university an entirely unnecessary amount of money. From the outside, Memorial Hall is a sight to behold: its dark coral bricks, coupled with yellow, navy, and red tiled stripes that wrap around its towering spires, give the building an aura of spooky fabulousness. (If Dracula had a flamboyant half-brother, he would definitely live here.) The spacious interior of Annenberg, meanwhile, evokes images of Hogwarts, with dozens of rows of long, hardwood tables and ornate chandeliers hanging from the lofty, vaulted ceiling.

The walnut-paneled walls are adorned with nineteenth-century oil paintings of Civil War heroes and marble busts of frowny-faced old men. Eighteen stained glass windows cap off the hall's stunning extravagance, leaving one to wonder if this magnificent space was not originally designed for the consumption of chicken nuggets.

During meal hours Annenberg's tables are always cramped with hundreds of hungry and chatty students, making it an altogether terrifying place for a forlorn freshman looking for an open place to sit. Even when the girl of his dreams doesn't suddenly appear.

Tray in hand, I had just emerged from Annenberg's serving area and was scanning the rows of tables for an acceptable seat when, quite unexpectedly, the smokeshow popped up on my radar. To my surprise, I could feel my feet shuffling as her magnetic beauty pulled me toward the empty seat at her table. But then I quickly veered off course, as I became self-conscious of the amount of calamari on my two plates. I didn't want to weird her out, so I sat a few tables away and chomped on fried squid as I admired her from a distance.

She was wearing some bulky sweater, which was kind of a bummer, but that didn't prevent me from confirming my initial impression that she was the hottest girl I had ever seen. What most attracted me to her wasn't her flawless smile or even the way she ate her banana, but the intangible aura of confidence that was reflected by her relaxed, emerald-green eyes. She seemed completely unaffected by the palpable anxiety that wafted through Annenberg like a contagious virus borne from Harvard freshman angst. Sitting to her right was a guy sporting a pair of earplugs as he reviewed a deck of flashcards in between bites of his beef stroganoff, while at the other end of the table was a boney girl, her hair secured in a tight bun, staring at her bowl of pasta like she was afraid an army of calories would jump out and latch onto her face, stomach, and upper arms. A redheaded guy a few seats away from her pulled a miniature bottle of Purell out of his pocket and offered it to the entire table with an alarmingly insistent look on his face. She politely accepted a squirt, and I thought I detected a restrained smile as she suppressed her urge to laugh at the kid's intense commitment to sanitization.

She spent her meal chatting with a couple of guys sitting across from her, sharing stories and giggling with the genuine laughter of a girl entirely comfortable in her environment. She sat tall and looked everyone in the eye as they spoke, like she really cared about what they had to say. Her face expressed a sincerity that was all too rare at Harvard, and she was giving the time of day to a couple of guys who were, in my unbiased opinion, total losers. (At least that's what I surmised from my strategic vantage point several tables away.)

All her movements, whether she was passing the salt or adjusting the position of her loosely tied ponytail, were made with grace and self-assurance. Her elegance was striking. Which is why I was so shocked when she reached for a napkin and knocked over her glass, spilling water all over the table and onto her neighbor's stack of flashcards.

"Oh no!" I said aloud to myself, causing a couple of people at my table to glance up at me as I stared blankly ahead. I felt so badly for the girl. Everyone at her table was staring at the mess she just created while the guy next to her stared blankly at his flashcards like his dog was just hit by a car. My heart was pounding and I squirmed in my chair as the second-hand embarrassment became overwhelming. What was she going to do?

I watched with anxious intrigue as she rolled her eyes at herself and reached for a handful of paper napkins from the dispenser in the center of the table. She then picked up the stack of index cards, which, I was relieved to see, were laminated, and easily wiped off any droplets of water that clung loosely to their plastic surface. She apologized to the owner of the flashcards who, after a thorough inspection of their condition, gave his begrudging approval before picking up his tray and moving to another table. As my crush dabbed at the remaining water on the table, she looked back up at the guys sitting across from her and continued her conversation, smiling and chatting as if nothing had happened.

And that's why I had to meet this girl. She wasn't perfect, but the way she handled herself was. I mean, I would've wet more than my tray if I did something embarrassing like that. I also would've made things worse by making some lame joke about the situation: "Sorry about the spill, everyone," I'd say. "I just figured my water would feel more at home in calamari!—I mean, I figured my *calamari* would feel more at water in *home*—I mean…shit, just forget it."

Before seeing my crush in Annenberg that night, my attraction to her was superficial and built on a foundation of my insecurities. She was physically flawless, so I came to think of her as a symbol of perfection that I could never attain. I imagined that she had perfect SAT scores to go along with her perfectly straight teeth, and that the only time she ever got a C was at Victoria's Secret. This outlook only deepened my sense of exclusion—the gates of Harvard Yard and this gorgeous girl: I didn't belong inside of either. Still, as unattainable as she seemed, I was convinced her beauty provided me with an opportunity. I believed if I could somehow get this impeccable girl to like me, I would prove to my classmates and myself that I could fit in at this paragon, that I truly belonged here. In a way, I figured Harvard would be far less intimidating if I could sleep with it.

After that night in Annenberg, my perspective on the girl changed dramatically. The primary object of my affection was no longer her body, but her attitude. I hadn't spoken to her and I didn't need to—her confidence was revealed in the conviction of all her actions, and I saw the rare image of an eighteen-year-old who seemed to know exactly who she was. Her self-assurance was remarkably alluring, and my desire for her only grew after I saw her reaction to the spilt drink. The way she was able to roll her eyes and laugh at herself showed me someone who wasn't trying to impress anyone, someone who was comfortable with her imperfections. She didn't take life too seriously, an outlook that I desperately needed to adopt if I was going to survive Harvard. The intensity of the school was beginning to suffocate me, and this girl seemed like the only antidote that could breathe some repose into my life. When I first saw her at dinner, my heart literally felt like it was burning. I hesitated attributing this sensation to the girl, knowing full well there's a fine line between true love and indigestion. But after she cleaned up her spill, I knew exactly how I felt about her.

———◆◆———

I spent the days following the sighting plotting a way to meet my crush. I soon realized that my room was the only appropriate venue for the introduction. I needed a controlled environment where I felt comfortable, a place where potential embarrassment was limited and pants were abundant.

With the location determined, my next task was to figure out how I was going to get her there. I couldn't exactly approach the girl with an invitation to hang out in my room. After what happened on move-in day, she'd more likely follow a bear into a cave.

Throwing a party, I decided, was a perfect idea because I could invite her somewhat anonymously. And it wasn't hard to throw a successful party if you offered the one thing Harvard students were most starved for: good food.

With a $37 billion endowment, one would assume the university would at least provide their students with an adequate dining service, but this was not the case at Harvard. You'd think we were enduring a national famine the way Harvard shamelessly recycled its food. Tuesday's turkey breast entrée would turn into Wednesday's turkey noodle soup. The ample leftovers from Wednesday night's baked squash would yield Thursday's squash bisque. And Friday night's clam casserole? You guessed it—clam casserole again on Saturday.

As if the quality of the food wasn't bad enough, Harvard doesn't offer meal plans to their students. The price of three meals a day for the entire year is automatically rolled into the yearly tuition, meaning I paid for about 250 breakfasts that I never ate. If the Mediterranean chickpea stew entrée looks like a rejected Purina recipe, or the portabella-lentil patty appears a little too radioactive for your taste, you could always order Domino's, but then you're essentially paying for two meals.

The food service was as unfair as it was nauseating, but despite the overflowing complaint boxes in each dining hall, Harvard administration would still boast about the "success" of the college's extensive dining options. They called it "brain" food, probably because that's exactly what it looked like.

Harvard students were desperate for alternate food options,

and this is exactly what I promised on the photocopied fliers I made for my party. I knew college students will do practically anything for free pizza, and visiting an unknown man-cave is a small price to pay for some quality grub.

Having established the incentive and location of my party, the only obstacle left was making sure that my crush got an invitation. I knew that she must live near my dorm, since she was unpacking her car very close to my room on move-in day, so I diligently left a flier at every room in the two small dorms closest to mine.

To be honest, I felt a little creepy sliding invitations under doors, trying to entice a girl to come to my room with promises of food. Change pizza to candy and my room to an unmarked van, and it wasn't that far of a stretch to compare me to a federal criminal. Was I taking all this too far? Maybe. But I was all in. And I couldn't help but feel that this quest for a girl would end either in a relationship or a restraining order.

———◆———

Dermot could not have been more fired up for this party. Which, as you might imagine, spawned a ravenous anxiety monster in the pit of my stomach. He desperately wanted to help out in the planning and organization of it. But this night had to be perfect and I couldn't trust him with anything. I didn't need Dermot's bizarre quirks embarrassing me in front of everyone—I was entirely capable of doing that myself.

"Oh, come on!" Dermot complained when I told him, politely, to stay the hell away from the party. "You have to let me do something! At least let me pick up the case of lipstick."

"Lipstick? What the hell are we going to need that for?"

"Well, how else are we going to play 'Fisty Kisses'? Second greatest party game there is! Oh, that reminds me, I also have to pick up a spatula so we can play 'Heave Ho.' There are going to be ladies at this hooley, I presume?"

I cringed. This is exactly what I was afraid of. I wasn't sure what "Heave Ho" entailed, but I didn't think my crush would be impressed if Dermot started catapulting girls at my party.

"Derm, listen to me carefully: there will be no lipstick, no spatula, and definitely no breast milk. You gotta hide that shit before everyone comes over tonight."

Dermot was happy to hide the rest of his powdered milk (he didn't want to share his nutritional bounty with others anyway) and he didn't even mind giving up his party games (apparently "Heave Ho" is better played outdoors with a pitchfork). But he wasn't about to let me carry out this entire operation solo. I finally made a minor concession, telling him he could help out by picking up the pizza from Pinocchio's that I had ordered. That was a simple enough task, right?

Dermot sighed and reluctantly agreed to his assignment, promising to collect the pizzas at 7:00 p.m. sharp. He grabbed his green windbreaker hanging from the top of our floor lamp and tossed it around his slumping shoulders before heading to the MAC for his daily session of jumping jacks.

I watched from the window as he slowly walked away from our dorm, and I felt a small twinge of guilt for reducing him to a delivery boy. The hardest part about living with Dermot—besides his reluctance to flush—was determining when I should be sympathetic toward his idiosyncrasies. Was his peculiar behavior in accordance with certain Irish customs, or was it exclusive to the Republic of Dermany? I wasn't positive, but I was pretty sure that it's not an Irish tradition to lick the frost off of windows. But who knows? Maybe I was being too intolerant, a bit of a xenophobe. Maybe powdered breast milk is a popular beverage in Ireland. After all, I hail from a nation whose gross domestic product relies heavily on the consumption of double-tall skinny pumpkin spice lattes.

Despite our cultural dissimilarities, Dermot and I didn't clash all that often. Part of our amity had to do with my unfamiliarity with Irish slang (was I supposed to be offended or flattered when he called me a "jammy client"?), but our harmony could mostly be attributed to the sense of comfort each of else felt when we looked at the other and thought, "Well, it could be worse." Dermot also served as a bit of an ambassador between foreign students and myself, bailing me out whenever I said something that may be deemed offensive by a non-American. "Excuse my mate," he'd say, "he's not xylophonic—just ignorant." Sure, Dermot would get under my skin every so often, but he was a good guy and I held no resentment toward him.

Of course, that would all change if he managed to screw up my party and humiliate me in front of my crush, the girl who was supposed to save me from Harvard.

Chapter Seven

PARTY IN THE USA

I checked my watch. It was 5:00 p.m., two hours before the advertised start of my party. I still had to clean our common room, but first I had to get in touch with Vikas so I could invite him to the party.

The poor kid had been depressed for the last two weeks after a tough break-up with his cyber girlfriend, whom he had been "dating" for six months over the online multiplayer computer game *World of Warcraft*. Their virtual relationship (which, according to Vikas, got "pretty physical" in private chat rooms) ended after Mage_Girl1989 was banned by *Warcraft* moderators for, among other things, using explicit language, casting an illegal spell on an undead warlock, and being a forty-five-year-old man named Dennis.

Like anyone who discovers that his girlfriend moonlights as a child predator, Vikas took the news pretty hard. So I thought it might cheer him up to invite him to a real live college party. I sat down at my computer and logged into Instant Messenger, Vikas's primary form of communication.

DarkWingDuck85: Hey vikas
3Point1Four69: sup?

DarkWingDuck85: nothing much. what are you up to tonite?

3Point1Four69: not sure yet. ive got a lot of peeps wanting to hang... im getting so many text-bombs it's like freaking pearl harbor on my cell phone! lol

3Point1Four69: i can't decide who to chill with, but im leaning toward catching a ride with my mom and hittin' up my mandatory astronomy class.

DarkWingDuck85: class on a saturday night? brutal. wanna come to a party in my room instead?

3Point1Four69: are you friggen serious?!?!!!!!!!!!!!!!!!!!!111

DarkWingDuck85: yeah, just sneak over to my room after your mom drops you off at the observatory.

3Point1Four69: oh snap, shit just got REAL! Are all your sweet-ass babes going to be in attendance?

DarkWingDuck85: my usual girls probably wont be there because they are too sore. but remember how i told you about that hot chick from move-in day?

3Point1Four69: you mean the one who saw you and asked seductively if you needed help carrying in your package but you said it was a three-person job and winked at her mom who then smiled and eye-sexed you?

DarkWingDuck85: yeah, she might be there, so you can't embarrass me. promise?

3Point1Four69: yes. okay my mom's yelling at me to get off the computer so I g2g, but ill see u l8ter!!!

DarkWingDuck85: later man

Auto Response from 3Point1Four69: gettin KRUNK 2nite!!!

So there was at least one person coming to my party. Vikas would be an ideal guest because he's easy to impress, but I knew if I wanted a similar reaction from others I would have to clean up our room, which had spent the previous weeks accumulating junk and grime at an alarming rate. Old pizza boxes, half-empty Gatorade bottles, miscellaneous shoes, and other forms of sticky, unidentifiable foods had joined forces to create a lumpy mess that had a smell and texture not unlike a compost heap. The cluttered floor was no longer safe to walk across in dim lighting, and with the plethora of strange growths thriving in our room it was starting to feel like we were living in God's experimental Petri dish. I had to do something before the school's environmental club started picketing outside my dorm.

After a lot of elbow grease and an entire bottle of disinfectant, I somehow managed to transform our room into a fairly acceptable living space. I was pleasantly surprised, in fact, to notice that our room was perfectly designed for hosting parties. The main door to our suite opened to a large common room with hardwood floors and a brick fireplace nestled in the back corner. One wall of the common room had two large windows that opened up to Harvard Yard, while the opposite wall had three doors: one led to our narrow bathroom, while the other two belonged to our tiny cells—excuse me—bedrooms. Two bedrooms for three roommates was a source of tension for us, as one person was blessed with a single while the other two were cramped into bunk beds like an army barrack. I was fortunate to have the single, though after a close two-to-one vote I agreed to rotate it with Dermot and Josh. We furnished the middle of our common room with a lumpy dark blue futon that sat in front of a black wooden coffee table and a depressingly small TV. We kept our desks in the common room, and in preparation for the party I arranged our desk chairs and futon in a circle around the coffee table, which would serve as the altar where the pizza would be sacrificed to the Hunger Gods. I also found a box for Dermot's perplexing trinkets, which had mysteriously moved back from our trashcan to his desk, like haunted artifacts in a horror movie.

———◆———

I learned later in my freshman year that this set of rooms, like many of the suites in Harvard's old nineteenth-century dorms, used to house only one student. Each scholar was given a large study area and a bedroom to himself, while a third small room was designated as his servant's quarters. I've always wondered what sort of duties were required of a college student's servant. The concept seems absolutely ridiculous. I can picture Tripp's great-great-grandfather, Winston, as a young Harvard lad relaxing in a leather chair, his feet resting comfortably on the back of his kneeling servant while he smoked a pipe and read *On the Origin of the Species*, laughing heartily at the work of his favorite fiction writer, Charles Darwin. I suppose this servant would be expected to satisfy every desire of his young Harvard master, from completing his homework to polishing his quail-hunting rifle. Keeping in mind that Harvard was an all-male university during this era and eligible women were scarce to come by, I hope for the servant's sake that "polishing the hunting rifle" wasn't a common euphemism.

Harvard's antiquated dorm rooms had their share of issues, but like grandparents, they were actually pretty interesting once you stopped complaining about them and learned a little about their past. True to their obsession with tradition, Harvard administration equips each freshman suite with a chronological list of every alumnus who ever lived in your room. I think Harvard provides this list to freshmen as a way to inspire them, like "Holy shit, the famed molecular chemist Dudley Herschbach lived here!", but I just saw it as a list of suspects responsible for the dubious stain on my mattress.

While I wasn't thrilled with the list of my suite's previous tenants, freshmen who were fortunate enough to live in a room with an impressive pedigree did not hesitate to share it. Stop by a Cambridge bar and you might overhear a Harvard guy hitting on a Boston University girl ("Want to see my dorm room? JFK had sex in it!"), while his unfortunate buddy drops a slightly less effective pick-up line a few tables away ("Want to see my room? Ted Kennedy masturbated in it!").

———— ◆ ————

When people began arriving at my party, I felt obligated to provide some background information about the history of my suite. "Welcome to my room," I said to the first couple of guests to arrive. "Current home of Dermot, Josh, and myself, and former residence of Robert Oppenheimer, the father of the atomic bomb!" The introduction didn't elicit much of a response from the early guests, except for Kiyoshi, who promptly left.

After Kiyoshi's departure, my party consisted of four measly dorks, and they were all dudes. Not exactly a party environment my crush would be impressed with, should she arrive. I tried telling myself to relax, that it was still early, that the party would rally once Dermot arrived with the pizza. But deep down I knew that girls as hot as my crush didn't spend their Saturday night's drooling over pepperoni pizza in freshman dorms—they went to the final clubs.

Generally speaking, there are three main social classes at

Harvard. Students who lock themselves in the library for seven days a week represent the lowest class, while the members of the exclusive, all-male final clubs make up the elite class (along with their female friends). I hovered in the middle class, which was for the type of kid who liked to party and have a good time, but who would spend five minutes trying to twist off a beer cap that required a bottle-opener.

At this stage I didn't know too much about the final clubs, as freshman nobodies like myself were locked out of their mansion clubhouses. There were plenty of rumors, though, of the type of absurd things that went on behind closed doors. I heard whispers of truly despicable activities (no surprise, considering guys like Tripp and Brady were members). But the thought of one day joining a final club was appealing to me, since membership would yield instant power and popularity. Before I could even be considered for membership, though, I'd have to at least get into a few of their infamous parties, and I had to climb several rungs on Harvard's social ladder if I wanted even the slightest chance at that.

My little party couldn't compare to a final club. But, as some of my statistically minded classmates would say, I believed there still was a "nonzero" chance that my crush would show up.

I began making awkward small talk about the library hours with one of the guys, when we were interrupted by a weak knock on the door. As with each time up to this point, hearing a knock made my heart race and my legs feel like jelly. *Was this her?*

I raced over to the door, paused a moment to collect myself, and opened it.

Shit.

It wasn't my crush—not even close. I stared ahead at a curly haired blond guy, smiling up at me from his wheelchair.

"Hi there. My name is Walker."

I must've misheard him, but I swear that's what he said. "Sorry, what's that?"

The kid chuckled. "I'm just messing with you," he explained. "I thought it was funny to start introducing myself like that, ever since the accident…"

It was a weird introduction, but I appreciated how the kid made light of his circumstance. I decided to make a little quip about it to show him I was cool with it too. "Well I bet I can guess what you wrote your application essay about!"

He frowned. "I wrote about how my mother died of Tocket's disease, you dickhead."

He glared at me and there was a prolonged silence, and I considered closing the door and pretending this exchange never happened.

"Ha! Tocket's disease doesn't even exist!" he exclaimed. "Now move aside and let me in, will ya? Is the pizza here yet?" Still flustered, I obediently shuffled out of his way while he rolled himself into my room. I never did get his real name.

With no food, no alcohol, and no girls, the first half-hour of my party was painfully uneventful. Everyone sat around the empty coffee table and fiddled with their phones, so I pulled out mine and started playing Tetris, inserting a few random laughs to give the illusion that I was participating in an engaging text conversation.

A few casual remarks about the weather were made here and there, and slowly our conversation morphed into Harvard students' favorite pastime: complaining about our classes. This was a topic on which I had plenty to contribute, and I fired off a brief tirade about my calculus class.

"Man, I hear you about integral calculus," responded one guy with buzzed brown hair and a large, circular Charlie Brown head. "It gave me a ton of problems when I took it a few years ago in high school."

It wasn't the most comforting response in the world, but hey, at least we had a conversation going. Still, any subject that could expose my moronic side needed to be avoided, so I deftly directed the discussion toward Harvard students' second favorite pastime: talking about themselves.

"What's my deal here? That's a good question." Charlie Brown paused and took a deep breath, like he was trying to build up the drama. "Well, I run the sixteen hundred meter for the track team, so I suppose that's the main reason I got into Harvard. Between track and SATs, you could say that 'sixteen hundred' was prominently featured on my application here."

I immediately regretted my question, as Charlie Brown launched into an entire speech about every accomplishment of his goddamn life. I should've known better: this compulsion to impress was not uncommon for a lot of Harvard students, who treated even casual party atmospheres like they were job interviews. I stopped paying attention somewhere around his ninth-grade summer when he volunteered as a cook at a Russian-American hydrology exchange program in Tahoe.

Even if I had actually cared about the finer points of hydro-meteorology, I still would've been distracted. *Where the hell is Dermot?* I kept thinking. He was now twenty minutes late and I was beginning to get worried. Pinocchio's is a short walk from the Yard, but it was entirely possible that Dermot somehow ended up on a train to Pittsburgh or something. At this point a few more people had showed up to the party, including a couple of girls, and they were all asking about the pizza. I reached for my phone to call Dermot, but then remembered that he always left his cell phone in his bedroom, out of fear of losing it.

As the only member of the suite present (Josh, the coolest of us three, was out with some of his hockey buddies), I felt responsible to monitor the health of the conversation, which was now focused on the recently launched website, Facebook. I sat quietly and listened in on the dialogue that was now zipping back and forth between several unknown faces.

"At first I didn't mind when they expanded Facebook to include some other schools. Like when they let Yale and Princeton join, I was like, 'fine.' But this week they invite Penn to join? Come on now…"

"Mark Zuckerberg was in my computer science class. Huge douchebag."

"You know Mark Zuckerberg?"

"I don't know him, but he sat in front of me and I could just tell."

"On the side, I do a little programming for this other networking site called Friendster.com. It's got a much more intricate user interface. Mark my words: in five years it'll be crushing Facebook. I'd bet anything."

"I can't afford any bets right now. Apple is suing me for hacking into their servers."

"I may take you up on that bet. How many people use Friendster.com now?

"Four-twelve."

"Hey, that was my GPA in high school!"

"My school didn't allow GPAs above four, but if you scale up my honors classes I would've been at four-nineteen. Unfortunately, I had to settle for a four-point-oh."

"My new razor has five-point-oh blades!"

My interjection kind of killed the conversation. Apparently these guys weren't easily impressed, so I quickly whipped out my phone and typed out a long text message to no one as I pretended not to notice their judgmental expressions of confusion and pity.

I had really hoped the conversation at my party wouldn't devolve into a prolonged one-upping contest, but it is unavoidable at a place like Harvard. The students have a fierce competitive nature embedded in their DNA; without it they wouldn't have gotten into Harvard in the first place. While this competitive drive yields incredible feats of excellence, it also sucks the fun out of social events. No one can truly relax at a party because they are always on guard to defend their honor and prove their superiority.

There are two driving forces behind this combative culture. The first is jealousy—when you're surrounded by classmates who have been awarded Rhodes scholarships; have been drafted in the NFL; have book, record, or movie deals; or have already made millions of dollars or are well on their way, you instinctively compensate for any feelings of inferiority through aggressive boasting. The other factor is a side effect of grading on a curve—you are automatically forced into competition with all your classmates over everything in your life, whether it be for grades in the classroom, playing time in football, a job offer at Goldman Sachs, or membership in a final club. It's difficult to form genuine bonds of selfless camaraderie when you benefit directly from the failure of your peers.

I'm convinced this is why Harvard has such little school spirit. At Harvard, it's every man and woman for themselves. Fame and unimaginable wealth are at stake for many of the students, which means even good friends can't be fully trusted, a painful lesson Mark Zuckerberg learned when his classmate and best friend sued him for allegedly stealing ownership of Facebook.

Pizza parties tend to lose some of their relaxed merriment when the guy sitting across from you might one day sue you for $600 million.

I kept my head buried in my phone for a few minutes, taking a break from the competition. I recognized the absurdity of these one-upping contests, but for some reason it still really bothered me. I hated how the social scene always harbored a certain competitive, humorless tension. I hated how much I got caught up in the atmosphere, and how much it affected my mood. There wasn't much laughing at Harvard. Wasn't college supposed to be more fun than this?

———◆———

When I eventually looked back up from my phone, my eyes were drawn to the window. I saw Vikas outside, approaching the entrance of my dorm. *Oh no, Vikas, you didn't...*

I sprang up from my seat, hurried over to the door, and opened it before Vikas could even knock.

"Vikas, what the hell are you wearing?"

"It's called a toga, bro. This is a college party, is it not?"

A white linen sheet was wrapped around Vikas's waist, climbing up one side of his torso and secured over his left shoulder.

"Dude, please tell me you have another set of clothes."

My question swept panic across Vikas's face. "I—I told my mom that it was 'Dress Up As Your Favorite Astronomer Night' at the observatory, so I had to come as Archimedes," he stammered. "I don't have any other clothes!"

"Jesus, not every college party involves togas!" There were occasionally toga parties at Harvard, though a much more popular dress-up theme was "CEOs and Office Ho's." "Whatever, just come inside. Where are your glasses?"

"I don't need that babe-repellent," Vikas explained. He took two steps forward and banged his head on the wall next to my door. I pulled him inside.

"Everyone, this is my friend Archimedes." The room fell silent as Vikas offered a sheepish wave. He squinted his eyes tight as he tried to make out the room, but fortunately Vikas couldn't see two feet in front of him, let alone make out the expressions of shock on everyone's faces.

The blond kid with the wheelchair and weird sense of humor was the first to break the silence. "Eric, quick request—"

"AHHH!" Vikas jumped backward several feet and tripped over the corner of Dermot's desk before grabbing the pole of the floor lamp to lend him balance. "Jeez, sorry," he said once he collected himself. "When you talked I thought Eric's desk chair had just anthropomorphized!"

I shot Vikas a dirty look and threw a subtle elbow to the ribs. He then apologized, not to the kid in the wheelchair, but to me, for his nerdy vocabulary.

"Um, as I was saying," wheelchair kid continued, "do you have a small, heavy object I can use as a block? The damn wheel-lock on my chair is broken, and look"—he lifted his hands from the wheels and his chair instantly rolled down the old, warped floorboards toward the center of the room.

"Yeah, in that box of junk under my desk there should be something you can use." I was pretty sure my hulking course catalog was in there.

As Charlie Brown, who was nearest to my desk, crouched down and began rummaging through the box, a horrible thought crossed my mind. *Oh god, that's the box where we hid Dermot's junk—including the powdered breast milk.* I tried to think of something to say to get his hands out of the box, but it was too late. My reputation at Harvard was about to defy gravity and reach a new low.

"Hey, take a look at this!" Charlie Brown announced. "Not at all what I expected…but it's perfect!"

I exhaled a relieved breath as he held up Dermot's short bungee cord. I nodded like the bungee was exactly what I had in mind, then watched with intrigue as Charlie Brown hooked one end of the cord to the chair and the other to the old, cast-iron heater beneath one of the windows. The wheelchair slid a couple of inches before coming to a rest, secured by the now-taut elastic cord.

"Wow, great call about the bungee cord, Eric," someone said.

"Yeah, that's a pretty useful piece of equipment to have around!" another agreed.

I smiled and shrugged my shoulders, soaking up everyone's suddenly approving eyes. "I like to keep that stuff around, in case it comes in handy."

Suddenly, I heard the door burst open behind me. I spun around, expecting to see Dermot, but to my disappointment it was Josh, who was leading in a small entourage. Josh was a typical eighteen-year-old guy, with the friendliness, sense of humor, and looks that would make him popular at any college. He hung out with hockey players and other athletes, and if he played his cards right, he had a shot at getting accepted into a final club once he reached his sophomore year. I had expected him to actively avoid tonight's party, as he knew me well enough to anticipate the disaster that this affair was quickly becoming, but here he was, ushering in a group of about ten people. I impatiently scanned the pack of girls behind him, and my heart sank when none of them was my crush.

Josh glanced at Vikas in his toga, then at the kid sitting in a wheelchair attached to the wall by a bungee cord. "Umm, where's the pizza?"

Where's the pizza? This became the topic of conversation of the party, which, at nearly twenty guests, had evolved into something real. As I surveyed the crowd in my now cramped room, I realized that this was a pivotal point in my social standing at Harvard. A few enjoyable conversations coupled with some quality pizza, and I could get a sizable group of students leaving my room with a favorable impression of me. Sure, being known as "the kid who throws sweet pizza parties" is better suited for elementary school than college, but still, this could be a good foundation on which to build a small but positive reputation as a guy you wanted to be around. For once, I'd be headed in the right direction at Harvard. I was still holding out hope that my crush would make an appearance, but I would certainly consider the night a success if I were able to impress a room full of Harvard kids.

Of course, Dermot was now a half-hour late. I made my way over to my bedroom to grab my coat so I could pick up the pizzas at Pinocchio's myself. I never got the chance, though, because at that moment Dermot barged through the door.

Hallelujah.

My relief, however, was instantly replaced by panic. Dermot was empty-handed.

"Oye, sorry for being late, everyone! This muppet at the tallypal was acting the maggot, and really made balls of my entire afternoon." Dermot weaved through the crowd as he made his way to the center of the room.

"What happened to the pizza?" I tried to make my voice sound strong, like I wasn't about to cry.

"They didn't have it! I told 'em I was there to pick up an order for Eric, and they told me there was no such thing."

"That's because I put the order under 'Dermot.'"

"Why'd ya go and do that? You're not Dermot, you're Eric!" Others nodded in agreement. "But don't worry," Dermot said calmly. "I got some quality scran for everyone, even better than pizza!"

Reaching deep into the pockets of his cargo pants, Dermot pulled out heaping handfuls of an unidentified substance and plopped them on the coffee table. I leaned forward to get a closer look, but the smell gave it away first.

Cod cakes. These clumps of processed fish, which had both the shape and edibility of a hockey puck, were served for lunch in the dining hall earlier that day. Dermot must've snagged some and carried them around all afternoon in his pockets.

"Help yourself, everyone! Come on, don't be shy! I've got plenty more in my knapsack...tartar sauce too!"

Groans bounced around the room, and I watched helplessly as people gathered their belongings and headed for the door.

"Hey, where's everyone going?" Dermot demanded. "Was it me? Sorry if I laid an air-biscuit. I had some milk and it's really tuggin' on the old fart-strings."

The majority of the room cleared out in a matter of minutes, leaving me with Dermot, Vikas, and the first five dorks that had arrived earlier. I could've gone to Pinocchio's to see if the order for "Dermot" was still there, but it was probably too late, so I didn't bother.

It was thoroughly depressing to see what my dream party had been reduced to: surrounding a mountain of stale cod cakes were five single dudes, a kid in a wheelchair tied down by a bungee cord, and a fourteen-year-old boy draped in a bed sheet with one nipple exposed. I had spent days worrying that my crush wouldn't come to this party. Now I was terrified that she *would*.

We sat speechless for a few minutes, the stillness interrupted only by intermittent crunches as Dermot, seemingly oblivious to despair, gnawed on a cod cake. I saw him eying his bungee cord, so I quickly spoke up before he had a chance to ruin what little credibility I had left.

"Like what we did with my bungee cord, Derm? I told you it would come in handy." I raised my eyebrows slightly at him, and he responded with a half-smile and brief nod, signaling that he knew what was up.

"You're one crazy langer with all that junk you keep around," he said casually. Dermot at least didn't mess that up, and my frustration with him for ruining my party briefly cooled.

Vikas seemed to be taking this megaflop the hardest—the disillusionment of his college dream had happened so quickly. I knew he had a difficult home life, with his parents being academically psychotic and all, and I felt guilty for ruining a chance to show him that there was a life of fun, pizza, and girls waiting for him in the future. It was like taking an inmate out of prison for one day, promising to show him a good time, and then bringing him to a DMV waiting room. He slumped in his chair and stared blankly at the wall.

"This party is about as cool as a boner in a Speedo," Vikas groaned.

The group murmured in agreement, with the wheelchair kid announcing that the only reason he even came to my stinking party was because it was on the first floor.

At this point it became clear to me that there was only one thing left to do, so I opened my desk drawer and pulled out a medium-sized flask of whiskey. I had been saving this container of liquid happiness for the postmortem of my calculus final, assuming I would certainly need it then. But I figured we might be able to salvage some of this night if we sat around and got drunk while enumerating all the ways in which we thought Mark Zuckerberg was an idiot.

Even though we were all underage, I certainly wasn't about to allow a fourteen-year-old to drink under my watch, much to Vikas's chagrin. It was just too easy to envision a scenario where, on his way home, a drunken Vikas vomits in his mom's minivan then calls Archimedes a loser. The only other person not drinking was Dermot, who remained steadfast in his belief that any American-made liquor was "poof-juice." He retreated to his bedroom as the rest of us passed around the flask and took exaggerated swigs of the lukewarm liquor.

As the supplier of the contraband I was suddenly the coolest guy in the room, a perception I intended to cultivate further by demonstrating my expertise in alcohol. After every sip I would declare my fondness of the whiskey's rich, oaky flavor, then identify the odorous cod cakes as the source of my gagging reflex. I flipped on some music, and within minutes smiles began to emerge; not because we were drunk yet, but because it was refreshing to break the rules. On the totem pole of collegiate coolness, the male freshman at Harvard was so low that we were buried underground. It felt nice to finally get some air.

The flask had only made it around once when we heard the faint knock on the door. It was short and hesitant and barely perceptible over the blaring music. I turned down my computer speakers while Charlie Brown approached the door and peered through the peephole.

"Eric, there's a girl standing outside...and she's hot!" He whispered this to me with hushed excitement, like he was my dad informing me that a rare bird had visited our backyard feeder.

My pulse skyrocketed. *She's here.*

A thousand thoughts ran through my head in about three seconds, including the idea of stuffing Vikas in the closet and tossing a bed sheet over the kid in the wheelchair. There was no time for these measures, though. I would have to perform under the current circumstances, which is really too bad because I was still about three shots of whiskey away from being cool.

"Let her in."

The person who walked into my room, it turned out, was the last woman in the world I wanted to see. Standing before us was a brunette lady sporting short curly hair and a pair of Tina Fey glasses. Counter to Charlie Brown's claim, she really was not much of a looker. Not unlike "beer goggles," Charlie was clearly under the influence of "crimson goggles"—a popular campus phrase suggesting that Harvard guys considered any girl with four limbs and two boobs to be hot. This woman's name was Judith, and she was in her late twenties. She was my resident advisor.

"Eric, you guys *have* to keep your music turned...what do we have here?" Judith snatched my flask off the coffee table, unscrewed the cap, and held it to her nose. Everyone in the room froze, and out of the corner of my eye I could see Dermot, who was hiding in his bedroom, slowly creep to his open window. Vikas squinted and rubbed his eyes as he tried to figure out what was going on.

Judith let out an audible sigh. "You guys, I was having a nice relaxing night, but now I have to report you to…"

"RUN!" The squeal came from Vikas, who rocketed out of his seat and made a blind dash for the door. His trajectory for freedom was off by about three feet though, and he crashed directly into Judith, landing a direct face-plant into her sizable chest. Vikas's head bounced off my RA's bosom, snapping backward like it had just been pelted by a rubber dodge ball. He tumbled to the floor and Judith staggered back in shock, allowing Vikas to hop back on his feet and scamper out the door. I watched through the window as Vikas sprinted away from my dorm and disappeared into the night, an enormous smile stretching from ear to ear.

The rest of us had remained motionless, resigned to our fate. Underage drinking wasn't an offense that yielded expulsion, but the Harvard Advisory Board only granted you so many strikes—horrible news for a guy like me, who had already anticipated an academic performance review at the end of the semester.

Judith recovered quickly from the collision, totally unfazed by the ancient Greek midget who had just motorboated her. "Alright guys, hand over your Harvard IDs. I'm taking down your names."

"Wooooooh!"

Everyone swiveled their heads to see Dermot burst out of his bedroom. His shirt was off and an Irish flag was fastened around his neck and streaming behind him like a cape. "Happy Pollywog Day! Hap-Hap-Happy Pollywog Day to one and all!"

Dermot pranced around the room, bouncing off the furniture like a pinball before settling in front of Judith. He swayed back and forth in his place and closed one eye as he looked her over. "Ah, don't look so gobsmacked, ya brasser, come 'ere and give the Derminator a goozer." Dermot extended his arms, inviting Judith for a hug, but quickly reeled them back in. "Whoa! You found me spirits!" he stammered, snatching my flask out of her hands. "Can't inebriate—ha, sorry—can't *celebrate* Pollywog Day without pissing up!" Judith recoiled as Dermot chugged the remaining whiskey and casually tossed the flask aside.

"What the *hell* is going on here?" Judith demanded, looking at me for answers.

"Uh, Pollywog Day? I don't really know, to be honest."

Unsatisfied with my explanation, Judith turned back to Dermot. "Did you drink that *entire* bottle yourself?"

"'Course I did! You think Eric or any of these langers had the clackers to get bolloxed off Oirish whiskey?

"Alright, Dermot, you've had way too much to drink. I'm taking you to health services," Judith said. "Eric, I'm sorry you had to put up with him. The Ad-Board will certainly be hearing about this. Will you help him get a shirt on so I can take him to UHS?"

I directed Dermot to his bedroom. As soon as the door closed I whispered, "Derm, why are you doing this?"

"Because you're my mate," he said, omitting the fake slur he employed in front of Judith. "Plus it was the least I could do, after you saved me earlier."

"What do you mean?"

"You know, for taking claim of my bungee when they found my junk." He said this with complete sincerity, and my stomach began to twist. "I'd much rather have a bunch of old Harvard farts think I'm a drunkard than a bunch of our classmates think I'm a loony hoarder who needs psychiatric help."

Dermot put his hand on my shoulder, and I averted my eyes from his appreciative stare. "I wish I had the stones to not care what those kids think of me. You're a good chum. A real mucker."

A real mucker.

He was off by one letter.

Chapter Eight

ARRESTED DEVELOPMENT

L ooking back, despite everything that had happened so far my freshman year, the singular moment that kick-started the rest of the chain of life-altering events that year was when I got arrested.

Well, I wasn't *technically* arrested, as the charge was later dropped. But getting stuffed into a police cruiser in front of a crowd of curious onlookers had the same humiliating effect.

I had been expecting karma to bite me in the ass after Dermot heroically accepted the blame for the underage drinking at my party. I just didn't think it would happen the very next day.

———◆———

I was having a shitty day even before my public incarceration. Coach Mac had chewed me out at our morning workout, sharing his philosophy that "life is a marathon, not a sprint…and you're running in the wrong fucking direction." Then Tripp ruined my post-workout nap by demanding that I meet up with him to review our cheating plan while he ran a quick errand.

Spending an extended period of time with Tripp is never pleasant, but today was particularly brutal as I accompanied him on his biweekly trip to the Cambridge sperm bank. The demand for Harvard sperm, I learned, is enormous (apparently prospective mothers are more than happy to put up with the initial discomfort of a big-headed baby as long as there is an oversized brain inside of it), and local sperm banks offer exorbitant compensation for Harvard DNA. Sperm donation was a prolific source of income for a number of male Harvard students and I was surprised, perhaps naïvely, to see how many guys took advantage of it.

"It's nine hundred bucks a month to jerk off," Tripp explained. "You'd have to be retarded *not* to do it."

This was a lot of dough for a typical college student. I was confused by Tripp's passion for "donation," though, since money is not an issue for him and his family. Maybe he just loved inflating his ego with the knowledge that in order to live above the poverty line all he needed was a Harvard ID, a *Playboy*, and a plastic cup.

Even non-narcissistic Harvard guys, though, become giddy when they first hear about the deal. It's like telling a guy that an unlimited well of valuable crude oil has been discovered in his backyard, and that the only way it can be extracted is by getting a massage while watching beautiful naked women dig it up.

As enticing as this scenario sounded, and as weirdly comforting as it was to know there were women out there who actually *wanted* my seeds, I could never bring myself to do it. Something about the process seemed deceitful. Women looking to buy my sample would see "Six foot two, brown hair, green eyes, varsity athlete, Harvard-educated." But that wasn't who I was at all. And I'm sure the sperm's market value would plummet if aspiring parents knew that guys like Tripp were among the providers. It was depressing to think of all the mothers who had paid extra to fill their tanks with high-octane premium unleaded, only to receive midgrade regular from a lead head. Equally sobering was the thought that the world was becoming saturated with Tripp's offspring. I hadn't taken biology since high school, but I was pretty sure the asshole gene was dominant.

"Does it ever freak you out that soon there will be enough of your kids out there to field an entire football team?" I asked Tripp as we made the short walk from Harvard Square to the sperm bank.

Tripp's eyes widened and he took a moment to think, giving me the impression that this was the first time he ever considered the fate of his sperm. "Well, I guess that would be the best-looking football team of all time!"

At least Tripp was quick once we got there. While he made his "deposit" in a special back room, I hung out in the waiting room and helped myself to a snack from the modest food spread. I had some coffee and toasted a bagel. (I recall chuckling at the implication of the sign on the table that read "Bagels are NOT permitted in the Private Production Rooms"). I also promptly spilled oily butter onto my khakis. Typically this wouldn't bother me so much, as condiments were frequent guest-stars on my clothes, but the sperm bank isn't exactly a place you want to walk out of with a stain on your pants.

On our way back to Harvard Square, Tripp updated me on the plan for our calculus exam. The entire scheme depended on one student who would feed us answers in the middle of the test, and apparently the guy was getting cold feet as the date of the exam approached. Tripp assured me this was a minor issue and that he would take care of it, but this news only intensified the anxiety that had recently taken over my life.

Easily the most frustrating consequence of my anxiety was my insomnia. Every night for the last several weeks I had lain awake in bed as my exhausted body helplessly yielded to an active mind filled with doubt, fear, and guilt. My days were packed with enough meetings and busywork to divert these menacing emotions, but they relentlessly poured down on me as soon as the lights went out and I was left with nothing to distract me from my inner thoughts. An ever-expanding list of anxieties would race through my head and get my pulse racing: *Will I ever meet my crush? If I do meet her, would I be composed enough to string together more than one coherent sentence? Am I even good enough for her? Am I good enough for any girl? Am I good enough for this school? Should I cheat on my calculus final? Is it worth it? What if I get caught?*

My heart would wrench as I imagined the pain and disappointment in my father's eyes if I had to tell him I was caught cheating. But then a moment later I would be squirming at the thought of having to inform my parents and friends back home that I, their golden boy who was destined for success, had flunked out of Harvard. I was too scared to cheat, but I was also too scared not to. It was driving me crazy.

I briefly considered visiting Harvard's ever-busy counseling offices. But I didn't want to be spotted there because, for reasons that made perfect sense in my teenage mind, my nonexistent reputation was more important to me than my emotional well-being.

Instead I developed a few nightly tricks designed to keep my mind preoccupied until my body would finally succumb to exhaustion. After completing my homework I would immediately turn on my computer and spend hours surfing the Internet for mindless websites and blogs that could divert my attention away from my anxieties. I'd check Weather.com, then ESPN.com for the latest sports headlines, then CNN.com for news updates, and then back to Weather.com in case the forecast had changed in the past fifteen minutes. If I was still awake after several cycles of my usual sites, I'd start rapidly clicking on link after link in a blind attempt to find new content to occupy my mind. As Vikas would always say, "There is no speed limit on the information superhighway," and before I'd know it, it would be 3:00 a.m. and I would be scrolling through a blog devoted to pictures of orangutans holding umbrellas.

When I wasn't killing time with some late-night perusing of the Internet, I was binging on video games. Games like *Halo* were the perfect escape for me because they offered a feeling of prowess that I sorely missed. In high school my esteem would be boosted fairly regularly by a good grade, a solid football game, or even something as simple as an encouraging word from a teacher. At Harvard, though, decimating hordes of artificially generated aliens was my only sense of daily accomplishment. I'd also play the crap out of *Madden*, and I used its "create-a-player" feature to design myself. I may have been a nobody on Harvard's football team, but this Eric Kester was six foot five, 275 pounds, and could be tackled by no less than ten people. He ran for seventy-two touchdowns in sixteen games, and had, I imagined, even more scores in bed.

With my mind so cluttered with apprehensive thoughts about my future, I became unusually forgetful. Once it took me three days to remember to switch my clothes from the washing machine to the drier. Just two days previous, to the delight of a lucky member of Annenberg's dishwashing staff, I left my iPod on my dinner tray.

And now, shortly after I parted ways with Tripp, I realized I had left my Harvard ID in the football locker room. I would return to the field house later this afternoon for practice, so leaving my ID card there wasn't a big deal. It did mean, however, that I couldn't easily get back into my dorm.

———◆———

Every entryway to a Harvard dorm is protected by an electronic lock that requires the swipe of a Harvard ID to open. This type of security system is fairly common at universities, though it's especially important for a school like Harvard, which is located in a lively city full of eclectic and occasionally deranged individuals. Harvard Square maintains a prolific homeless population which, when combined with its nerdy residents, yields a startling juxtaposition of demographics. It's one of the few places in the world where a genius can settle under a tree with a metaphysics textbook while a vagrant defecates in the bushes fifteen feet away. Despite obvious differences, Harvard students and hobos actually share a number of qualities as well. A student may scoff at a homeless man begging for change, and then an hour later find himself sitting in an office begging his professor to change the poor grade on his essay. And indeed, mumbling to oneself and smelling horrible were not traits limited to just one group.

I'm not sure how Harvard Square, home of the world's most renowned university, also became a Mecca for drifters, but it must have to do with the fact that some Harvard students are easy targets for scams and other forms of swindling. The best example of a Harvard student getting fleeced comes from a naïve freshman girl who lived in Wigglesworth, a dorm located on the southern edge of the Yard. According to campus legend, the girl was writing an essay by an open window of her third-floor dorm room when a homeless man called out to her from the street below. "Hey you, gimme dat computer!" he said.

The girl could have easily denied the request and closed her window and continued her essay in a quieter part of her room, but instead she panicked at the threat of the scary man with no shoes and poor diction. She told him to give her a second, and then spent the next ten minutes assembling a makeshift rope out of knotted sweaters and pants. She secured her laptop to the end of the rope and carefully lowered it down to the astonished man before closing the window and thanking god for her spared life.

It's stories like this that corroborate the popular belief that Harvard students have "book smarts" but no "street smarts"— that their brilliant minds are only useful in an academic setting and can't be utilized in practical, real-world scenarios. While I can't entirely dismiss this stereotype (I once saw a kid volunteer his wallet as a prop for a street magician, who then pulled a disappearing act), I feel like it is an unfair generalization. Harvard students come from vastly diverse backgrounds and, in many cases, their real-world experience is far more advanced than the average young adult. Dermot felt the same way, once saying, "I don't understand how anyone can say we have no 'street smarts' when Harvard has the most roads scholars in the world."

Whether Harvard students mind it or not, homeless people have a noticeable presence in the community. With a first-floor bedroom with a paper-thin wall adjacent to a public street, I grew quite familiar with a few of these unfortunate people. I recall one night struggling with a pesky calculus problem while overhearing two guys outside partaking in what sounded like a fight to the death over a salami sandwich. You'd think an act of such desperation would put my trifling calculus homework into perspective, but really I just wanted to trade places with them. Other students would get even more exposure, as occasionally homeless people would sneak into dorms and make themselves at home. Once a freshman girl returned to her room to find her shower occupied by a stranger. When she asked the person to identify himself, a disheveled hairy man popped his head out from behind the curtain, smiled, and said, "Hi, I'm Steve."

Call me old-fashioned, but first-name familiarity should be enough to share your loofah with a guest in need. The girl thought otherwise, and called the cops on poor Steve.

Swipe-card locks at the entrance of dorms are an annoying but necessary measure for ensuring that all our hot water isn't used up by homeless folks. Of course, on this day it was more of a nuisance to me because I couldn't get to my room until another student swiped me in. Fortunately it was the middle of a busy weekday, and I didn't have to wait long before a short, brown-haired girl wearing a purple cable-knit hat approached my entry-way. I wasn't too familiar with her, so I stood politely to the side and waited in silence for her to enter. As the door closed behind her I deftly slipped in the dorm and proceeded to my room.

I had an hour to kill before calculus class—plenty of time to check my email and refresh Weather.com several hundred times—so I took off my butter-stained pants and tossed them in my hamper and sat down at my computer.

About ten minutes later, I was interrupted by an aggressive knock on the door of the common room. Neither of my room-mates were around, so I begrudgingly unglued my eyes from the glowing screen and headed over to the door to see what all the fuss was about. I was only mildly concerned when I looked through the peephole and saw two rather large police officers. I hadn't done anything wrong, so I doubted this visit was relevant to me. Maybe they're here for Dermot? I was pretty sure that bottle of whale-oil he kept in his desk has been illegal in the U.S. for, like, fifty years. In fact, the only thing that concerned me at that moment was my lack of pants, a fashion state that was becoming a frequent and highly unfortunate theme of my freshman year.

"Police! Open up!" I suddenly realized these guys weren't messing around. They had guns and Boston accents, so I made a point to swiftly comply with their request. I grabbed a random pair of pants off the floor of the common room, slipped them on, and opened the door.

"We received a report of a suspicious person entering the dorm," one of the cops told me. "Have you seen anyone or anything out of the ordinary?"

I paused a moment to think, but couldn't remember anything that struck me as strange. I told them I hadn't noticed any irregular activity.

"Alright, well please let us know if you see any—"

The officer was abruptly cut off by a loud voice over his radio: "Officer Jenkins, we have a description of the intruder. The student reported him as a white male over six feet tall, with dark brown hair and small, duplicitous eyes. He's wearing a red hooded sweatshirt."

Both cops narrowed their eyes as they inspected my face, then all three of us simultaneously looked down at the red hooded sweatshirt I had on.

Oh shit.

"Sir, can I see your Harvard ID?"

Oh shit.

The officers really could have been a bit gentler when they dragged me to the cruiser parked outside my dorm. As they aggressively led me by the arm, I took a moment to silently curse the person who was surely responsible for this predicament that would ruin my afternoon, if not my life. I couldn't believe that girl in the purple hat had called the cops on me. I didn't know her name, but over the semester I had definitely passed her in the hallway a number of times. Was I really that forgettable? And did I really seem that suspicious to her? I was a showered, college-aged guy who had lathered himself in masculine body wash earlier that day. Vagabonds don't typically smell like midnight thunder.

In retrospect, though, I can kind of see her concern. To her I was an unshaven stranger loitering by the entrance while eating stray animal crackers out of my sweatshirt pocket. The stain on my pants probably didn't help matters either.

The vehicle's flashing blue lights had attracted a dozen or so curious students, and that number quickly swelled once the officers triumphantly emerged from the dorm with the culprit. I would've offered anything to avoid this public spectacle, but I had no money for a bribe and I doubted it would help matters if I offered the cops a cup of my sperm.

I wasn't resisting the officers, though I had some difficulty moving in the ultra-tight pants I had hastily picked off my common-room floor. They clearly belonged to one of my roommates, as they were about two sizes too small and severely cramped my overflowing ass and waist.

The officers shoved me in the direction of the car and ordered me to place my hands and the side of my face on the hood.

Officer Jenkins clicked on his walkie-talkie. "Patrol, we've apprehended the suspect. About to bring him back to the station. He says he's a Harvard student…" he hesitated a moment to look me over, "…but I'm not so sure."

As I waited for my next instructions I frantically scanned the growing throng of onlookers for someone—anyone—who might be able to vouch for me.

And that's when I saw her.

She couldn't have been more than ten yards away from me. Wearing a black fleece, dark-wash jeans, and a green handbag over her shoulder, my crush was as stunning as ever. She was standing in almost the exact same spot as the first time she saw me on move-in day. I couldn't tell if she was looking at me with disgust or pity. Either way, it was not an expression a guy wants to see from the girl of his dreams.

This cannot be happening.

"Do you have anything sharp in your pockets?" Officer Jenkins barked as he positioned himself behind me for the pat-down search.

"I…I don't know." I left my statement at that because, "They're not my pants," isn't the type of thing innocent people say.

The officer patted me down by my ankles then moved up my legs before reaching into my pockets. Suddenly, I felt the cop back away from me. The crowd erupted in varying exclamations.

Keeping my hands planted on the hood of the cruiser, I craned my neck around to get a glimpse of the commotion. Officer Jenkins was standing in shock and staring at his hand, which was clenched around a deformed and slightly mushy cod cake. The stench of old fish must've been overwhelming, as the officer dropped the cake, put his hands on his knees, and began dry-heaving.

The other cop, raising his voice over the clamorous buzz of the crowd, ordered me to look forward as he swiftly moved in to finish the unenviable task of searching me. He dug his hands deep into my pockets, and to my relief the only thing he extracted was a crumpled-up piece of paper. He unfolded it and read it over, then turned to his revolted partner. He held the paper up high and spoke to him in a suspiciously declarative tone.

"It's a printed receipt from BreastMilkMommy.com," he announced. The crowd reacted to this in unison, bellowing a loud "OOOHH!" like they had just witnessed an accident that looked too painful to be funny. The cop circled back to me. "What the hell's the matter with you, son? Get your ass in the car."

Before unassuming the position, I reluctantly glanced up at my crush. Yup, no doubt about it now—it was a look of disgust. She was surrounded by a group of three girlfriends, and one of them turned to her. "Ewww, Jen, this is gross. Let's go."

———◆◆◆———

It's funny how sometimes in moments of crisis you don't process just how badly things are going. Don't get me wrong—this little disaster caused me to skip ahead several stages of depression. But as I was driven away to the police station, my brain kept returning to one uplifting thought, over and over: finally, I had her name.

Chapter Nine

THERE'S SOMETHING ABOUT LARRY

Is there something wrong with him?" I whispered to Ryan.

"I don't know. Maybe he just has a bad speech impediment...and vertigo...and narcolepsy." Ryan's lips barely moved, his eyes locked straight ahead.

"But he's making no sense at all," I continued. "It's like he's drunk or something. Isn't he supposed to be a super-genius?"

"Will you shut up?" Ryan hissed. "You're going to get us in trouble."

Ryan was right. This was a special moment for our football team, having a celebrity give us an inspirational speech on the eve of the big Harvard-Yale game. And the coaching staff had specifically instructed us to "not fuck this up." I really should have been showing more respect for such an accomplished and powerful man, but it was difficult to contain my curiosity as I watched Larry Summers, the former U.S. Treasury Secretary and current president of Harvard swaying in his place, rambling on about nonsense while spewing out words from a dyslexic Scrabble game.

"Ever since I was installiated as the president of, uh, Harvard, nearly about sixish years ago...or was it three? It was three...yes.

Of this I am sure now. So, for the last six years I have always been a hugest fan of the football team...that being, uh, you guys. So..."

Larry interrupted his own speech by breaking into a solo applause. It was a lackluster salute, I recall, as the resonance of his applause was muted by his black leather gloves and by the fact that he completely missed his hands on the majority of his attempted claps. My teammates and I looked around at each other in confusion, unsure whether we were supposed to join him. A few guys contributed a couple of hesitant claps, but Larry suddenly halted his ovation, now separating his hands and holding them out to the side in an effort to stabilize his wavering balance.

Today was our last practice of the year—a joyous occasion for human tackling dummies such as myself. But Larry's speech was an unwelcome extension of what had been a very long season. Dusk had settled on the practice field behind Harvard Stadium, and towering lights illuminated our breaths as we inhaled the frigid November air and converted it into puffs of smoky vapor. My entire team was kneeling in a semi-circle around Larry, who held his arms out at a downward forty-five-degree angle with his palms facing toward us. To rush-hour commuters careening past Harvard's practice field, the scene must have resembled a crowd of disciples glorifying Jesus—that is, if Christ ever preached at the fifty-yard line and his blood had been turned into wine.

"Just the other day I was on the, uh, phone the other day with the president of Yale, Ricky Levin, who's the president of Yale." Larry spoiled this exquisitely constructed sentence by slurring it into one long word. "He claims he's got a better, uh, football team. Can you—can you believe that? What's next? Is he going to claim they're more well-endowed?"

This was meant to be a joke, I think, but not a single one of my teammates echoed Larry's nervous laughter. Thankfully our coaches erupted in forced hysterics, except for Coach Mac, who shook his head angrily, wrung his hands, and said, "That fucking liar Levin can suck my endowment!" Coach Mac's outburst was muffled by the whipping of a fierce breeze, and Larry took a break from his incoherent monologue to button his long cashmere overcoat.

This was the first time I had actually seen President Summers in person, though I had read a lot about him and had deleted plenty of his campus-wide emails. He was different from what I imagined a Harvard president to look like, sharing hardly any qualities with my only point of reference, the famous John Harvard statue located in the middle of the Yard. The effigy of Harvard's founder portrays a man of imposing authority—a chiseled jaw, prominent brow, and well-defined cheekbones establish his stately countenance. He's posed on a throne-like chair and clutches a book in his right hand, though my eyes have always been curiously drawn to his left hand. His long, flowing hair and hard, confident gaze seem to enhance the potential of that empty left hand, which sits poised, like it's ready to strike the face of an insolent schoolboy or the ass of an attractive coed. His appearance reflects a womanizing intellectual, the type who could just as easily find g in a variable equation as he could inside a woman. It was exactly the look of refined ruggedness that I expected from the most powerful man at the most powerful university.

Larry Summers did not fit this mold. His amorphous face lacked any defining characteristics, other than a pair of sharp blue eyes that were a little too far apart and a receding chin that was on the verge of being swallowed by his other chins. He wasn't obese, but seemed short enough and round enough to be cast as an extra in *March of the Penguins*. An oversized forehead offered plenty of real estate for Larry to scratch, which he did compulsively throughout his speech. His fidgety movements and slumping posture didn't communicate a man of great authority, and it didn't help that his voice sounded a bit like a post-pubescent Kermit the Frog. It was clear to me that Larry's physical appearance and social grace had very little to do with his ascension to power—luckily for him his résumé was attractive enough to arouse quite a few members of Harvard's governing boards.

From birth it seemed Larry was destined to become one of the world's top economists, having two uncles who had won the Nobel Prize in that field. Larry himself showed remarkable intelligence from a very young age. He wisely pursued his education at the only two schools where you can pick up chicks by using the line, "My uncles are Nobel laureates": he enrolled at MIT at the age of sixteen, then received his PhD from Harvard shortly thereafter. Following a short but impressive career as a scholar (at age twenty-eight, he became one of Harvard's youngest tenured professors), Larry joined the Clinton administration where he bucked the office trend by making advances on his career, not on interns. He was named Secretary of the Treasury in 1999.

Sitting on a $15 billion endowment and in need of a new president in 2001, Harvard couldn't help but be interested in an accomplished economist like Larry Summers. Harvard's endowment was a sum of money larger than the GDPs of nearly 120 countries—surely it couldn't be trusted in the hands of a humanities scholar who thinks "capitalism" is what happens at the start of a sentence. No, Harvard needed a moneyman, someone who could inflate that endowment and allow Harvard to fulfill its century-old ambition to acquire a nation of its very own. Perhaps forgetting that Harvard was actually a school and not a bank account, the Harvard Corporation named Larry Summers as CEO—excuse me—*president* of the university in the summer of 2001.

"This game tomorrow…When you take the fields tomorrow…This game is of great importance to the universe…city. I don't—I don't think this. I…know…this."

Larry's eyelids, which had been dangling half-closed throughout his speech, finally drooped completely shut. It was too bad, because the guy was really on a roll.

There was an awkward silence as Larry took what appeared to be a five-second nap, and I took advantage of the intermission to massage my forearms, which were bruised and bloodied thanks to Coach Mac. I could no longer practice in pads with the rest of my team because, a couple of weeks earlier, I had managed to injure my right knee while returning an interception for a touchdown. Or at least that's what I told girls. I had actually slipped in the mud and severely twisted my knee.

Of course, just because I couldn't run didn't mean I couldn't stay in shape, so during practice Coach Mac forced me to perform endless army-crawls around the field, dragging my body along the ground using nothing but my forearms and elbows. He would tail me every inch of the way, and I considered myself lucky that Harvard had outlawed whips on campus back in 1797.

Larry's eyes flickered back open, though his mind seemed momentarily frozen, like he had just restarted his computer and now had to wait for that damn spinning hourglass to go away. A moment passed before he began again.

"Ever since I was installed as the president of, umm, Harvard, four years ago, I have been a huge fan of the, uh, football team…"

He started to bring his hands together for applause, but his *déjà vu* instinct overrode the action and cut it short. Thankfully, Larry took his rambling address in a new direction. "Can you feel the excitement? Do you? Tomorrow you can make history!"

Now this actually made some sense, given the ramifications of tomorrow's big game. The Harvard-Yale game (or simply, "The Game") is always one of the most anticipated events on the school calendar, dating all the way back to 1875. Predating the NFL, The Game was annually the biggest football event of the early twentieth-century—kind of like the Super Bowl, if it was played by a bunch of 160-pound white guys wearing argyle socks. In 1925, Yale coach T. A. Dwight Jones famously summed up the importance of The Game in a speech to his players, stating, "Gentlemen, you are about to play football against Harvard. Never again may you do something so important."

Contemporary iterations of The Game aren't nearly as hyped (I sincerely hope the most important moment of my life isn't sitting on the bench with my freezing hands stuffed down my jock) but this year's game held special significance. Led by league MVP and NFL-bound quarterback Ryan Fitzpatrick, we had devastated our schedule and boasted a 9–0 record. Tomorrow we had a chance to secure the Ivy championship and complete the perfect season on our home field against our most hated rivals. The buzz for the game was mounting and media coverage had reached the point where even my local town newspaper wrote a story about my role on this historic team (headline: "Practice Makes Perfect: Kester's Effort in Practice Helps Starters Hone Skills").

We were anticipating a packed stadium for the big game—a major departure from our typical game-day crowd, which consisted mostly of my parents. To be honest, I wasn't entirely sure why my parents kept dutifully attending our games. I guess they weren't going to miss the opportunity to proudly watch their son step on Harvard's legendary field and perform groin stretches during pregame warm-ups. I appreciated their support and all, but I was looking forward to finally having a crowd loud enough to prevent my dad's voice from echoing throughout the stadium whenever he announced to my mom that he was going to the bathroom (an all-too-common event in a man of his age).

The increased attendance of the Harvard-Yale game would certainly go a long way in improving my team's self-esteem, but I think none of us could shake the feeling that, despite its historic implications, the football game wouldn't even be the biggest attraction tomorrow. That would be the tailgate.

———◆◆◆———

Our undefeated season had done little to reduce the student body's apathy toward football. Tomorrow the stadium would be filled mostly with older alumni, while just outside its walls thousands of students from both Harvard and Yale would participate in the annual tradition of skipping the big game to get shitfaced at the rowdy tailgate. The Harvard-Yale tailgates are always hyped as the social event of the year, and the seemingly endless rows of kegs and barbeque grills ensured that the massive outdoor party lived up to its billing. These Harvard-Yale tailgates are attended by even the most timid and abstinent of students, who emerge from the inner depths of the library to witness the debauchery and occasionally revel in it. It was a rare opportunity for many of the repressed geeks to let loose and feel badass for acting like those "regular" college kids they had seen in movies. Nerdy guys would line up for their turn to operate the keg, eager to use their overdeveloped wrists and forearms to pump something new for a change. They'd blast "Gin and Juice" by Snoop Dogg on their portable speakers and start gulping foamy beer, only to puke from alcohol poisoning by the end of the song.

Friction between Harvard and Yale students is virtually non-existent during the tailgate, despite their perennial and well-publicized rivalry. In fact, the only evidence of hostility between the two colleges is found on the fronts of student-produced T-shirts, which contain disparaging and sometimes witty slogans aimed at the opposing school. Everyone at the tailgate would know that these shirts were in good fun, though I know a couple of sensitive Harvard guys who took it personally when they spotted a Yalie sporting a shirt that read, "What do Harvard and poop have in common? They're both No. 2." Such sophisticated wit is to be expected from the academically elite, but unfortunately not every shirt reflected its creator's brilliance. One year, Yale, displaying an immense lack of creativity, came up with an offensively lame catchphrase for their anti-Harvard T-shirt: "Huck Farvard." Harvard, of course, felt compelled to respond the following year with an infinitely more scathing T-shirt that proved once and for all that not only were we more clever than Yale, but more imaginative as well. The "Yuck Fale" shirts sold out in a single day.

Not surprisingly, these "savage" T-shirts did not generate much actual acrimony between Harvard and Yale students. In fact, most of the undergrads seemed to enjoy the drunken inter-mingling, viewing their counterparts not as rivals but as social opportunities. For some the Harvard-Yale tailgate served as a reunion with old friends from that unforgettable sixth-grade summer they spent studying marine biology at The Center for

Talented Youth. Others would take advantage of the tailgate's carnal possibilities, as the festivity brought a fresh crop of like-minded coeds who hadn't yet rejected them. After a few drinks and a couple of subtle hints at your lofty GPA, you may be able to entice a Yale girl to retreat to your dorm room. From here the hookup is inevitable—lights off, music on, move in, make out, pants down, ankles up—and before you know it you've had casual sex with a girl who was just wearing a shirt that reads, "You can't spell 'Harvard' without V.D." Of course, even hard-core college football rivalries might see occasional intercollegiate hookups, but those are of the praying-mantis variety, where an Ohio State woman may kill her Michigan partner after sex. A Harvard guy and Yale girl would hook up and then exchange their blog addresses.

———————◆————————

The entire university was excited for tomorrow, but at this rate I was concerned that Larry was attempting to filibuster us into forfeiting the game. His address, which contained maybe about three minutes worth of words, had been dragged out to nearly ten minutes as his thoughts kept getting lost on their brief trip from brain to lips. The drawn-out post-practice speech allowed the freezing November air to stiffen my sweat-soaked hair, and my throbbing forearms ached to take refuge in our warm locker room. Larry began to explain his love of the football team for a third time when he mercifully ended his speech midsentence and waddled away from us, which we happily interpreted as a signal that he was finally giving up on this painful exercise.

"Hey! Wh—where are you guyses going?" Larry asked when he sensed the start of our exodus from the field. "I'm not finished!"

The entire team froze midstride around the twenty-yard line while Larry sauntered over to the sideline and picked up a football. "You know, I used to play a pretty good football back in the days," he explained as he made his way back toward our nucleus. "Watch, I'll prove it."

Larry put down the ball and slowly unbuttoned his black overcoat, wiggling himself out of it with a few spastic shakes of his arms. He then handed it to Coach Mac, whose face reflected confusion and disgust, like someone had just passed him a dirty diaper. Coach Mac promptly slipped the coat around the dirt-stained shoulders of a nearby tackling dummy as Larry grabbed the football and paced around the scattered clusters of my teammates.

"Now, who's a quarterback?"

Larry had settled directly in front of me and I froze, praying that his impaired vision was only movement-based. I was flanked by two of my teammates, Treshaun and Jamaar, and he paused to eye us over. "You look like a QB," he stated, tossing me the football. "Hit me with a pass in that end zone. Are you familiarized with football plays?"

I paused a moment, trying to figure out if this was a serious question.

"Yes."

"Excellent. I'm going to run the old 'pick and roll' play, and you hit me in the corner of the touchdown zone."

Before I had the chance to tell him that he had called a basketball play, Larry was scampering toward the end zone. He moved fairly well for a penguin in a pair of loafers and a button-down shirt, though his random zigzag pattern made it difficult for me to anticipate where the hell he'd end up. Given the circumstances, my nerves were surprisingly calm. I knew that as a linebacker neither my teammates nor coaches expected me to throw a good pass, and I didn't feel pressure to impress Larry with a play that he may not even remember in the morning.

I tossed a wobbly spiral in his direction, and as the ball hung in the air I realized the throw was just about perfect.

It was a little too perfect, it turned out. Larry zagged directly into the ball's flight path, catching it with his face. *SLAP*. The distinctive sound of leather colliding with flesh was followed by a yelp from Larry and then a round of gasps from my teammates. They slowly backed away from me, probably to give the sniper a clear shot at the guy who just assaulted the president.

My eyes instinctively darted around the surrounding area, in search of an escape route or, if I was lucky, a portal to another dimension. I caught Coach Mac's eye and he gave me a single nod, as if he considered my bombardment on Larry Summers's face to be both intentional and noble. I then turned my attention back to Larry, who was staggering around the end zone with one hand pressed firmly against his right cheek, just below his eye. One of our trainers approached him, but Larry rejected the help. He tottered over to the black Town Car that waited for him behind the end zone, eventually flinging the door open and slumping inside. Seconds later, the car drove off into the November skyline.

———◆———

Outside of *Halo*, I can't think of a time I would feel good after nailing someone with a headshot. But for some reason I felt especially shitty after this particular blast. Later that night I lay awake in bed and mulled over my guilt, trying to make sense of this unpleasant feeling festering in my conscious.

Why was I feeling so sympathetic toward Larry Summers? He had ordered the pass, and he was maybe even drunk, for Christ's sake! It wasn't my fault that his impaired vision turned a harmless ball into a bloodthirsty projectile.

But the more I thought about it, the more I realized there was a chance Larry wasn't even drunk. It was clear that he was exceedingly nervous speaking to us. Perhaps he was afraid of Coach Mac, who looked like he was ready to steal Larry's lunch money and then jam his head in a toilet. So maybe it was Larry's anxiety that caused him to fumble his words and botch his sentences. As for his coordination, well, I had seen plenty of sober Harvard nerds move with the grace of a three-legged elephant, so maybe he was just the type who was chosen last for pick-up basketball games at recess. It was still difficult to explain the compressed catnaps he took midspeech—though I had read reports that in his previous job Larry was notorious for falling asleep during meetings in the Oval Office. So it wasn't out of the question that I was mistaking Larry's aggregate awkwardness for intoxication.

Larry was a brilliant man, that was for sure, but his lack of social grace may have been impeding his effectiveness as president of the university. His presidency started off on the wrong foot in 2001, when he moved into his office and promptly called a meeting with Cornel West, Harvard's famous professor of African American Studies. Larry didn't pull any punches with West, telling him that he skipped too many classes, contributed to grade inflation, and perhaps worst of all, that his rap album sucked.

Larry's actions may have been brazen, but his intentions were sensible. Ask any Harvard student and they'd tell you how disappointing it is to sign up for a class, only to have the celebrity professor give merely the first and last lectures, leaving the rest in the hands of a pimply-faced grad student. The end of the semester would leave you feeling ripped off, especially since you couldn't return those seven required course books that happened to be authored by your celebrity professor, who you later discovered spent most of the term doing "independent research" off the coast of Cabo San Lucas.

The prolonged absences of professors were a legitimate issue at Harvard, but Larry probably should have approached the Cornel West situation with more tact. It doesn't take a genius to realize that, as a roly-poly white guy, it isn't such a good idea to kick off your administration by castigating one of the world's preeminent African American scholars. Cornel West split for Princeton, and Larry was left with backlash and dissention among factions of the faculty. He stood firm to his vision for a better Harvard, but his personal skills weren't refined enough to mitigate faculty discontent whenever he made a difficult or unpopular decision.

I hadn't even been at Harvard a full semester and I could already feel the anti-Larry sentiment gaining serious momentum among the faculty. I recall lying in bed that night and thinking, "Man, this guy isn't going to survive Harvard for much longer."

And that's when I realized the source of my guilt: I had injured and humiliated one of my own kind. On the surface, Larry and I could not have been more different. He was a short, unathletic genius who was once in charge of the national debt, while I was a tall football player who had to have his bank account monitored by his dad. At Harvard, though, we were just a couple of guys who couldn't fit in.

He just couldn't find his place at this university, which was an absolutely terrifying thought for me. I mean, if the *president* of

Harvard, the most important individual at the school, couldn't even fit in, then how the hell was I going to? Despite what my parents kept telling me over the phone, each passing day left me feeling more isolated, not less. I wondered if Harvard was worth the trouble, and for the first time I seriously considered dropping out.

The only thing that kept me going was my insane hope that I could somehow convince Jen that I wasn't a total creepshow, and that she would then save me from my depressing insignificance. But it was difficult to stay optimistic when even someone like Larry Summers was devoured by Harvard.

Little did I know that far worse times lay just around the corner for both Larry and me. And though we would hit rock-bottom through different means, the source of our downfalls would be the same: girls.

Chapter Ten

SOMEBODY AT HARVARD LOVES YOU

I n Harvard's infinite wisdom, the school elected to hold final exams *after* winter vacation. Most students hated that we had post-holiday exams, and it's hard to blame them. A couple of days before Christmas, Harvard would send us home for a ten-day break, which is precisely enough time to forget everything you learned over the course of the semester. Of course this ill-timed hiatus wasn't a big disadvantage for me, because I had little in my head to begin with. It was like having an empty wallet stolen.

So following my final class in late December, I packed my suitcase full of dirty laundry and fake smiles and headed home.

I had decided to do my Christmas shopping at the official Harvard merchandise store, The Coop, because I was tired of giving out iTunes gift cards with values uncomfortably less than the ones I was receiving. Located just outside the Yard and directly across from the Harvard Square subway station, this three-story megastore has realized that it can sell practically any item by slapping the word "Harvard" on it, a shameless tactic perfect for truly lazy individuals. The Coop carries the standard gamut of university-branded apparel, as well as an arsenal of novelty items like Harvard dog bowls, Harvard scrunchies, Harvard carabineers, and Harvard letter openers (so that when applicants open their rejection letters they can instantly stab themselves in the heart). And for those who like a little extra class up their ass, the Coop sells a variety of Harvard thongs.

Other than Harvard cufflinks, the most pretentious merchandise you can find at the Coop is the teddy bears. Initially, these stuffed animals appear to be the perfect gift for a loved one. They seem cute, sweet, and totally unassuming, devoid of the Harvard shtick that plagues many of the Coop's other items. Then you read the smug words scrawled across every bear's chest: "Somebody from Harvard Loves You." Despite their barely contained self-satisfaction, the bears are one of the Coop's most popular items, since jackasses like me buy them in bulk.

I experienced unprecedented popularity when I handed out these teddy bears to family members on Christmas. People went bananas for that shit. It was like I was giving out my personal seal of approval. "You know, Aunt Karen, not just anybody loves you…somebody from *Harvard* loves you." Deep down, I was a little disgusted with my gifts. I was also slightly appalled by how much I was enjoying myself. It's not often you can give someone a present designed to validate their existence.

I was the center of attention over that holiday break, which felt good. Everyone was eager to hear about my Harvard experience, and it was easy to see that my friends and family regarded me differently. People would still ask me what channel the game was on, but now they would also ask me what my opinion was on the latest international trade tariff, how many quarts are in a gallon, and if I had any good hunches about what the stock market would do in the first quarter. My mom even lifted my lifetime ban on oven use. In group settings, any questions were immediately deferred "to the Harvard boy." Clearly, I was now defined by my school. People were automatically impressed with me, proof that they had no idea what was actually going on back on campus.

Coming back to school after Christmas break was incredibly difficult for me. My anxieties and fears, both real and imagined, had completely hijacked my mind. I couldn't stop thinking about failing calculus, couldn't stop thinking about Tripp and the sordid path I was headed down, couldn't stop pining for a girl I hadn't even officially met. I spent so much time worrying about my future that I became practically immobilized—too tired to study but too anxious to sleep.

The inside of my mind is like one of those funhouses full of mirrors: it's mildly interesting and humorous at first, but spend too long in there and you'll start to feel terrified. I needed help getting out, which is why I reluctantly began searching for mental health services.

For a small school, Harvard has a ton of options for mental health support. The Bureau of Study Counsel primarily helps students find better study techniques and appropriate tutors, but they also offer many services to help cope with mental stress. The Study Counsel has specific support groups for almost every issue a Harvard student can have. There is a support group for international students having a tough time adjusting to a new culture, a group for students embarrassed that they have a learning disability, and a group called simply, "What Are You Doing with Your Life?"

By far the most common mental issue Harvard students face is "perfectionism." I know it doesn't sound like a particularly harmful condition, but perfectionism can be extremely difficult to live with. (For instance, many Harvard students will be physically unable to read past the previous sentence, since it ended with a preposition.) The Study Counsel has an entire section of their website devoted to perfectionism. They offer several resources to assist students who suffer from this terrible affliction, including books and academic studies on the topic, and of course a weekly support group called "Perfectionism: The Double-Edged Sword."

What I needed most was a support group called "Incompetence: The Singled-Edged Sword," but alas no such therapy existed at Harvard.

I began to search for options outside of the Study Counsel. It wasn't that they didn't have any support groups that were a good fit for me. Hell, they offered a support group specifically for students having a hard time coming back to Harvard after vacation. But all these groups involved other students. I wanted something much more anonymous.

Fortunately, Harvard has a number of mental health resources that adamantly guarantee your privacy. One place that actively promoted their commitment to privacy was Room 13, a peer-counseling group located in the basement of the freshman dorm, Thayer Hall. Despite its mission to offer a comfortable environment, Room 13 can be pretty intimidating. They are only open overnight, so you have to slink down there late at night under a shroud of darkness. Even the name Room 13 is more creepy than it is inviting (in fact, *Room 13* is the title of a 1989 horror novel). They try to be welcoming by placing separate baskets of free cookies and condoms near their entrance, which was appealing to me since I was a prolific consumer of half of those commodities. Still, even with their promises of free goodies and complete confidentiality, I couldn't get past the fact that the "counselors" at Room 13 were current Harvard undergrads. What if I went down there and discovered that one of the counselors was a classmate or teammate of mine? What if Jen was down there? I'd probably leave immediately while mumbling a very audible complaint about their basket not containing Magnums.

There was only one answer for me, and that was the professional therapy offerings from the university hospital. My counseling would be one-on-one with an adult stranger, someone whom I would never see at a party and someone whom I (hopefully) would never want to hook up with. I was still not completely comfortable with this solution, however. University Health Services is a busy building filled with students on doctor visits, and I was concerned about being spotted entering the mental health wing. For at the time, I didn't view my therapy as a mature decision to foster self-improvement, I considered it a last-ditch effort to survive Harvard. I was ashamed that one semester here had led to such emotional deterioration.

In retrospect, I probably shouldn't have been so worried about people knowing I was seeing a therapist. My friends wouldn't have been too surprised. Thinking it was entirely natural to see a guy like me entering the psychiatry department, they would've quietly nodded to themselves, the way you might when you see a cop entering a donut shop. And I vaguely understood that lots of students at Harvard (and at colleges everywhere) were in some form of counseling, and there were even more who probably should have been. I didn't judge these people at all, but for some reason I was an incredibly harsh judge of myself. I was overly aware of the competitive nature of Harvard students, and I hated exposing myself as having a weakness, making me prey for a ravenous pack of wolves. This wasn't an entirely fair assessment of my classmates, but when you spend long enough in an ultra-competitive environment, you begin to think that everyone is out to destroy you. It never once occurred to me that most students were too busy worrying about themselves.

———◆———

I wish I could tell you that I left my first therapy session feeling refreshed and ready to tackle my challenges with renewed vigor and optimism. I'd to love to say that I had a profound rapport with my therapist, and that I felt compelled to reward her good work with a "Somebody from Harvard Loves You" bear. Unfortunately, the only thing I took away from the session was a sore ass. Literally.

To be fair to my therapist, Dr. Braden, I should confess that my miserable experience was partially my own fault. I had a bad attitude going in and was even more pissed off when I stepped into her office and realized that real therapy is nothing like it's portrayed on TV. I had expected to conduct my soul-cleansing while comfortably stretched out on a plush chaise longue, a box of tissues within arm's reach as well as a bowl of jellybeans to ravage in between tears. What I got instead was a warped hardwood chair so uncomfortable that it left my aching butt preferring a year in prison before another hour in that seat. There were tissues, but they were for Dr. Braden to blow her nose, which she did often following my more heartfelt moments of candidness.

Instead of jellybeans there was stale candy corn, which is essentially a "fuck you" in confectionery form.

Dr. Braden looked to be around my mother's age. I was okay with that, although it did make me worry that she would cite violent video games as the source of all my problems. She had a few stripes of gray weaving through her dark brown hair, and a butterfly pin attached to her turquoise blouse. Her office was small, windowless, and sparsely decorated, save for a series of framed medical diplomas that meant she was officially certified to call me a crazy person.

She sat behind a large desk and began our conversation by immediately peppering me with a series of questions in a disinterested tone. She asked me if I had mood swings, or problems controlling my anger, or issues with my roommates. It seemed like "Hello" would've been a better conversation starter, but it occurred to me that she may have been trying to determine whether I needed to be relocated to one of the single dorm rooms in Canaday Hall. These special rooms were known around campus as the "Psycho Singles," because they were supposedly reserved for those students who were having problems living with others. (It's hard to blame the university for taking precautions, especially after the tragic events of May 28, 1995, when a Harvard undergrad stabbed her roommate forty-five times in a gruesome murder-suicide.) Still, Dr. Braden's interrogation seemed like a waste of time since I liked my roommates and had demonstrated no belligerence toward them, unless you counted the passive-aggressive way I would rearrange Dermot's food to the back of our fridge.

Apparently satisfied that I was not a threat to anyone's safety, she finally asked me why I had come to see her. I wasn't used to talking about my feelings so openly, so I paused a moment to gather my thoughts and communicate them as concisely as possible. "When I first came to Harvard, I was terrified that I may not belong here," I explained. "Since then, there's been overwhelming evidence that my fears were spot-on. Now I'm convinced that I won't last here, and that anxiety is affecting my daily life. I'm having a hard time sleeping, eating, and studying. I've tried a few different solutions, but nothing is working."

"Ah, trouble studying," Dr. Braden nodded and spoke in a revelational tone, giving me hope that she may have already pin-pointed a solution to my issues. "Are you interested in taking some tests to see if you'd benefit from a psychostimulant like Adderall? Many students here find it very effective."

Dr. Braden was so quick to offer Adderall I half-expected her to ask if I preferred my pills precrushed. I knew the medication really helped some people, but I didn't have a problem staying focused. My problem was that I focused too much on the things in my life that sucked, like my calculus ability, my football performance, and candy corn. Was Adderall the solution to everything here? The office suddenly felt a lot like Tripp's room, and I wanted to leave.

"I'd rather try to figure out a way to control my anxiety. That's my biggest problem right now."

Dr. Braden glanced at her computer screen and made a few clicks with her mouse. "Just taking a few notes," she mumbled quietly, as if speaking to herself. She was clicking her mouse throughout the session, and I was confused because she never actually typed anything. I assumed "notes" was her codeword for "computer solitaire."

"Tell me about the first time you remember feeling overly anxious," she asked in between clicks.

The truth was that my first feeling of sheer panic happened when I was about seven years old. My mom had made a trip to the supermarket, but she was taking longer than forever, so I asked my dad where she went. "Mom went to Jupiter," he joked to the child with strong knowledge of outer space but limited understanding of sarcasm. This planet was, in my estimation, at least a thousand miles away. Getting home from the supermarket would take her at least a few hours, and I believed with every fiber of my being that I couldn't survive that long without string cheese.

I couldn't tell this to Dr. Braden, of course, because it's polite to ease someone in before revealing you're a complete psychopath. So I took her to a more logical genesis of my anxiety: high school and the college process.

"I guess I was pretty anxious my senior year in high school. The whole college process really took a toll on me. Going into my senior year, everyone assumed I would get into an elite school because I was pretty good at stuff. But my guidance counselor told me I was just short in academics, SATs, and football to get into an Ivy.

"I felt a ton of pressure to become a better applicant, so I went crazy trying to improve in those categories. The summer before my senior year I went to numerous football camps, then a bunch of hockey camps in case football recruiting didn't work out, then a few baseball camps as a double backup plan. In school I enrolled in AP Computer Programming, even though I typed with two fingers. On Sunday mornings I had four-hour sessions with Mrs. Barnstable, my SAT tutor. She smelled like she lived with double-digit cats."

I don't know why I added that last part, but it seemed relevant somehow. I waited to see if Dr. Braden had any response to my oration, but she just looked at me like she was trying to figure out what she was going to get for lunch after this. When I continued, I somehow stumbled on an interesting consideration.

"The amount of mental and physical stress I put on myself in high school was overwhelming, but I thought those feelings would at least go away once I actually got into an elite school. It's worse, though. I'm scared that if I blow it here, then all that effort and stress goes to waste. All those hours playing football, all those superfluous vocab words Mrs. Barnstable stuffed into my head, all of it flushed down the toilet."

"I've got just the thing for you," Dr. Braden interjected, and she opened her desk drawer and began to rummage around. I thought she might hand me a gun and tell me to end it all, but instead she gave me a pamphlet on perfectionism. "Many students here struggle with perfectionism," she added.

I opened the pamphlet and read the first headline. *Your B+ is A-OK!*

I tried to restrain the annoyance in my voice. "Maybe I'm not articulating myself well. I don't want to be perfect. I just want to feel normal here, like I belong."

Dr. Braden smiled softly. "It sounds like you're saying that you just want to feel normal here, like you belong."

"That's exactly what I'm saying…literally."

Dr. Braden sat back in her chair in satisfaction. Clearly this was going nowhere, so I began to spew whatever came into my head. "I thought the college process was hard enough, but it doesn't even compare to the way students at Harvard handle the job process. Everyone is obsessed with getting internships at the best investment banks, or getting accepted into the best graduate programs. GMATs, LSATs, job interviews, networking…it's like the college process all over again. But now there's a lot more at stake, because now we're dealing with careers, money, and our future happiness. How am I going to compete for those things if I can't even make it through my freshman year?"

We spent the final twenty minutes of the session chatting about nothing in particular. At one point Dr. Braden suggested that I might be suffering from seasonal affective disorder (SAD), an observation that actually had some merit since I hated the dark days of winter. We then returned to my earlier point about the job process and wrapped up our session by talking about how money doesn't buy happiness, a life lesson I could have just as easily found in a fortune cookie. She didn't prescribe me any medications, but strongly recommended that I pick up one of those fancy lamps that replicate the UV rays of the sun, which should fight my SAD and bring happiness back to my life.

The lamp cost $299.

Harvard designates the week following vacation but prior to final exams as a "Reading Period," where all extracurricular activities are halted and students are expected to do nothing but study, eat, and (if you're the slacking type) sleep. In a surprising move that belied my typically casual approach to academics, I actually used Reading Period to study a fair amount for my calculus test. In fact, in general I found it slightly easier to repress my anxieties after my therapy session. My newfound focus wasn't because of anything Dr. Braden said—I just had motivation to shape up so I wouldn't have to visit her ever again. Also, I figured it would be important to study as much as possible so if Tripp's cheating plan unexpectedly went to shit, I could still have a slim chance of surviving the apocalypse on my own. This was like wearing a helmet in case your parachute doesn't open, but it was better than nothing.

I spent most of Reading Period studying inside Lamont, which was easily the most popular library in the Yard. Widener was too intimidating with its fragile three-hundred-year-old books and its even older librarians, and most students found the Pusey to be too small and musty inside. Lamont, though, was far more inviting with two large reading rooms equipped with comfy chairs, wide hardwood desks, and ample windows to help entrenched students determine when one day had ended and another began. For those seeking more privacy, carrels were dispersed throughout the stacks of the five-floor library (these private desks were in such high demand that they required reservations and an application process).

Throughout my first semester I had rebuffed Lamont Library in favor of my dorm room, preferring to conduct my meager studying within arm's reach of my stash of animal crackers. But Dermot's recent earsplitting discovery of "electrofunk" music forced me out of my dank cave and into the library for the Reading and Exam Periods.

I thought I had a full understanding of the intensity of my school's academic culture, but I was not prepared for the savage domain of the Lamont Library. When I first stepped inside and surveyed the scene, I felt a rush of hopeless terror grip my soul. I was entering Harvard's wretched underworld.

The inside of Lamont looked like a postapocalyptic shanty town, with hundreds of exhausted and unshowered students converting every inch of real estate—from desks to couches to open patches of carpet—into a personalized workspace. For the foreseeable future they would study in their individual workspace, which typically evolved into a makeshift shelter equipped with a blanket and an assortment of other survival provisions: Red Bull, eye drops, earplugs, white noise machines, caffeine pills mixed in a bag of granola and raisins like some kind of 'roided-up trail mix, extra batteries for the white noise machine, etc. While the students diligently reviewed their notes and wrote their term papers, the library resonated with sniffles, anxious foot tapping, overaggressive keyboard typing, coffee slurping, and the sporadic echoing of faint moans from over-worked students slipping into advanced stages of dementia. It was a soundtrack that made you consider lighting yourself on fire, but still quite a bit better than electrofunk.

At first glance the Lamont Library, with its disheveled dwell-ers and its stench of abandoned hygiene, appeared to be a place where hopes and dreams came to die. But despite the chaos, most of the overwhelmed students still managed to work with amazing efficiency. The mass of students executed their tasks with a certain focused desperation, like a war-ravaged nation urgently preparing for one last stand against the relentless forces of Academia. Weary students teetering on the edge of collapse would find motivation by reaching into their pockets and pulling out crinkled pictures of loved ones, reminding themselves that this sacrifice was ultimately for a greater cause.

Despair was pervasive, though, as unshaven, bleary-eyed stu-dents huddled around the depleted vending machine and waited in line for their daily rations, speaking to each other in solemn voices with stories of fallen comrades:

"Hear about Jeremy?"

"Aye…massacred by the Physics 312 exam."

"I heard he was cruising through the multiple choice sector when he was blindsided by an ambush of quantum superposition questions. He took 'em like a man, but then his calculator jammed up and…well…the kid didn't stand much of a chance after that."

"The rook didn't pack an extra calc?"

"Freshman didn't know any better. They found him afterward staring blankly into the distance and mumbling the Heisenberg Uncertainty Principle over and over."

"I warned him not to take Physics 312. He was too green, man. Too green…"

Armed with only a textbook, a pencil, and an apple, I timidly took a seat at a table across from a guy gulping coffee as he buried his head in a study guide. Study guides are a popular time-saving technique at Harvard, in which a dozen or so students from the same class form an alliance and divide up the semester's work. Each person would be responsible for typing up a helpful overview of his or her assigned topic, which would then be compiled into one complete review package from which all the group members could study. I was never asked to join any of these study groups, likely because of this weird glitch with my email client where the POP3 would temporarily switch to an unknown IP address, resulting in a resynchronization that may have prevented me from receiving study group invitations. Either that or I just wasn't very popular.

Anyway, I always questioned the so called "efficiency" of these study guides, as overachieving Harvard students would occasionally write an overview of a course book that somehow ended up *longer* than the course book itself. Still, these detailed study guides were invaluable resources during Reading Period and inevitably they would wind up in the hands of students outside the study group. Extraordinary measures were taken to prevent these undeserving students from benefiting from a study guide to which they hadn't contributed; password protection and data encryption for Word files were not uncommon, and I know of at least one instance in which a legal contract was signed by the group members.

Of course betrayal is prevalent in the cutthroat world of Harvard academics, as some ruthless students would aim to lower the curve by intentionally slipping bits of false information into the study guide. These deliberate inaccuracies would have to be miniscule to slip past the discerning eyes of Harvard geniuses (though it's been rumored that Tripp once tried to lie about the year of the War of 1812). As you might imagine, shit really hits the fan whenever a study group discovered such acts of deceit. Harvard may be the only place in the world where lying about the number of electrons in polonium is regarded as an act of terror.

The guy at my table was so enthralled with his study guide that he didn't even notice me until I removed the shrink-wrap from my textbook. The crinkling noise caused him to glare at me with his bloodshot eyes, and I could tell he was suppressing murderous intentions as he scowled at this noob who showed up to the Lamont Library with nothing more than a dull pencil and a perishable snack. He pulled out his laptop and started to type with disturbing aggression, no doubt pretending the keys were my face. Loud typing is among my top three pet peeves, along with loud gum-chewing and people who study with a piece of paper on their desk that reads "DIG DEEP." This kid was checking off all three of my aggravation boxes, so I collected my possessions and ventured to the top level of the library, totally ignorant of the fact that this floor was Lamont's own version of Dante's second circle of hell.

When I reached the top floor of the library, I settled down in the seemingly innocuous Farnsworth Room, a small reading area that was filled with books but surprisingly devoid of students. The Farnsworth Room was a gift from the family of a fella named Henry Weston Farnsworth, class of 1912, who was killed in the First World War. According to the library's website, "The Farnsworth Room was dedicated on December 5, 1916, four full months before the United States officially entered the Great War, making it quite possibly the country's first memorial to an American who lost his life in WWI"—in case you had any doubts which university was the *very best* at turning tragedy into books.

The Farnsworth Room houses four thousand "eclectic leisure" books and was the "very first extracurricular reading collection at an American college or university." After just fifteen minutes of browsing the dusty collection of old books, it was clear to me that "eclectic" and "extracurricular" was just Harvard's fancypants way of saying "totally fucked up." *A Handbook on Hanging* sounded a little outdated, while *Black Bonanza* sounded like a movie in the adult pay-per-view section. The worn condition of *The Rich Man's Guide to Europe* indicated that this book had been utilized by many Harvard gentlemen over the decades, and I wondered if it was one of Tripp's relatives who went through and underlined all the best European brothel locations listed inside. No topic is off limits in the Farnsworth Room, and I spent nearly an hour browsing books about freaks, secret societies, whore houses, dark magic, bestiality, and other quirky, poorly written titles that had a print run of precisely one (in fact, it is quite likely that, at this very moment, you are reading *That Book about Harvard* in the Farnsworth Room).

This room was beyond bizarre, but as I was about to find out, its adulterated contents were tame compared to the shit that was going down inside the fifth-floor men's room.

———◆———

I sat in the Farnsworth Room for several solitary hours, alternating chapters from my textbook and a paperback entitled *The World's Wickedest Women*, a topic that I found to be a little more interesting than calculus. It was past midnight and the top floor of the library was so desolate it was kind of spooky. My intestines were starting to rumble as that second helping of "Carnitas Burrito Surprise" I had for dinner was coming back to bite me in the ass. So I put down my books and made my way through the deserted hallways to the nearby restroom. Which I was soon to learn was Harvard's headquarters for anonymous gay sex.

Yes, that's right.

Apparently everyone at Harvard knew about this scandalous bathroom but me. As early as the 1960s this particular men's room, tucked away in the upper recesses of the vast Lamont Library, has served as a hub for frisky gay students looking for a little action. These clever students devised an efficient way not only to satisfy their sexual appetite, but to do so anonymously. Small holes, about two inches in diameter, were drilled waist-high in the partitions of the bathroom stalls. It's a dirty little secret that the administration continually had to deal with but could not easily stop—it wasn't like they could send out a university-wide email begging the students to stop drilling glory holes in the fifth-floor Lamont bathroom. Instead the restroom was constantly closed down for "routine repairs" while the holes were boarded up. Eventually the bathroom would reopen and the glory holes would mysteriously reappear within days.

You can imagine my surprise when I entered the bathroom at one in the morning and saw that a stall was occupied. Weird, but not entirely crazy; it had been burrito night in the dining hall, after all. I didn't pay much attention to the small hole in my stall, figuring that it was there for ventilation purposes or whatever. Still, my intuition was telling me that there was something a little off about this bathroom. I couldn't quite put my finger on it, but I thought it a little unusual when I sat down on the toilet and a voice in the stall to my left said hello to me. I shrugged and continued about my business, but then the guy chirped up again.

"So do you wanna go first or second?"

Now this *really* confused me—I saw no need to synchronize bowel movements.

"Do whatever you want, man. I'm good," I replied.

"Are you sure you want to do this?" my nosey neighbor asked.

"It's not so much a 'want' as it is a 'need,'" I explained.

"That's true. I've been so stressed with exams lately that I need to release all this tension. I come here way more often during Reading Period. What gets you going?"

"Mexican."

"Ooh, Mexicans. Kinky."

Five seconds later I was sprinting out of the stall, never to return.

Amazingly, this wouldn't be the last time some unexpected penis trauma would pop up before the calculus exam.

Chapter Eleven

THREE BATHROOMS AND A FUNERAL

nytime you wake up at 7:00 a.m. and have to whip out your dick in front of a guy with a mustache, you know it's going to be a bad day. Another truism is that a three-hour calculus final will leave you feeling violated and questioning the existence of good in the world. Unfortunately for me, both of these traumatic events occurred on the same day.

Only fifteen of my teammates were randomly selected by the NCAA for steroid testing, and, of course, I was on the list. I don't know what I did to piss off God so much my freshman year, but it seemed like He was determined to ruin my life. What did I do to deserve this? Maybe He knew that the majority of the five thousand songs in my iTunes library were not obtained through legal means, or maybe He had access to my Internet Explorer history, or maybe He knew that I knocked Dermot's toothbrush into the toilet then put it back without telling him. In truth, I wasn't surprised when I was chosen for steroid testing, because up to that point *everything* that could go wrong for me had. God was tormenting me with catastrophes, stopping just short of turning my johnson into a lightning rod. And He wasn't done yet.

The night before my calculus final I received an email informing me that I had to report to the athletic training room sometime tomorrow between 7:30 a.m. and 10:00 a.m. so the NCAA could collect a urine sample. My calculus exam was at 9:15 a.m., so I set my alarm for 7:15, chugged about sixteen glasses of water, and tried to get some sleep.

It was a futile exercise. On top of the immense anxiety I had over my calculus exam, now I had yet *another* test tomorrow that required restless tossing and turning. Over the previous weeks I had been guzzling an array of suspicious strength cocktails with such unabashedly robust names as "Muscle Milk," "NitroTech Hardcore," and "Primordial Performance." It wasn't like these post-workout shakes were oozing with anabolic steroids and horse testosterone, but I harbored the sneaking suspicion that their secret ingredients weren't simply spinach and Vitamin C. I had gained ten pounds of muscle over the past six weeks, and it sure as hell wasn't from gorging on "Stir Fry Tofu Delight" in Annenberg.

I was particularly concerned about one drink called "Diesel Venom," which came in "AdrenaLIME" flavor. Each serving supposedly contained "15 grams of whey protein and 20 bolts of lightning," which might explain why it burned my throat on the way down and left me with the ability to breathe fire for several distressing yet empowering minutes. A flashy sticker on the bottle claimed that this supplement was COMPLETELY LEAGAL*, which had to be the least reassuring declaration in the history of guarantees. I couldn't find the corresponding footnote to that pesky asterisk, but I had an unsettling feeling it would say something like *IN PARTS OF CUBA.

These questionable supplements caused my urine to adopt a few unearthly chemical attributes, and it disturbed me that my body was producing a fluid that was best described as "sizzling" (seriously, the bathroom mirror would fog up when I took a leak). I was worried that tomorrow the NCAA would suspend me on the spot, citing the fact that normal human urine shouldn't have fluorescent properties or, for that matter, the ability to disintegrate a plastic cup.

I finally drifted off to sleep around 3:00 a.m., only to be roused a few hours later by nature's alarm clock, the bladder. It was a freezing January morning so I threw on a pair of cargo pants and a heavy winter coat. With one hand clutching the strap of my backpack and the other secured on my crotch, I sprinted through Harvard Square and across the Charles River, arriving at the training room about ready to explode. I checked in with an NCAA official, who handed me a small plastic cup. I asked her if she had a larger vessel, like maybe a wine vat, but she said no and ordered me to take a seat and wait for my name to be called.

Three excruciating minutes later, a short man wearing a white lab coat emerged from a curtained-off section of the training room and told me they were ready for me. He was middle-aged, mid-forties I'd say, with small beady eyes that were magnified by a pair of wire glasses. He was balding but compensated for his hair loss with a thick graying mustache with bristles sturdy enough to polish a shoe. I followed him out of the training room and into the hallway where he directed me to a private bathroom. I swung open the door, bolted to the toilet, swiftly unzipped my fly, and held my plastic cup out to receive its rancid elixir. But just as I was about to free my body from its acidic burden, I was interrupted by a cough. I glanced up and to my surprise there was Mr. Mustache, crammed in the bathroom with me. *What the hell?* He just stood there in awkward silence as he fidgeted with the crooked nametag pinned to his lab coat, so I initiated.

"Hi."

"Hello."

"I think I'm all set from here, thanks. I'll just be a minute."

"Okay." This was the part where the guy was supposed to nod politely and leave, but he made no movement for the door.

"Umm, can I help you?" I asked.

"Nope. Just make sure you fill the cup all the way to the dotted line."

That's when it dawned on me. "You...you need to watch?"

"It's policy. Have to make sure the urine is actually yours."

I sighed. When I came to Harvard to play football I thought I was headed down a path of glory, not one that ended with me holding my dick in front of a guy named Norman.

"Please proceed." Norman's eyes were wide and unblinking as he locked them on my junk. My heart now racing, I took careful aim at the cup and tried to go.

Not a drop. I closed my eyes and pushed again. Nada.

This was fucking unbelievable. Thirty seconds ago I was on the verge of wetting myself in prolific fashion, but now my bladder had completely locked up under the scrutiny of Norman's piercing glare. My pipes were frozen, and there was absolutely no chance of them regaining their pressure anytime soon. I'd have a better chance squeezing water from a stone. We stood there in awkward silence for another five minutes as I aimed my malfunctioning pistol at the empty cup. Norman must've been dominant at staring contests as a kid, because I don't think that son of a bitch broke his penetrating gaze even once.

My other teammates waiting for their turn out in the hallway were starting to lose their patience. "Come on, Kester. Hurry up!" one of them shouted as he pounded the bathroom door. "Dude, it's a urine sample, not a stool sample!"

My desperation mounting, I gave my stubborn appendage a stern pep talk. "Come on, you motherfucker!" I hissed. It didn't appreciate the oedipal reference, though, and it continued to mock me with its abstinence. I stood there for a couple more painfully fruitless minutes before Norman finally suggested that we take a break.

"It's okay," he said solemnly as we left the bathroom. "This happens to a lot of men." This was meant to be a sympathetic remark, but he said it with a hint of restrained frustration, like a girlfriend talking to a guy with erectile dysfunction.

I couldn't believe this was happening to me. I had suffered from stage fright only once before, but it was in the literal sense of the term: I had panicked when I forgot the lines to my monologue in my elementary school's production of *William Tell* (though in that instance, unfortunately, the pee flowed freely). This was a different type of stage fright, and it was going to cause my inflated bladder to burst like an overfilled water balloon.

The steroid testers came prepared for guys like me, and Norman sat me down in the training room next to a cooler full of bottles of apple juice. For the next half hour I would drink a bottle, head back into the bathroom with Norman, come out shamefaced five minutes later, and then repeat the harrowing process all over again. Despite the ocean of juice that had been force-fed to me, I wasn't any closer to going. In fact, my stage fright was only getting worse; the longer this process took the more pressure I felt to produce, which just constricted my muscles even more. It was like my bladder had turned into a Chinese finger trap.

After nearly an hour of failed attempts, this had officially turned into a spectacle. Every time Norman and I emerged from the bathroom with an empty cup, the other NCAA officials would huddle together and whisper among themselves in decidedly judgmental murmurs. It was at the point now where they were referring to this as "a situation." The training room, meanwhile, was filling up with other sleepy-eyed athletes receiving morning treatment, and they instantly became transfixed by this real-life drama (or depending on their level of empathy, dark comedy) unfolding before their eyes. Everyone was very supportive, but I would have preferred them to keep their words of encouragement to themselves. I don't think they realized how unnerving it is to hear a dozen hardly known acquaintances shout "good luck!" as you are ushered into a private bathroom with a mustached adult.

In addition to the unwanted volleys of encouragement, everyone in the training room seemed to have different opinions on advanced urination tactics. "Try running the faucet!" suggested one guy; "distract yourself by reciting the quadratic formula in your head!" offered another; "try squatting and tucking it down at a 180 degree angle!" advised a girl who was, I was mortified to see, kind of cute. One skinny cross-country runner with a sinus infection tried to offer some hope as I sipped on my third bottle of apple juice. "Don't worry," he said in between sniffles, "you're bound to go eventually. You don't have a choice—it's the law of displacement."

Apparently even the laws of physics were against me that morning because no amount of fluid was powerful enough to flush out my stage fright. My bladder was throbbing and

Norman, perhaps fearing that I had turned into a human time bomb with a considerable blast-radius, suggested that we try an "unorthodox but highly effective" solution to my dilemma. At this point I was willing to try anything to release the concentrated evil that was building up inside of me, though it was with great reluctance that I followed him to the communal shower in the football locker room. At his instruction I stripped off my clothes, turned on one of the showerheads, and impatiently waited for the water to heat up.

Norman apparently still didn't have much confidence in me to produce quickly, as he made a point to bring a folding chair into the shower room. His shower idea did show immediate promise, though, as the comfortable surroundings of the football locker room and the soothing stream of hot water against my back relaxed me considerably. The shower room and adjacent locker room were (thankfully) empty this morning, and it was only a matter of seconds before I began to fill my plastic cup.

Thank god.

I didn't even care that my stream had the luminescence, destructive power, and audible hum of a lightsaber. My hellacious trial was finally coming to an end.

"Kester?!"

The raspy voice was unmistakable. I looked up to see Coach Mac standing in the locker room, just outside the open entrance to the shower room. My stream immediately came to a stinging halt.

"Did you get in some morning Arm Farm?" he asked excitedly. "That's what I like to fuckin' see!"

Before I had a chance to respond, Norman poked his head around the corner. Coach Mac jumped back, startled by the sight of the fully-clothed adult in the shower with me.

"Actually," Norman corrected, "we're collecting a urine sample. Mr. Kester here has a case of bashful bladder."

"You gotta be fucking kidding me." Coach Mac took a few aggressive steps toward the shower room. "For Christ's sake, Kester, just fucking relax and do it!" he barked. "Let's go! Siphon that python!"

Now I had four eyes (actually six, if you count Norman's glasses, but I was in no position to judge) staring at my wang, which at this point had practically recessed into my body out of humiliation. The cup was partially filled, though it was about an inch short of the dotted line. I was so close, but there was no way I could go now that Coach Mac was staring me down. He had been pleased with my recent improvement in the weight room, but this situation was certainly going to knock me further down the depth chart. How could I be counted on in the fourth quarter of a big game when I couldn't even perform the most basic bodily function under pressure?

In an attempt to draw some attention away from my nether region, I asked Norman for the time. He told me it was nine o'clock.

Son of a bitch! My calculus final!

My test started in fifteen minutes, and the walk from the field house to the exam room in the Science Center would take at least that long. The NCAA wouldn't allow any of their subjects to leave until they provided a full urine sample, so unless I miraculously opened the floodgates this instant, there was no way I could make it to my test. I clenched my teeth and tried to go one more time, but, predictably, it was to no avail. I explained my conflict to Norman, and that I needed to call my calculus professor to inform him that, due to an unexpected glitch in my digestive system, I would have to take the exam at a later time.

As I dried off and put my clothes back on, I realized that my traumatic onset of stage fright might actually be a blessing in disguise: missing my calculus final this morning also meant that I would miss out on my opportunity to cheat with Tripp. The moral conundrum that had been consuming me these past weeks was now simplified. Up until this very moment I had been grappling with a choice between two miserable scenarios: cheat or fail. I was screwed in either case, but what made the decision particularly difficult was my fear of future regret. If I decided to go through with the cheating, I would undoubtedly suffer from remorse and self-loathing for disposing my morals just so I could survive a school with a sexy name. If I chose not to cheat, I would likely flunk out and spend the rest of my life knowing I could've been a refined Harvard graduate if only I hadn't pussied out of a low-risk transgression. My post-exam devastation was unavoidable, but it would have been made even more torturous had it been accompanied by a lifetime of wondering if I would've been better off choosing the *other* evil. Now I no longer had a choice of what to do. It wasn't a major improvement of circumstances, but at least my inevitable downfall was completely out of my hands. There would be disgrace, but no haunting regrets.

Professor Phlegm, in a demonstration of idiotic benevolence, had handed out his cell phone number to the entire class, in case students wanted to call him with last-minute questions as they studied for the final. I shudder to think what his phone bill looked like after waves of overanxious and frazzled students assaulted him with nitpicky questions about minutia that could mean the difference between a score of 92 and a 92.5 on the exam. I thought I would never call this number ("Hi Professor, I

was wondering if you could explain the concept on page 327…
and every page preceding it"), but my involuntary reluctance
to take a piss left me no choice but to fish around my backpack for the slip of paper with Phlegm's contact information.
Norman wouldn't allow me to use my cell phone, citing some
more "policy" that was surely devised by a major prick, so I was
ushered back to the training room to use its office phone.

Upon seeing the fluid in my plastic cup the crowd in the
training room erupted in an enthusiastic cheer, like I was a
toddler who just triumphantly emerged from the potty. Norman
then quickly notified the room that, as you can see, Eric had not
yet completely fulfilled his uric requirement, thus squashing the
celebration and any chance of a parade in my honor.

I was directed to a phone on the wall, which was typically reserved for calling the hospital about injuries a little more rugged
in nature. Professor Phlegm didn't pick up his phone until my
third try.

"Vat do you mean, you hov stooge-fright?"

I was describing my situation in the simplest terms I could, but
it was nearly impossible to relate the concept of "stage fright" to a
non-English speaker—I might as well have been trying to explain
the finer points of existentialism. After several minutes of desperate explanation ripe with mathematical analogies ("it's like there's
a negative number in my log—the output is undefined!"), Phlegm
seemed to capture two basic takeaways: that Meester Keester didn't
want to take his calculus exam this morning, and that he was suffering from some kind of shortcoming in his masculinity.

"I am zorry, but I cannot grant you a dee-lay on de teast just
because you are impotent. Dee-lays are only granted for life-
treatening medicinal emergengees."

So the next call was made to University Health Services. The nurse I spoke to checked to see if my situation qualified as a medical emergency, but apparently "acute stagefrightocious" wasn't listed in *The Index of Deadly Maladies*. It probably would be after today, I thought, but that wouldn't help me in the short term.

I notified the NCAA officials with me that I couldn't get out of my calculus exam, prompting a flurry of phone calls to various higher-ups to hear their thoughts on this unprecedented state of affairs. Norman did most of the talking, beginning each call by loudly stating my full name followed by a vivid explanation of my penile deficiencies. One high-ranking official at the NCAA headquarters in Indianapolis declared that there are no exceptions to their drug-testing policy, and that Harvard, for all he cared, could get bent. Norman relayed this information to Professor Phlegm, who scoffed and dialed up Harvard's registrar's office and put them on a conference call. They politely informed the NCAA officials that I could not miss my exam, and that their little "policy" couldn't overrule a college ordinance that had been in effect for centuries. When the NCAA refused to concede to Harvard's resolute assertion of seniority, the registrar's office was left with no choice but to bring the freshman dean into the debate, which had now evolved into a vicious custody war over me. The dean astutely pointed out that in the hierarchy of tests, "calculus" beats "urine" ten times out of ten—"this is not an opinion…it's a fact."

Professor Phlegm agreed. "Yes, I vould like to zee you find a rebut-hole to dis fag."

The NCAA countered by adamantly declaring that if I left the premises without finishing my drug test, they would permanently revoke my NCAA eligibility. Honestly this was fine by me, as long as it meant the termination of any further debate centered on the stubborn disposition of my johnson. Harvard really couldn't care less whether or not I would be allowed to resume my duty as benchwarmer for another three years, but this had turned into a dick-waving contest between two institutions who took themselves way too seriously, and there was no way the World's Greatest University was going to come up short.

That's when they dropped the hammer. "You know," said one of Harvard's attorneys participating in the five-way conference call, "I think it's about time we get President Summers's opinion on the matter."

"What?!" I shouted in unison with several NCAA officials. This was likely a bluff, but the NCAA didn't want to take any chances messing with a man who definitely had friends in the IRS. Norman quickly offered a compromise that he had clearly thought of at the very start of this whole mess.

"What if I escorted the subject to his exam, allowing him to take the test while still under the watch of the NCAA?"

Norman and I speed-walked through Harvard Square, partly because I was late for my exam but mostly because it was fucking freezing out. The bottom of Norman's lab coat poked out from under his puffy winter jacket and he was wearing a yellow wool cap with a pompom that made him look positively idiotic. He wrapped both of his hands around the plastic cup that was partially filled with my sizzling sample, gleaming in the winter sun.

"Don't even need to put on gloves to keep my hands warm!" he joked.

I accelerated my pace to try to separate myself from Norman a bit, but the dude shadowed me with relentless efficiency. During the walk, Norman suddenly became far more talkative, asking me annoying questions about what it's like going to Harvard ("Is it true you can rent pieces of art to decorate your dorm room?"), but his nettlesome inquiries hardly registered with me as I frantically reviewed my calculus textbook. Though I could now take my exam with the rest of my class, Norman's suffocating presence would foil any chance of me utilizing Tripp's cheating scheme.

My nerves were out of control as Norman and I approached the Science Center. The calculus final was the primary source of my apprehension, but in the short term I also had to worry about the bustling crowd in front of the Science Center. With Norman tagging along beside me, the potential for epic public embarrassment was astronomically high. Knowing my luck, I was convinced I would cross paths with Jen on this walk. I managed to calm down a bit when I reminded myself that it wouldn't be the worst thing in the world if Jen saw me walking into an academic building holding a calculus textbook. At least that would confirm to her that I was an actual Harvard student and not some deranged homeless man with an affinity for synthetic breast milk.

Sadly, I realized, I had reached the point at which Jen seeing me being escorted into the Science Center with a cup of my own urine would actually be an *improvement* of her perception of me.

Luckily the final leg of my journey was Jen-free. We made good time through the Yard, with the only delay coming when Norman slowed down to get a good look at the famous statue of John Harvard, who was getting his daily bath from a hose-wielding groundskeeper. I avoided eye contact with founder, but I could still feel the cold judgment of his stern glare. Though

Norman was the one carrying the urine, I had a feeling John Harvard knew who it really belonged to.

My exam had already started by the time I walked into the amphitheater lecture hall, and I grabbed a free seat in the second-to-last row. Harvard uses a "one seat between you and your neighbor" rule as a sophisticated anti-cheating mechanism, for-getting that human eyeballs had evolved to the point where they can still read a paper three feet away. Norman left his goddamn puffy jacket on and clumsily wedged himself into the open seat between me and a poor Korean girl. Her eyes grew wide when she saw the plastic cup.

I quickly surveyed the room as Professor Phlegm climbed the auditorium steps to hand me my exam. Tripp was sitting two rows below me to the left, his pen resting on a blank exam as he crossed his arms and closed his eyes. I saw Vikas all the way down at the front of the hall hunched over his test and furi-ously scribbling answers like a boy possessed. He was wearing his lucky Cleveland Indians baseball cap (the irony of this was lost to him). Phlegm passed the exam to me and shot Norman a dirty look, but my mustached escort didn't notice. He was too busy observing the horde of number-crunching Harvard geniuses as he took in this behind-the-scenes glimpse like a fascinated child observing the frenzied yet ultimately pointless activity of an ant farm.

There were several extenuating circumstances that were going to make this test difficult for me: in addition to the minor dilemma that I knew jack-shit about calculus, I also had to cope with a pulsating bladder that was now shooting pain to all my extremities. I was barely breathing when I turned over the cover page and read the first question:

$$\int \frac{23}{y^2 + 1} + 6\csc y \cot y + \frac{9}{y} dy$$

The pee started to flow immediately.

"It's time!" I hissed to Norman, who snapped out of his trance with a start. I did the best I could to hold it in as we hustled out of the back of the auditorium, and I managed to make it to the men's room with minimal leakage. I filled up the rest of the cup and then continued into the urinal, unleashing a quantity which could have single-handedly replenished the world's nitrate supply.

"Jeez, should I put out a flash-flood warning?" Norman quipped.

The feeling of relief was so profound during those four glorious minutes that I completely forgot about the daunting exam waiting for me in the other room.

Perhaps it was sad, but it was also true: this was my greatest moment in Harvard so far.

———◆✦◆———

After I was done I said goodbye to Norman with a supremely awkward handshake then returned to the lecture hall. I took a moment to scan the rest of the test to see what kind of twisted acts of torture Phlegm had in store for me. I vividly recall that crushing feeling of helplessness as I stared at the jumble of numbers and variables and Greek letters that might as well been alien symbols. I felt especially devastated because this time around I actually had studied really hard for the test. My past failures in this class could be partially blamed on my inadequate preparation, and I am convinced that my lack of effort was a subconscious defense mechanism to protect my esteem. By not giving my greatest effort I was able to provide myself with a convenient excuse for my failings. But this time there were no excuses, and now I was discovering the true limits of my intellectual capacity. There's no worse feeling than trying your hardest and *still* failing, especially when hundreds of your peers are succeeding, and prolifically so.

I bit my lip and began to write down a few "solutions" (I use that term very loosely), but I felt like I was writing my own obituary. After a few frustrating minutes I put my pencil down and looked around the room in exasperation. I noticed Tripp walking down the auditorium steps. I checked the clock: ten o'clock on the dot. The cheating scheme was on.

Tripp handed his test to Professor Phlegm, then exited the room for his permitted bathroom break. He returned in four minutes, according to plan, and retrieved his test from Phlegm. Now it was my turn.

I hated myself with each step I took down the aisle, but really what choice did I have? Cheating was the only solution I could come up with—it was a "damned if you do, but completely fucked if you don't" situation. The short-term goal was to pass my calculus class and eventually graduate with a Harvard degree so I could get a good job. That's why people go to Harvard, isn't it? Just get through it by any means necessary then pay a shrink to deal with your guilty conscience when you're older. At least that was my uneasy way of justifying it.

Phlegm was a little suspicious that I needed to use the bathroom again, but then he recalled the intestinal "condition" that I told him about when we had met for tutoring in the Pusey Library.

"Loose stools again?" he asked a little too loudly for a dead quiet room.

I nodded grimly.

Phlegm put his hand on his lower torso and winced. "I know de feelings."

My heart was beating through my chest when I returned to the bathroom and entered the third stall from the right, as Tripp had instructed. I closed the door and sat on the toilet, then made my signal—two short, soft taps on the partition of the adjacent stall. One faint tap responded. According to Tripp our co-conspirator had a photographic memory (not too uncommon at Harvard, I learned) and he was going to use his bathroom trip to write his solutions to Part II of the exam. Prior to the test Phlegm told our class the exam's format: Part I was multiple choice worth 40 percent of the grade, while Part II was word problems that accounted for the final 60 percent. Tripp figured that if he could get a math whiz to help us ace Section II, then even random guessing on the multiple-choice questions would yield a passing grade. Our accomplice would slip us his solutions to Part II and we would type the answers in the data input section of our TI-83 calculators, which we transported to the bathroom in the oversized pockets of our cargo pants. We could then return to our seats and transcribe those answers onto the test simply by looking at our calculators. The plan seemed fail-proof.

I didn't know our accomplice, but I felt a little bad for the guy. He didn't know it, but there was an excellent chance Tripp was going to screw him over and not live up to his end of the deal. I wondered what Tripp promised him that would be worth risking expulsion over. Women? Drugs? Money? It really could've been anything—Tripp's resources were as limitless as a college guy's desires. Women on drugs with money in their mouths? It was a possibility.

What's taking this dude so long? Tripp had gone before me so the solutions should have already been written on a piece of paper; all the kid had to do was pass it to my stall by slipping it under the one-foot gap between the floor and the partition. Had something gone wrong? Was he getting cold feet? This delay gave my contrite heart one last opportunity to appeal to my desperate brain. I was having a hard time breathing, and I noticed the four walls of my stall suddenly seemed to close in on me. It's not uncommon for a guy to experience feelings of regret while sitting on the toilet, but usually they are aimed at things like "Carnitas Burrito Surprise." My thoughts concerned a subject with a little more gravitas, and like most teenagers toeing the line of immorality, I couldn't get my parents out of my head.

I had been thinking about my parents a lot in the weeks leading up to my calculus final, and two memories kept coming to mind. The first was that incredible, almost surreal moment when I opened my acceptance letter to Harvard and my dad hugged me tight and told me how proud he was. I came to realize that my *entire life* was like my parents' test, and me getting into Harvard was confirmation that all their hard work had paid off. They had tried their best and received an A+ for their efforts. The pride radiating from my parents was palpable and the memory of that moment remained precious and vivid to me.

But then I think about those quiet moments when I rode in the passenger seat of my father's car, listlessly watching the blurry world whiz by my window, and Dad would break the string of silence with a pat on my leg.

"I'm proud of you."

What was the source of his pride then? Was he thinking about Harvard, or was he reflecting on something more profound, something ineffable? It's difficult for teenagers to understand these moments, so we shove them to the back of our minds and strive to impress our parents with achievements that yield tangible pride. Grades, touchdowns, college degrees—these are concrete sources of pride and easier to grasp than an abstract sense of character, morality, and honor. And it's not like parents aren't exceedingly gratified by these material accomplishments. In a way, it almost seemed selfish of me *not* to cheat. My parents would be intensely disappointed and saddened if I failed out of Harvard; shouldn't I be willing to cope with a guilty conscience to ensure their blissfully unaware happiness? My parents cared deeply about my morality, but they would likely never find out about my sin, and I'm sure they would rather tell their friends about "Eric, our son who goes to Harvard," than "Eric, our virtuous college drop-out." I would hate myself for taking away that pride I saw in my father's eyes when I received my acceptance letter. But if I went through with this, would Dad's next unsolicited pat on my leg feel like a gut-wrenching punch to the stomach?

My head was spinning as the contracting walls had turned my stall into a suffocating coffin. I had to get out of there.

I left the stall silently and proceeded to the row of sinks across the room. There were several guys milling about the bathroom, and I washed my hands vigorously even though they were clean. Despite my innocence, my pulse quickened when the restroom door flew open and Professor Phlegm stepped inside. I continued to wash my hands as I stared at the mirror and watched Phlegm approach the row of stalls. My former stall was the only one left unoccupied.

I was the first to see the bodiless hand reaching under that stall's partition, holding out a piece of paper for an absent recipient. Phlegm saw the slip of paper too, and I casually turned off my faucet and dried my hands as he bent over, snatched the note, and slowly unfolded it.

Game over for that guy, I thought gravely. As I made my way to the exit I couldn't resist looking back at the dead man's stall. The door was still latched closed, and I looked down at the open gap by the floor. My heart skipped a beat when I saw a tiny pair of untied Air Jordan sneakers.

Vikas.

Chapter Twelve

THE ACE OF CLUBS

I can always gauge my overall anxiety level by how terrified I am to check my email. When things aren't going well I start to regard my inbox as nothing more than an efficient system for delivering terrible news. So it's needless to say that, in the week following my calculus exam, I was nearly shitting my pants every time I logged into my account.

So far I had only received two semi-damaging emails: one was a "home update" from my mom, in which she accidentally referred to my bedroom as "the new storage area," while the other was a brief passive-aggressive message from Grandma (*Eric, have you been getting my emails? Because I haven't been getting yours.*). As impressed as I was that an eighty-two-year-old lady knew how to use email, it struck me as a little unnecessary for her to CC the entire family, cousins and all, on our correspondence.

But the only email I was truly dreading was one from the academic office, which I imagined would be a notification that my GPA was too low for me to continue on with Harvard, and possibly with life.

———————◆————————

The news, it turned out, wasn't delivered via email, but in person. Judith, my resident advisor, knocked on our door one snowy afternoon in late January.

"Sorry, Judith. I told Dermot to turn down his music, but then he did the exact opposite."

"This isn't about the music, Eric. Have you seen your first semester grades yet?"

"No."

"Well, you made the Dean's List…"

"What?! Oh my god!"

"…of students on academic probation."

"Oh."

My emotions fluctuated from terror to jubilation to disappointment before finally settling on relief.

Inherent in the word "probation" is "second chance," which is exactly what I got. It probably doesn't surprise you that I survived into my second semester (at least for your sake I hope it didn't, given the length of this book). But it was utterly shocking to me.

I had struggled in all of my classes and that calculus exam in particular had defiled me. Still, I somehow managed to compile final grades good enough to barely squeak by Harvard's cutoff for the unworthy. I won't go into specifics, but at least my GPA was high enough to be expressed without the help of negative exponents.

I had received a C– in calculus, a miraculous feat that I was sure would yield an intense bidding war between *Ripley's Believe It or Not* and *Unsolved Mysteries*. Phlegm must have liked me more than I thought because there was no way the average of my homework and test scores worked out to a C–. I made sure to send him a quick email that thanked him for essentially saving my academic career. His response was short. And weird.

Mr. Kester—I am very happy to have pleasured you. Hopefully I will see you again soon? Maybe at the Student-Faculty luncheon next month? It would be enjoyable indeed to spend an evening outside the Pusey :)

Great, so now I have to invite Phlegm to the student-professor event at Annenberg next month?

———◆◆———

At least I was back at Harvard for a second semester, which was more than Vikas could say. He wasn't technically expelled after Phlegm caught him, because he wasn't a full-time student. But he would no longer be allowed to audit the math and science classes at Harvard.

Immediately following our calculus exam, I rushed over to Tripp's room to punch that asshole in his fucking pretty-boy face. My fist was clenched when I walked into the room, but I ended up just sitting on the couch, like a pussy, while Tripp congratulated himself for pulling off another successful scandal "with minimal losses." Tripp beamed with pride as he explained how he convinced Vikas to cheat by appealing to two soft spots in the kid's heart: the fact that Eric (that is, me) and Beth (the rugby player Vikas was hopelessly in love with) desperately needed his help. "Eric will be eternally grateful," Tripp told Vikas, and Beth only needed one good word from Tripp to fall head-over-heels for the fourteen-year-old. With an incentive like that, Vikas didn't even need to run the proposition through his qualitative risk-assessment matrix. He was in.

The only concern Tripp had had following the exam was whether Vikas would rat out his co-conspirators. But of course my loyal buddy never ended up turning me in. He didn't finger Tripp, either. And the poor kid *definitely* didn't finger Beth.

I could've easily beaten the shit out of Tripp that day, and his customized croquet mallet lying on the floor seemed to beg me to do so. But I was too busy concentrating all my hate and blame on myself. Not only did my last-second withdrawal from the bathroom stall directly lead to Vikas getting caught, but I was also the reason he was involved in the scheme in the first place.

Leading up to the test, I had lengthy conversations with Vikas in which I revealed my anxiety about the exam and what was at stake if I didn't pass the course. I subtly hinted that it would be the end of the world if I didn't make it at Harvard ("armageddon times a million" I believe was the terminology I used), and Vikas honestly believed the same thing. The little guy had been flourishing in his classes here, yet he risked everything to help me. Now Vikas was the one who didn't survive Harvard.

It wasn't right. My obsession with getting a degree from this school (at all costs) had been disintegrating my morals, which was bad enough, but now I was hurting others too, and that guilt was becoming impossible to bear. I hadn't heard from Vikas the entire week following the exam. His cell number had been disconnected, emails bounced back, and ThreePoint1Four69 had stopped patrolling the Internet. I could only imagine the type of punishment his crazy parents had dropped on Vikas—they might've killed him, or worse, cancelled his *World of Warcraft* account. It was a shitty situation, but I felt some comfort knowing Vikas was smart enough to succeed in any environment. Plus, I was beginning to wonder if leaving the Harvard bubble wasn't such a bad thing after all.

Despite the relief of passing calculus, my guilt led to many more sleepless nights in my Lionel dorm room. I found myself surfing the Internet for hours. And by "surfing the Internet" I mean "exploring Jen's Facebook profile" and by "exploring" I mean "stalking."

After I learned Jen's name during my public arrest, it didn't take long to finally find her Facebook profile—there were only a handful of Jens and Jennifers in my freshman class. Her profile picture was a black and white photograph of (presumably) her chocolate lab, which explains why I had difficulty finding her in my initial searches. I was encouraged by the cute dog photograph, as adorable pet pictures are typically the calling card of a single lady.

Jennifer Wesker. I liked that name. It was pretty. Admittedly her beauty caused me to be a little biased; I probably would've thought Doris Dingleberry was a cute name for her as well.

Her profile didn't exactly have the type of information I was hoping for (namely, a list of her turn-ons), but the similarities between our Facebook pages were striking: we both were born in September, we both liked movies, and we both had genders. If that's not a match made in heaven, I don't know what is.

The only big difference in our profiles was the activity on our walls. Hers was plastered with inside jokes from hot friends and flirtatious messages from tanned guys, while mine had only one comment. It was from Dermot, who wrote a kind message on my birthday: "hey ya plonker—I got the scutters and the bog is outta toilet paper. mind grabbing some at the mart? time is factor."

I considered sending Jen a friend request, but how would I preface it? "Hey Jen, you've seen me in my underwear and you've seen me in handcuffs. Maybe one day you could see me in both at the same time, if you're into that sort of thing ;)" I was totally lost when it came to Facebook etiquette. Like, could I be "friends" with a stranger? My understanding of opposites told me probably not.

And what the hell was this "poke" feature? Up to this point I had been using it only for nefarious purposes. Back in November, for instance, this kid called me a fuckface for accidentally knocking over his pencil case, and since then I had been poking him three times a day for eleven straight weeks. But while Facebook poking was a great tool for harassing your male enemies, I wasn't sure how females would react to it. I've had bad luck with poking girls in the past. In elementary school I got in big trouble for poking Sally Jensen in the eye, then in junior high I got in even more trouble for poking Sally again, this time in the boob. It seemed to me that this Facebook "poke" feature was just asking for trouble, as it was little more than a virtual "fondle" button.

Since sending Jen a friend request appeared a little aggressive and poking her seemed borderline illicit, I finally came up with the perfect plan. I determined that the least creepy course of action was to use her tagged pictures to identify her most frequented areas on campus, and then start loitering in those same areas myself. I would then casually bump into Jen and impress her with a charm that would hopefully come out of its lifelong hibernation at that very moment.

There was just one major problem: I was forbidden from all the locations where she liked to socialize.

If you were to ask a Harvard student about Greek life on campus, they'd probably shrug and point you in the direction of the local gyros joint. That's because Harvard's social scene doesn't revolve around fraternities or sororities—it's centered on "final clubs." The moniker for these exclusive all-male social clubs originated many years ago when only seniors—those in their "final" year— were allowed to join. Final clubs at Harvard now allow members from all classes—excluding, of course, the animal kingdom's lowest life form, the freshman male.

To many on campus, the eight final clubs—the Porcellian, the Delphic, the Phoenix, the Fly, the A-D, the Owl, the Fox, and the Spee—are the epitome of "Pretentious Harvard." They reflected the elitist, sexist, intensely hierarchical, and all-around snobbish nature of the old-money school. All the clubs were established before the twentieth century, and while I didn't know any of the founders personally, having just missed over-lapping with them by a hundred years or so, I think it's safe to say these gents were of the "affluent white" demographic. The Owl, for instance, was founded in 1896 by eight chaps named Reginald Mansfield Johnson, Preston Player, Charles Clifford Payson, Austen Foxx Riggs, Malcolm Scollary Greenough, Jr., Frazier Curtis, and Dudley Hall Bradlee, Jr. Somehow I'm not surprised that Mookie "The Mook" Swinehand was left out of this social circle.

Each club has their own multimillion-dollar mansion in Harvard Square (the A-D's house is valued around $3.7 million dollars, or about *ten times* Tripp's yearly allowance). They are equipped with lavish amenities essential to the development of a young Harvard man: squash courts, saunas, full-time chefs, ball rooms, severed heads of antlered mammals attached to the wall, billiard rooms, chess rooms, poker rooms, pork-her rooms with king-size beds and ceiling mirrors, chandeliers, multimedia centers, original Picasso paintings, and walled-in outdoor court-yards that are perfect for garden parties or for taking a leak when the bathroom line is too long at a party.

The wealth of these clubs seems as limitless as that of their alumni, who range from U.S. presidents to movie stars to white-collared criminals. These alumni send money in a regular stream, to ensure that their old final club always has enough to keep the kegs filled, the kitchen stocked, and the moose heads stuffed.

And the power of some clubs is the stuff of legend. For in-stance, the Porcellian, the most exclusive and wealthiest of the final clubs, is said to own 70 percent of the land in Cambridge and several wheat plantations in northern England. There is also the well-known rumor that any member of the Porcellian who has not earned his first million by the age of thirty is given that sum by the club. I don't believe that for a second, because I am jealous.

Final clubs are filled with social guys—mostly athletes and wealthy legacies—who know how to throw a good party. The opulent clubhouses are perfect locations for some Gatsbyan debauchery, and with the alternative Saturday night option at Harvard being the intramural spelling bee, it's no wonder that these final clubs are the center of the traditionally "popular" social scene at Harvard.

But despite the endless line of well-dressed students clamor-ing to get into these exclusive parties, there is a certain stigma attached to the final clubs. Entitled, preppy douchebags can be found in every club, and their conceited disposition does nothing to change the perception that the clubs are swarming with elitist assholes. Whether these guys represent the majority or minority of members can be debated, but either way it's their demeanor that dictates the universal reputation of the clubs. In a crowd of five dudes you're not going to remember the four normal ones—you're going to recall that dick wearing seersucker pants and a pair of sunglasses inside while he complains about how his family's "Latina" shrank his tennis whites.

Rather than try further to explain the nature of one of these guys, I'll let one of them do the talking, in the form of an actual Craigslist ad that was posted by an anonymous final club member. I'm quoting word-for-word from the original post. I wish I were making this up:

Harvard senior seeking female companion—22

My final club has a reunion this fall, and my relationship of two years ended disastrously earlier this summer. I have an invitation for myself plus one, and am willing to show you a great time. It is a private party, in an extremely classy setting. There is no real way to describe how ornate the club is, but I guarantee that it will be the most upscale experience of your life. Think back to your high school prom, take away the terrible music, and multiply the experience by ten.

You must be white, 5'6"–5'9", young, blonde, attractive, and intelligent. You must be in school, preferably Tufts or Wellesley but BU and BC are acceptable (definitely not MIT).

You should be able to hold a conversation, know when to be quiet, and be polite in all your behavior. I have seen unruly guests embarrass members before, and I hope this won't be a problem. This event is black-tie, and I am willing to procure an evening gown for you. I hate to sound so harsh, but I have expectations to live up to. No Asian, overweight, or unattractive women please. Ages 18–22 only.

Picture required.

As far as I know, the identity of this prick was never discovered.

When the guy realized his post was being ridiculed in email chains across campus he immediately took it down, figuring he should remove it before some loser with too much time on his hands copied it to his hard drive and reprinted the message in a future book.

Even before this, though, all final clubs, fairly or not, were blanketed with a reputation as being dubious at best and straight-up heinous at worst. There were many whispers that date-rape drugs were ever-present in these clubs. In response to these allegations, some final club guys would refute their misogynistic image, explaining that they respected all women very much, and that these accusations were merely malicious rumors started by "your typical ugly rugmunchers."

But for all the grumbling on how final clubs treated women, it seemed like the greater issue might be the way they treated their own members. Similar to pledging or rushing a fraternity, final clubs have a "punch" process for all prospective members (mostly sophomores), which begins in October. Unlike open rushing at other colleges, you must be invited by a current member to "punch" a particular club, meaning you have to be lucky enough to pass an initial selection process just for the opportunity to get officially rejected later. Once you are "punched" to a club, you are known as a "punch" and you attend a series of events so the members can meet you and internally judge you on important qualities like your friendliness, sense of humor, and proclivity to tattletale. These punch events range from formal open-bar cocktail parties in the club's courtyard to day-long expeditions to a random farm in western Massachusetts where you crush a few kegs while telling dirty jokes and proving your manliness through some shirtless, but totally completely 100 percent hetero, mud-wrestling. Starting off with about fifty punches, cuts are made after each event, until the big "Final Dinner" where the members and the dozen or so remaining punches eat steak and get wasted in formal attire. This night is followed by a final vote, where members evaluate the prospective members on the following criteria, in order:

1.   Is he a legacy of the club?
2.   Is he the heir to a Fortune 500 company?
2a. If not, is he one "unfortunate accident" away from becoming the new heir?
3.   Does he hold any potentially damaging information against any current members?
4.   Is he a tattletale?
5.   Was his tuxedo at the Final Dinner owned or rented?
6.   Does he have a hot sister?
6a. Is *she* a tattletale?

    .

    .

    .

57. Is he a good guy?

Clubs have different ways of delivering the good news to accepted punches, though the most popular method involves some good old-fashioned chicanery. A few members would arrive at the punch's room and tell him that, unfortunately, he didn't get into the club because he got "blackballed" by one member who hated his guts. This news is typically followed by tears as the punch realizes that he wasted so much time and dignity attempting to get into this club, at which point the members tell him, "Psych! You've been accepted and we actually love you—now come here while we congratulate you with some ceremonious kicks to your balls."

The abuse is kept pretty tame at this point, though, as some guys get accepted into more than one club and have to choose which one they liked best. The clubs pull out all the stops in trying to impress their accepted punches, treating them to lavish dinners, bringing them to a luxury box at a Celtics game, escorting them to strip clubs to see some not-so-luxurious boxes, and even flying them across the world for weekend trips to fancy, non-English-speaking cities like Paris, Rome, or Prague. It's quite the lifestyle for a bunch of hedonistic nineteen-year-olds.

But they deserve this period because, man oh man, they're about to get their shit rocked. For in the winter, once the accepted punches have made their final choices, the hazing begins.

Before the "neos" (short for neophytes) can become official members, they must demonstrate that they possess the loyalty, class, and sophistication to join such an elite club. A weeklong initiation period allows the neos to prove their merit through a number of mundane yet essential tasks, such as memorizing the club history, acquiring the official club necktie, and taking a dump on the floor of Boston College's student center.

There is basically no time to attend class during initiation week, as your schedule is packed with a series of mandatory events: a noontime sprint through the Yard in a leotard while singing the "Na-Na-Na-Na-Na-Na-Na-Na...BATMAN!!" song; an afternoon visit to a middle-school girls' basketball game to run onto the court and violently reject little Susie's lay-up attempt; and an all-night group bonding activity where the neos are locked in a pitch-black basement with an impossible quantity of alcohol that must be consumed before the trashcan overflows with vomit.

Typically the most torturous hazing activities involved demolishing your liver with medical-grade alcohol, though there have been horror stories about other nauseating incidents, like one game that I'll just say involved Tabasco sauce and anuses. (Clue: it's not the classic children's game, "Keep the Tabasco Away from the Anus.")

Late one night in my room, I was working on a group project for my dinosaurs class with a guy named James, who was a neo. We were frantically throwing together a shoddy poster-board that would've hardly merited a "Participation" ribbon in an elementary school science fair when we were interrupted by a rapping on my door. I'm not sure what freaked me out more: that the Porcellian knew to find James in my room, or that the guy summoning him was dressed in all black with a top hat and a terrifying mask featuring a long, sinister beak.

"Can I help you?" I asked, even though no, I definitely could not.

The Avian Reaper was silent as he ominously pointed at James and beckoned him outside with a wave of his index finger.

James was gone for two hours, which sucked because he was the smart half of our two-person group. When he finally returned at three in the morning, James walked into our common room and, without saying a word, made a beeline straight to the bathroom. He washed his hands for a solid five minutes before rejoining me in the common room. He then slumped onto my futon and sat in silence. I did the same, figuring it probably wasn't a good time to tell James that while he was gone, the only thing I accomplished was spilling the glitter.

"Don't ever ask me what I did tonight," he finally said.

Sensing that he just went through a very traumatic and emotionally scarring ordeal, I nodded and asked several times what he did. James never did tell me what happened that night, presumably to protect his reputation. But he probably would've been better off being upfront with me because I have forever since assumed that it involved homoerotic murder.

Almost every final club member I know unequivocally declares that the abuse he endured during initiation was completely worth it—the benefits of the brotherhood were that special. Of course this might be an example of that psychological phenomenon where if you sacrifice so much for something you will justify it no matter what, like when I spent my entire allowance on a mini tadpole ecosystem and concluded that it was the sweetest effing thing in the history of ever, even though that lazy pollywog did nothing but float around the tank belly-up. Some members would rationalize their suffering by noting that one had to pay his dues before earning the right to one day be the hazer himself, as if watching a game of "Tabasco Up Your Ass-ho'" was a delightful evening activity. But regardless of their basis for loyalty, members clearly maintained an undying, almost freaky love for their club, and they really didn't give a shit that everyone on campus seemed to have a strong opinion on these polarizing social institutions.

Personally, I believed final clubs were for a bunch of elitist shitheads and wondered why anyone would ever want to go to one of their retarded parties. This thought often came to mind as I walked back to my dorm, after trying in vain for two hours to get into one.

Facebook led me to believe that Jen preferred to socialize at the Delphic, one of the more athletic final clubs that specialized in soccer, baseball, and hockey.

I had walked past the Delphic on Linden Street many times on my way to the athletic facilities, though I had never come close to actually stepping inside. A bright blue door almost seemed to welcome visitors into the stately brick clubhouse, but the perpetually closed window shades served as a sharp reminder that this sanctuary was only for the privileged, not for the lowly freshman who thinks "I-Banking" is what happens when you manage your checking account online.

The intimidating mansion didn't deter me in the first semester, though, as I attempted several times to attend one of their weekend parties. It was like a game of *Duck Hunt*, I was shot down so many times. But knowing now that Jen would probably be inside, my determination to get in was indomitable. This semester I would be better prepared.

Now I lacked several attributes that could get a nonmember into the Delphic, primarily a pair of boobs. But that didn't mean it was impossible for a freshman guy to talk his way into a party. I would have to convince the member working the door that I brought something to the table, that I belonged in this social circle.

Looking the part would be essential. So this time around I was going to go heavy on the preppy garb (in my initial attempts I committed a huge preppy faux-pas: not only was the collar on my shirt not flipped up, it was nonexistent). Having once attended a private school myself, I was knowledgeable in preppy dress, though I didn't own much in that style. I had to look better than a million bucks, because that was pocket change for some of these guys, so with that in mind I assembled an outfit that was oozing wealth, power, and class.

Embracing emblems of polo players and alligators could only

get you so far, though. You also had to know a member if you wanted to get in. I wasn't friends with anyone in the Delphic, so this would be a major hurdle. My plan for that problem was not as concrete.

———◆◆———

It was snowing lightly on the night of my infiltration of the Delphic. As I plodded down Mount Auburn Street, I was filled with the rush of being there, finally in the moment ready to pull off my carefully constructed plan.

But as I turned the corner onto Linden my excitement gave way to nerves. It had suddenly occurred to me that I had spent all this time concocting a way to get into the Delphic, but I had no plan if I actually saw Jen.

How would I impress her? I wasn't sure my looks were enough, considering my mom was the only woman who had called me handsome lately. Intelligence was certainly out of the question, so what was left? My sense of humor? It had been destroyed during the first semester, as it was difficult for me to have any sense of humor about the endless parade of embarrassing calamities that kept befalling me. It was also hard, almost impossible, to adopt a sense of humor at a school that took everything so goddamn seriously. I was trapped in a hypercompetitive bubble, focusing my obsessive thoughts on how I stacked up to, and how I was perceived by, my superhuman peers. There was little room for a sense of humor with the stresses of academic pressure, football performance, and parental expectations occupying so much of my mind.

But I had no other ammunition in my arsenal of charm. So I would have to give it my best shot.

The narrow side road that the Delphic resided on was quiet,

and with the snowflakes slowly meandering through the dimly lit air, I was able to briefly push aside my stress and appreciate the peacefulness of the moment. It would've been a picture of absolute tranquility if not for the deranged homeless woman on the sidewalk shouting racial slurs at a fire hydrant. Before approaching the Delphic, I took a moment to dust the snow off my new Sperry Top-Siders and pull up my Nantucket-red pants. It was game time.

To the left of the Delphic's main entrance is a short concrete path that leads down to the basement door. It was here that a member stood guarding the door, imposing his authority.

The guy was tall and blond and looked more likely to own a baseball team than actually play on one. The sleeves of his white button-down were rolled halfway up his forearms, revealing an offensively large nautical watch. I could see that the watch face also served as a compass, which I guess would come in handy if he ever got lost at sea in the middle of Cambridge. His shirt was tucked into a pair of light brown corduroy pants, and a yellow cable-knit sweater was draped over his back, with its arms tied in a loose knot just below his neck.

Some guys enjoy being the doorman, as it feeds their ego to shoo off undesirables. But in reality, the position is often delegated to the omega wolf of the club. Well, to the members inside this kid may be merely a guardian troll, but to me he was a freaking Supreme Court justice.

He eyed me over when I approached the basement door. "Sorry, you're not on the list."

"You didn't even check the list."

"And you didn't even check to see if your fly was zipped."

I glanced down. *Touché, motherfucker.*

"Come on, it's freezing out here. Can you please let me in?"

"Can't. Fire regulations. We're over capacity." The well-groomed troll paused. "Maybe if you brought some girls we could find some room."

"You realize that makes literally no sense, right?"

"Do you know any club members who could vouch for you?"

"Yeah, uhh, he's on a leave of absence so you might not know him. His name is Theodore...Francis...Humphrey...Vanderdick...the Fourth."

The kid looked skeptical, and at that moment a crowd of people formed a line behind me. I started to get desperate.

"No? Well how about, umm, Chadwick Beef Wellington, Jr.? Sir Allistor Atticus Anderson? Sebastian Cornelius Whipplecrotch?"

"Okay now I *know* you're lying," he interjected. "His name is Sebastian Whistletrot, and he graduated two years ago! Stop wasting my time."

"Father is going to be disappointed when he hears about this," I said in my most pretentious tone, as if Dad was some duke or earl who could levy beheadings and castrations at his discretion.

The kid looked at the crowd and grabbed my arm. "Come on, stop embarrassing yourself and get out of here. Look, your girlfriend is waiting for you." He chuckled and pointed toward the street where the homeless lady was now beating the shit out of the fire hydrant with a stick.

"Relax, Christopher. He's fine." The voice came from the small crowd gathered behind me.

The doorman paused and looked suddenly puzzled. And then he said the last thing I ever would have expected: "Jen, you *know* this kid?"

Jen?

"Yeah," she said, "and don't make him angry. You wouldn't like him when he's angry."

It's kind of a blur after that. I had to concentrate all my faculties on not fainting. But I vaguely recall Jen grabbing me by the arm and leading me down into the Delphic basement.

I do remember how proud of myself I was when I finally managed to utter not one but several sentences to her in comprehensible English dialect: "Thanks for the help. I don't know what that guy's problem was. I think the sweater tied around his neck was cutting off the circulation to his brain."

"You're assuming he actually has one," Jen said. Then she headed upstairs, a place only for members and girls. But not before glancing back at me. Was that a smile?

———◆———

It had been freezing outside, but it was much warmer in that packed basement. About 489 degrees warmer, to be exact. I surveyed the crowd of people stuffed in the basement, which had a very unique atmosphere, like it was the weird lovechild of a frat house and a country club. Dark oak paneling and a large fireplace gave the room a refined old-school feel, but the wood floor was so sticky that it sounded like you were unfastening Velcro each time you lifted a foot. Several people were engaged in a raucous game of flip cup, but they were playing on an antique piano. There were girls rocking oversized pearls and plenty of Lilly Pulitzer dresses, with pastel shades of pink, green, and yellow twirled into patterns that appeared to be designed by the Easter Bunny tripping on LSD. There were a handful of important-looking guys in seersucker, Polos, and cable-knit sweaters. Then there was the shirtless bro passed out in the corner with his hand down his pants.

After my impassioned moment with Jen (*she touched my arm!*) I could feel adrenaline shooting through all my extremities. My confidence was at an all-time high, especially since I had applied a copious amount of midnight thunder body wash in the shower before hand (the bottle said that men who used this product were 50 percent more likely to pick up a girl, so I wisely used double the amount).

As I made my way into the center of the room I brushed against a couple of hot girls, and I overheard them mention my fragrance.

"Eww, do you smell that? It smells like blue Gatorade burning on a hot sidewalk."

Her friend sneezed. "I think my nostrils just vomited."

So with my confidence meter back down to neutral, I spent the next half hour being that guy who hangs out on the periphery of conversation circles laughing at jokes I couldn't really hear. I was mostly invisible—the only time girls looked at me was when I accidently breathed on the back of their necks. When I wasn't orbiting around strangers' conversations, I would lean up against the wall and repeatedly check my text messages, as if all my bitches were begging me to tell 'em where the party's at.

Of course I also kept my head on a swivel so I could keep an eye on Jen, who had returned from upstairs. I was looking for an opportune moment to approach her. She looked incredible, and it was no surprise that a gaggle of morons were following her around in the hopes she would pay attention to them or even touch their arm.

I noticed one guy pull out his phone and start showing Jen some pictures on it. A couple of other dudes were also surrounding them, so I figured it wouldn't be weird if I joined the viewing party.

"It's a 1964 Porsche 911. Isn't she a beauty? My father gave it to me for my twenty-first birthday. Her name is Stephanie."

As the guy flipped through different angled photos I feigned automobile expertise and echoed everyone's enthusiastic praise, agreeing that yes, Stephanie's independent rear suspension was indeed sexy.

"So what about you guys? What do you drive?" This last question was directed at me specifically. All eyes turned to me, including Jen's.

"Oh, umm, I drive a vintage 1992 Volvo station wagon. Her name is 'White Lightning.' Not the most accurate name for her, but calling her 'Slightly Off-White Slug' makes it difficult to impress girls." Jen was the only one who laughed, which was fine by me.

Before the others could share their vehicles' epithets and vitals, a guy wielding a loaded beer funnel entered the basement. Apparently it was time for the birthday boy to "stop being a fag and shove this tube down his throat." A dozen guys encircled him, leaving Jen and me standing next to each other while we witnessed what seemed to be an age-old tribal ritual. The birthday boy first removed his sweater vest ("it's dry clean only!"), then took a knee underneath the funnel. As the tube was lowered and the beer began disappearing into his gullet, one guy led the group in a call-and-answer chant that filled the room with their century-old mantra:

> "Who fucks bitches?"
> "PHILLIP FUCKS BITCHES!!"
> "Who fucks bitches?"
> "PHILLIP FUCKS BITCHES!!"

I glanced at Jen, who looked mildly disgusted. Now was my chance.

"Well thank god *that* question has finally been answered," I said. "Now I can sleep at night."

My heart swelled as Jen revealed her perfect smile. "You know, for a guy who worships *The Incredible Hulk*, you're kind of funny…"

I probably should've quit while I was ahead, but that would've required a certain amount of social grace.

"Well, you can't spell 'jokester' without 'Kester'!"

"What?"

Shit. I forgot that she hadn't spent nineteen hours on my Facebook profile. She didn't know my name yet.

"Sorry, never mind. I'm Eric. Eric Kester."

She extended her hand. "Jen Wesker."

It was such a surreal moment; here I was, inside an actual final club, having a one-on-one conversation with the girl of my dreams. We talked for a while, and everything was going well. But then, when I was in the middle of explaining and apologizing for my move-in day nudity, someone grabbed me from behind and put me in a headlock.

"Hey, who let *this* guy in here?"

My stomach churned as I heard Tripp's obnoxious laugh. He planted a noogie then released me from his "playful" headlock. "How ya doing, Kes? Jen, good to see you, as always." Tripp flashed his blinding white teeth in a wide grin. This was a friendliness I had never seen from him. "Man, Kester, you look fantastic!" He took a step back to get a full view of my outfit, then pointed at my plaid ribbon belt from J.Crew. "I love the belt. That's the exact same design as my dog's collar."

I forced an awkward chuckle. "Well, he's got good taste."

"He's got worms."

"What kind of dog?" Jen interjected.

"Golden retriever. His name's Mister Winston, but we mostly call him 'Twain' because he has a terrific sense of irony. He's my special little guy." Tripp looked directly at Jen and softened his voice. "He keeps me grounded while I shoot for the moon."

I wanted to puke.

Tripp turned back to me. "I really like your blazer, kid. I think I have the exact same one but in khaki. Is it from the Brooks Brothers Quintessential Autumn Collection?" Tripp reached behind my neck and inspected the tag. "Oh, Men's Wearhouse." He patted me on the back. "Well, it looks *great*."

God, I wanted to kill him, but I just shrugged my shoulders. Poking weaklings in cyberspace was about as confrontational as I got.

When I found a cigar butt in the bottom of my beer and hardly cared, I knew it was time to call it a night. I had been at the Delphic for nearly three hours when I stepped outside into the snowy world and drunkenly wandered back to Lionel. It was typically a short walk, but it took twice as long since I was teetering about two steps sideways for every one step forward.

Despite Tripp's unwanted appearance, it had been a great night. I finally met Jen, and I managed to make her laugh not once but twice. Sure, I made that one awkward joke, but at least this time it had nothing to do with my genitals. *Progress*, I told myself.

Jen had departed shortly after our three-way convo with Tripp, but I stuck around when I saw a couple of guys who I knew from class. They introduced me to a few of the club members, and to my surprise they weren't douchebags at all. In fact, some of the Delphic guys were pretty good dudes. Yeah, there were some pretentious guys who wore silk boxers and referred to their houses as "estates," but there were also a bunch of regular guys who liked to drink some beers and talk about sports. No one ever brought up academics, or the latest scientific discovery, or that second semester's final exams were exactly 119 days away. In a way the Delphic was a more casual environment than a typical Harvard gathering. It was relaxing to party with guys who didn't calculate their blood alcohol content in their head. And not one person said "nice parabola" after I sunk a shot in beer pong.

A weird thought hit me: were final clubs the solution to my inability to fit in at this school? There were elements about them that I still found repulsive, but I might be willing to overlook them if it meant I found my place socially at Harvard.

I couldn't join a final club until next year, but I figured I would need that time anyway. If my current social status remained the same, I was unlikely to get punched anywhere. I was lacking some of the qualities that guaranteed you'd be punched: my family's driveway wasn't paved in crushed seashells, I didn't have multiple estates (or blazers, for that matter), and my bitch-fucking skills were nonexistent. I did have two golden retrievers, but they weren't exactly "classy," unless you considered peeing on my neighbor's car a refined form of diplomacy. So how could I get my name recognized enough so I could get punched next fall?

"You just gotta throw yourself out there, do something a little crazy," said one member when I asked him earlier that night. "Like one kid in our club managed to complete the Three Harvard Acts in his freshman year."

And these are…?

"The Harvard Acts are legendary. It's what every student is supposed to do before they graduate. A lot of people try, but not many people pull it off. The first Act is peeing on the John Harvard statue. The second is the hardest: you need to have sex in the stacks of Widener library. And the third Act is running in Primal Scream, the school-wide streak across Harvard Yard the night before final exams."

I had actually heard of these "Acts" before, so I knew the kid wasn't playing with me.

As I stumbled back to my dorm room, I passed the John Harvard statue.

"I'll…I'll be dealing with *you* later," I stuttered threateningly to the inanimate object.

When I finally arrived back in my dorm room I was more than ready to pass out in my bed. But somehow I ended up sitting at my computer, like a fly attracted to the bright glow of the monitor. Jen's Facebook page was still open from earlier that day.

You know when you're drunk, and you come up with a genius idea, only to realize a moment later that it was fucking retarded? That's how I felt as I stared at the tiny image of that creepy blue hand with its little molesting finger extended.

"You have poked Jennifer Wesker."

I stared at the message in disbelief. *Oh dear god, what have I done?* It might as well have said, *"You gave Jennifer Wesker the shocker."*

My blurry vision zipped around the computer screen. There was no "unpoke" button, and no "commit violent suicide" button. This could turn out horribly. How was she going to respond?

I found out in only a matter of seconds. A message from Jen popped up in my inbox.

"I felt it."

My mind was blown.

Chapter Thirteen

BEAUTY AND THE BEAST

J udging from the untouched basket of free condoms in my
dorm's basement, the dating scene at Harvard leaves something to be desired.

I always found it curious that, in addition to your standard
prophylactics, the basket was filled with an array of novelty
rubbers, including a glow in the dark "Rise 'n' Shine" brand and
even a few edible ones ("Like a free vending machine!" Dermot
noted). Clearly, whoever was responsible for the supply of contra-
ceptives made variety a priority, as if the nymphomaniac women
of Harvard were having so much sex that they would eventually require a special ribbed "Ruff Ryder" condom just to get
off. Maybe this was where our bloated endowment was going?
I could picture a bow-tied Harvard administrator pounding his
fist onto a desk at a financial planning meeting: "The food may
taste like puppy-chow and the dorm ceilings may be imploding,
but god dammit, our students are going to have the kinkiest sex
this side of Amsterdam!"

Unfortunately, the sexual activity on campus was not as scintil-
lating as our health services had so optimistically predicted. If you
were to ask one of my freshman year buddies, who shall remain

nameless because I've forgotten it, the scarcity of sexual activity was entirely the fault of our female population. "Harvard chicks are busted," he complained. "Like, there are only a handful of good-looking girls here. For a school with nearly three thousand women, it has me doubting the legitimacy of statistical theory."

It was a conundrum that Harvard guys spent hours upon hours debating: why was there an inverse correlation between intelligence and attractiveness?

"It's a variation of nature versus nurture," my unmemorable friend explained. "Are the girls who are naturally unattractive excluded from social activity, and thus turn to reading and studying and developing their intellect? Or did many of these girls actually have the potential to be pretty, only their precocious minds kept them focused more on schoolwork and less on things like exercise, style, and grooming? In other words, does ugliness beget intellect, or does intellect beget ugliness? Either way it sucks for us, getting stuck with a bunch of undateable gargoyles like this."

It was a valid point, I thought, and pretty eloquently delivered for a guy wearing a retainer. In addition to this particular rant, the only other things I remember about this kid were his hometown and that I had little sympathy for his sexual frustration. If you're a guy from Beaverton, Oregon, and still a virgin, then shame on you.

Harvard guys would love to complain about the girls, as if the lack of hot coeds was the real reason we were sitting around on a Saturday night grumbling about chicks and watching *Spiderman 2*. Part of the Harvard man's dissatisfaction with the female "talent" was due, I think, to unfulfilled expectations of the college experience. I'm going to go ahead and assume that in high school most Harvard guys were not among the league leaders in hookups; that their definition of "getting some ass" involved a bully sitting on their faces. But for any teenager concerned about the apparent immortality of his virginity, college seems like a timely answer to his carnal prayers. With the way college is portrayed in movies, how could a dork not get excited about the endless sexcapades that surely awaited him?

A high-school nerd dreams of college. He envisions a place where a hot blonde, after breaking a sweat in a frisky pillow fight, asks her equally hot roommate for a little help soaping her down in the communal shower because, shit! she's late for that wet T-shirt contest in the quad. But then the nerd arrives at Harvard and realizes it's more likely for a girl to break a sweat practicing her violin, and then skip a shower entirely because she's tardy for a lecture entitled "The Phallic Fallacy."

There were plenty of Harvard girls who had potential, but many of them seemed to sacrifice their appearance for scholastic pursuit, as if finding a cure for cancer and using hair conditioner was an either/or tradeoff. Though I suppose you can't blame them for choosing academics over geeks whose tongues unrolled at the mere sight of a girl sunbathing in the Yard. The bottom line is that both Harvard guys and Harvard girls thought they were too good for each other. And you know what? Both sexes were kind of right. Girls were looking for a mature romance worthy of a Jane Austen novel, and guys were looking for a girl with the unmatched sexiness of Jabba the Hutt's slave Leia. And you weren't going to find either at Harvard.

That's not to say there wasn't hot, steamy, awkward, scandalous, awkward, sultry, (did I mention awkward?) sex on campus.

Harvard's incoming students have got to be among the most

sexually repressed freshmen in the nation going into college. There may be plenty of fish in the sea in high school, but when your primary interests include Riemann surfaces and hyperbolic geometry, it ain't easy to find a lover to have pillow talk with. But at Harvard you may actually find that person who appreciates your long-division capabilities, your CD-ROM collection, and your hatred for Klingons.

But while it's nice to see a guy finally find the "poin" to his "dexter," the result can be rather messy. Excited that they can finally use all the copious notes they took in their sixth-grade sex ed classes, the couple can't resist smothering each other in an explosion of PDA that most people get out of their system in junior high. Too often I would pass by a couple using their tongues to probe the inner depths of each other's esophagi—just two lovers who share the same heart, the same soul, the same bifocal prescription.

Harvard did have a few "traditionally" hot women—girls who would be just as desirable at a college with a normal male population (you know, one that ranks "body" above "vocabulary" on their list of turn-ons). And those girls, like Jen, were pursued with relentless aggression. Even the pickiest Harvard guy agreed that their ample mammary glands and advanced cerebral cortexes made them quite suitable for procreation. The competition for these rare beauties was so fierce, though, that attaining one of them seemed hopeless.

But fortunately for Harvard guys we had another source of women: nearby Boston-area colleges that were rife with attractive coeds. Often these girls were easier for a Harvard guy to hook up with, not because they were sluts, but because they maintained the terribly misguided notion that a Harvard man was a guarantee of future success and an extravagant lifestyle. Like after graduation, we would simply use origami to fold our Harvard diploma into a four-bedroom beach house.

Not surprisingly, the final clubs took full advantage of this phenomenon, busing in sororities and female social groups from Wellesley, Boston College, UMass, Northeastern, and Boston University. On weekends the "Fuck Trucks," as they were affectionately called, would pull up in front of a clubhouse and deploy a parade of scantily clad girls ready for a themed soiree like "Golf Pros and Tennis Ho's," or "Victoria's Secret Fashion Show," or some other "let-us-rob-you-of-your-dignity" gimmicked party.

"Dropping the H-bomb" on a non-Harvard girl would typically grant you some extra time to impress her, as your school's reputation will initially buy you the benefit of the doubt (*Well, he got in to Harvard—he must be good at something other than mumbling and staring at his shoes, right?*). But eventually you have to live up to the hype.

I always felt extra pressure talking to non-Harvard girls because they seemed to have such high hopes for me, like any moment now I was going to put the "stud" back in "study." I made a conscious effort to come across as self-assured, tall, and interesting—a guy who was in control, who had grabbed life by the balls. I tried to make lively, stimulating conversation that showed off my supposedly lofty intellect, but my fancy, expensive classes weren't helping (believe it or not, dinosaurs, gladiators, and aliens weren't coming up in conversation).

There is the illusion of the "Mr. Perfect" Harvard man, and we would do our best to maintain the charade, but inevitably the girl would have a "*wait a minute—this guy is full of shit*" moment. For me this would occur as soon as I brought a girl back to my room, as my Boston Red Sox bedspread didn't exactly scream "future CEO." Other guys would be exposed as undateable creeps shortly into the first date when they drop a cringeworthy pick-up line: "Are you differentiable? Because I want to be tangent to all your curves."

A line like this and your target flees back to her own college, leaving you back at square one, pining for unattainable Harvard goddesses like Jen.

———— ◆ ————

I must've read the Facebook message a hundred times.

"I felt it."

It could've meant so many things. Dermot concluded that it implied Jen was "horned up somethin' fierce" and "ready to play a three-part concerto on your flute." Josh thought she was drunk. I liked thinking it was a layered message, referencing both the flirtatious poke and the intangible connection we shared at the Delphic. Or maybe she was drunk. Either way, it couldn't have been a bad thing, right?

I was lucky Jen received my poke positively because I saw her *everywhere* after that night. In the dining hall, walking around the Yard—she was even in my second-semester social anthropology class. After seeing her only three times in the first semester, I had run into her at least a dozen times in the first week of March alone. It seemed more than coincidental, like the Facebook gods were conspiring to get us together. (It also didn't hurt that I was spending more time out in public and less time under my covers, biting the heads off my animal crackers and feeling sorry for myself.)

Where first-semester-Eric would've seen Jen and thrown up

a little in his mouth, second-semester-Eric actually went up and talked to her. It wasn't like I had suddenly transformed into Mr. Smooth (I would hardly qualify "not puking" as the mark of a confident man), but my positive interaction at the Delphic gave me a foundation with Jen on which I could build. It started off as a couple of dinnertime conversations where I somehow managed to put a smile on her face and keep the food off of mine. Then one morning she sat next to me in the back row of our anthropology lecture. Then it happened again…and again… and again. Whether she sat next to me because I provided witty in-class commentary or because I always gave her a piece of gum, I wasn't sure.

The class met three times a week at 11:00 a.m., so afterward we would walk to Annenberg and eat lunch together, where she would extrapolate on the lecture and I would nod my head. Our anthropology class was a catalyst for friendship, and soon I was stopping by her room a couple of times a week to borrow her textbook, having accidentally lost mine after dropping it in a trashcan.

Since we were sharing textbooks, it was only natural to form a study group, and during these review sessions we talked about many things, almost none of them relating to our anthropology class. Our weekday study rendezvous were soon augmented by weekend meetings at bars and parties, and before I knew it, Jen and I were doing almost everything together.

Honestly, I had no idea why Jen was so interested in spending time with me. Compared to other Harvard guys, my résumé was pretty boring: I wasn't an intern for the CIA, nor the heir to the Heineken company, nor headed to the NFL. And she wasn't tagging alongside me to satisfy some court-ordered charity work, as far as I could tell. So what did Jen see in me? Did she have a secret fetish for guys who could fit fifty-seven Skittles in their mouth?

In trying to wrap my mind around the reason for our sudden relationship (or friendship? I didn't know what to call it), one possible explanation kept popping up. Jen often complained about all the Harvard guys being "fake." And I sort of got the sense that she didn't include me in that group. Trying to impress a girl at Harvard was a discouraging process because it always felt like your competition was more accomplished than you were, and Jen hated how guys overcompensated for this inferiority complex by flaunting a false aura of excellence and refinement. Guys would sit down next to Jen at breakfast and pretend to give a shit about their copy of the *Wall Street Journal*, complaining to her about things like declining interest rates when they should've been more concerned with Jen's declining interest in them. She didn't want to hear exaggerated stories of academic conquests, or not-so-subtle jabs at the qualifications of fellow male classmates. She just wanted something genuine.

With the hypercompetitive atmosphere of the school, I could've easily fallen into the trap of adopting a "fake" personality to impress others. Believe me, I certainly tried. But as both Jen and I discovered, I was just too damn awkward to be phony. I would do everything I could to come across as suave and brilliant and sophisticated, but eventually I would screw things up and my true nature would be exposed. For instance, while at dinner with Jen one night, I contributed to the table discussion by claiming that, in my humble opinion, Johann Sebastian Bach's Brandenburg concerto in D major was heaven in musical form. Then a moment later, during a fatal lapse of concentration, Jen caught me whistling the chorus to Sisqo's "Thong Song." My social goofiness was like an irrepressible beast that seemed to tear apart my polished façade, revealing my authentic self. It wasn't a self I was particularly proud of, but at least it was genuine. So I guess I had that going for me.

It was a lot easier to understand why I loved hanging out with Jen. First of all, she was hot. Like, real hot. When she wore sunglasses, it was crazy how much she looked like Jessica Biel. One time we were shopping together in Harvard Square when an excited teenage girl, ignoring the improbability that Jessica Biel would be hanging out with a guy wearing tapered sweatpants, asked for Jen's autograph. The girl even requested to take a picture of us, to commemorate the day she saw Jessica Biel buying Hot Pockets at a 7-Eleven. Jen laughed and played along, grabbing my arm as we posed for the picture. I felt like the faux-boyfriend of the faux-celebrity, provoking an exhilarating sense of faux-importance that I hadn't felt since hanging out with a certain easily impressed teenage buddy.

Before I sound shallower than a kiddie pool, I should point out that I was attracted to more than just Jen's looks. After getting to know her, I was still drawn to that confidence I had first noticed from afar, back when I was observing from the sidelines. I soon learned, though, that Jen maintained a different type of self-assurance than I had imagined. To my surprise, Jen was like me in that she was having a difficult time figuring out who she was and what she wanted to be. (We would joke that we were the only students left at Harvard who hadn't yet switched our browser's homepage from google.com to cnbc.com). But unlike me, she was confident enough in her abilities to conquer doubt and take on Harvard with optimism, holding on to a faith that eventually everything would work out. Where I saw the uncertain future as a demoralizing black hole, Jen saw a blank white canvas.

Jen's attitude left her far better equipped to handle the unavoidable embarrassments and failures one must face at Harvard, and it was eye-opening when she applied her perspective to my life. She viewed every one of my self-proclaimed "disasters" as an opportunity: "Coach Mac says that if you don't reach your bench press goal, he's going to a stab himself in the pancreas with a samurai sword? Well, you have the chance to save someone's life!" "Your freshman year has deteriorated into an epic comedy of errors? Record them in a journal—maybe one day you can write a book about it!" It was such a refreshing way of looking at adversity. I hoped that Vikas, wherever he was, had a similar attitude.

I know it's a cliché, and I feel like an idiotic contestant from *The Bachelor* when I write it, but I loved hanging out with Jen because we just had so much fun together. Finally, my ratio of LOL to FML moments was starting to climb. Jen was such an upbeat and vivacious girl that it was difficult to remain in my gloomy, humorless Harvard world when I was around her. I could laugh with Jen, and the momentary lift I would feel as we cracked up over something like a bird shitting on my head would help me forget about a recent bad grade and its seemingly life-altering implications. She was a welcome antidote to a school that was drowning me in its gravitas.

On the surface, Jen seemed like a typical Harvard girl. She was remarkably bright, an exceptional writer and public speaker, an all-star in the school's Mock Trial Association. But it only took a few minutes with her to see how she differed from the majority of her female classmates, and it was this side of her that I found most compelling. She wouldn't correct my grammar midsentence, or twist some mundane comment I made about burnt toast into an argument about race in America. She went to class with only one color of pen. She always ordered medium rare at Mr. Bartley's Burgers, and never sniped any fries off my plate without asking. She preferred hot chocolate over coffee, ponytails over buns, Advil over Adderall, Pixar over documentaries. She wasn't too good for *Us Weekly*, or some trashy yet wonderfully addictive reality TV. And she wasn't too good for me, even though she definitely was.

As if these qualities weren't appealing enough, there were also some external benefits from hanging out with Jen.

It seemed like everyone at my school had a "thing"—a specialty or identifiable trait that could explain their presence at Harvard in one tidy sentence. "Thomas, the guy who sold his Soccernet website to ESPN for $40 million when he was seventeen years old." "Kaavya, the freshman girl who just signed a lucrative multi-book contract with a major publishing house." "Laura, the Guinness world-record holder for fastest crawler."

For a couple of weeks I was simply "the guy with the Hulk underwear," but since then I had slipped into a depressing obscurity. Now I was known as "Eric, the guy Jen always hangs out with," and it felt freaking awesome.

People were starting to take notice of me: my football teammates, who were used to seeing me lying on the field writhing in pain with my eyes looking in two different directions, now held me in higher esteem; final clubs let me in the parties more often (though only with Jen by my side); even Dermot started to look at me as something more than a toilet-paper delivery man. I was making a name for myself. *I mattered.*

Of course the ceiling for my popularity was even higher. I began to wonder: if I was getting this much attention just for hanging out with Jen, imagine if I actually dated her? I know "dating the hottest girl at Harvard" may sound like "climbing the tallest mountain in Kansas," but Jen was legit, and if I could be her boyfriend, I would be too. Like my classmates who were spelling-bee champs and Olympic stars, I'd have a trophy too—and I could make out with it without being creepy.

The mere thought of dating Jen made my stomach churn, though, as I realized I was delving into dangerous territory. I was no expert in the dating world, and screwing up my relationship with Jen would yield devastating consequences. Yes, I would lose my newfound social relevance, my place at Harvard. But the threat of squandering my reputation hardly mattered to me, compared to what else I could lose: what started as an irrational freshman crush on a nameless babe had developed into a genuine emotional attraction to a girl for whom I cared deeply.

It was terrifying.

———————◆•◆———————

I met Jen outside her dorm, Hollis, which was located directly in front of my dorm, Lionel, on the west side of the Yard. She looked fantastic, wearing a pair of dark-wash jeans, a black peacoat, and a light beige headband that matched a pair of boots that gave her a few extra inches. We were headed to an a cappella concert in the famous Sanders Theater, which is connected to the back of Annenberg Hall, a little beyond the gate on the north end of the Yard.

Jen and I walked slowly through the Yard, braving the cold winter air as we navigated the precariously icy footpaths. I noticed Jen cup her hands together and blow into them, so I offered her my gloves. She said no, she was fine, but I insisted I didn't need them. There was enough warmth inside the pockets of the puke-green ski jacket my mom had bought me. Jen still declined, so I took them off and placed them in her frozen hands. She finally conceded and slipped on the fleece-lined leather gloves. I was staring at the ground, on the lookout for slip-inducing, back-breaking, date-ruining black ice, but I could tell she was looking at me and smiling.

"Wow, these are really warm," she said.

"Aren't they? I found them on the subway."

"You did?"

There was a brief silence and Jen surveyed the empty Yard, like she was taking in the night. The moon was bright, illuminating the thin, frosted branches of the barren trees lining either side of our path. Jen inhaled a deep breath. "A lot of people complain about the winter here, but I really like it. It's quiet. Peaceful."

"Yeah, it's like the winter comes in to cool down this over-heated school. The winter reminds us how to be still. It's like this Robert Frost poem I read in high school—"

My thought was interrupted by a muffled noise reverberating from my pocket. I stopped talking to get a better listen, and the theme to *Inspector Gadget* ruffled the still night air with its sophomoric whimsy. My heart jumped. I knew whose ringtone this was. My ice-block fingers fumbled to grab my phone and flip it open.

"Vikas?"

"Dude!"

"Hey! What's up? How are you doing? Where are you?"

"Boarding school."

"Your parents sent you to boarding school? Shit, I'm sorry, man. About everything."

"Don't be. It's not so bad. Lights out in the dorm isn't until 11:00, two hours later than at home!"

I covered the mouthpiece of my cell phone and turned to Jen. "Sorry, just a sec." I spoke back into the phone. "So what's up?"

"Dude, I've got a freaking emergency! I need your help!"

"What? Are you okay?"

"Was Napoleon okay after Waterloo? No, I'm not okay!"

"Oh Jesus. What happened?" Upon hearing me say this, Jen's expression adopted a look of concern.

"Last night was my first dance here. I wanted to impress the ladies, you know, show 'em that V-Gup was for real. So I did what you always said worked for you. I walked into the room and was like, 'Yo' and started jiggling the zipper of my fly. But instead of girls running toward me and drooling like Pavlov's dogs, they just looked at me like I was a freak!"

"I wouldn't worry about it, Vikas. High school girls can be tough at first. Just be patient." Jen, realizing the triviality of our conversation, relaxed.

"That's easy for you to say!" Vikas exclaimed. "You once had a freakin' threesome during your bathroom break at the SATs! I'm totally effed. And now I just instant-messaged this girl who's hotter than Aphrodite and Helen of Troy combined, and I don't know what to say!"

"Settle down, big guy. We'll help you through this. What's been said so far?"

"Me: Hey girl, what up?
Her: Nothing much, you?
Me: Not much, you?
Her: Nothing."

"Hmm...good start, good start," I said. "Now try asking her some more specific questions. Like, what are her hobbies? Girls love to talk about themselves." Jen giggled in apparent agreement. There was a break and I could hear Vikas typing.

"Okay, she said she likes to ride horses and do puzzles," he finally said.

"She likes puzzles? Perfect. Now tell her you like puzzles too, and ask her if she wants to 'get jiggy' later."

Jen snatched the phone out of my hand. "DO NOT say that to her!" She punched me in the arm playfully. "Just be yourself, be honest," she said to a probably very confused Vikas, "and compliment her."

I wrestled the cell back from Jen and clicked on the speakerphone. "Oh, and try to be funny," I told him. "Use self-defecating humor, that usually works." Jen started to crack up, and it took me a moment to realize my slip of words.

"Alright," Vikas announced proudly. "I just told her that she looked so good last night I almost crapped my pants."

Through the speakerphone Jen and I heard the familiar AOL "door slam" sound effect, indicating that the girl had signed off. "Mother effer!" Vikas squealed.

Jen practically collapsed into my arms, she was laughing so hard.

———— ◆ ————

Harvard will use any tragedy as an excuse to build a magnificently expensive edifice. So following the Civil War, the school had more than enough reason to construct a big-ass concert hall. Completed in 1875, Sanders Theater is a grandiose, magnificently crafted hall dedicated in honor of the Harvard alumni who fell fighting for the Union. (In 1995, several plans to commemorate the Confederate war dead were struck down by the university. Not because of the South's slavery implications, but because Harvard refuses to honor failure.) A grand chandelier illuminates the polished wood paneling that coats the majority of the hall's elegantly carved interior. The large stage opens to three tiers of seating, and the balcony hovering over the orchestra and mezzanine levels gives the theater a much more intimate feel than you'd expect from a 1,166-capacity theater. The wall behind the stage is covered with an enormous slab of white marble, which is engraved with, like, two thousand words of Latin inscription, in case the language ever comes into vogue again. And, of course, the theater indulges Harvard's fetish for marble statues of old white guys who look constipated, with two such sculptures guarding either end of the stage. The hall is mostly used for larger lectures, but it still hosts concerts and other performances at night.

As we approached Sanders Theater, I asked Jen for a little background on the concert. There were a few details of the group I didn't know, like who the hell they were.

"They're called Chorus Credit," Jen told me. "They're a coed, non-audition singing group."

Oh Christ. That "non-audition" part had me seriously worried. It sounded like we were about to watch an assembly of singers who had been rejected from all of Harvard's other 567 a cappella groups. But Jen's roommate, Debbie, was in the group so Jen wanted to go because she was a good friend. And thus I wanted to go, because I had hormones.

Before we stepped in the theater Jen looked me over, then adjusted my collar and patted down a tuft of hair that had been separated from the group.

"Ready?" she asked, smiling.

"Of course," I replied as I opened the door for her.

It turns out I wasn't ready. At all.

I hate to sound so judgmental, because if I tried to join Chorus Credit with my voice they would likely become "audition-required," but the concert quickly warped into a brutal test of endurance. I think the main problem was their song selection, which consisted entirely of show tunes and Disney ballads. It also didn't help that their notes were like little invisible demons jabbing pitchforks into unsuspecting eardrums. Okay, maybe that's a bit of an exaggeration, but their singing did seem better suited for other purposes, like last-resort interrogation tactics in Guantanamo Bay.

The guy supplying the beat box was making guttural clicks and explosions that resembled the sound effects I vocalized as a kid for my G.I. Joe combat sequences. To make matters worse, Sanders Theater's famous acoustics filled the entire hall with music, so sound waves bounced from every angle and riddled my body with piercing shots, like I was caught in the middle of a ferocious crossfire in 'Nam. The performers were having fun at least, dancing and grooving to the tunes, but watching their spastic bouncing and bobbing made me feel seasick. It was impossible to tell whether their dancing was more embarrassing or offensive, but it was very unsettling to know that, on the very spot where Martin Luther King, Jr. himself once spoke, there were now two kids slow-grinding to "Hakuna Matata."

Chorus Credit seemed determined to get through the Broadway and Disney catalogues in their entirety, so the concert lasted for two hours, with no intermission for me to take a leak or a sip of cyanide-laced chloroform. Any hope for a miraculous cessation to this horror show was lost when the chandelier above me didn't crash down during the fifteen-minute *Phantom of the Opera* remix bonanza, so I tried to focus my mind on positive thoughts, which wasn't too difficult with Jen sitting next to me.

I couldn't help but notice (and incessantly obsess over) the position of her right leg. It had wandered ever so slightly into my personal space, and now rested against my left leg.

Holy shit! Was this move intentional? Was it Jen's attempt at sparking a more physical relationship between us? Or had my brain's exposure to these malignant sound waves triggered an early stage of schizophrenia, with my mind now inhabiting an imaginary world of sexually charged leg-placements?

The question of whether our leg contact was incidental or intentional distracted me for a good portion of Chorus Credit's rendition of "Greased Lightning." When they started to sing "Greased Lightning" again, this time in Spanish, I felt Jen begin to squirm in her seat. She leaned over and whispered something to me, but due to the newly acquired permanent damage in my ear canal, I didn't quite hear her. She either said "sorry about this" or "suck my tits." As enticing as the latter sounded, I chose not to act on it. I was still trying to decipher this leg situation.

———◆◆———

None of my classmates or professors would ever accuse me of overthinking, but when it comes to making moves on girls, I am an egregious offender. When is the appropriate time to attempt progressing the relationship to a physical level? Throughout my amateur career of courting women, I could never get a good read on body language. Like one time I apparently missed an opportunity with a girl because I failed to notice the flirtatious way in which she slapped a mosquito on my arm. ("It was sooo obvious," she said later.) But then at another party I got rejected trying to kiss a girl who I thought liked me, when really she was just sitting on my lap because "the only other seat left was next to that smelly kid, Stuart, who breathes too loud."

The flirting habits of girls made less than zero sense to me, so in college I chose to err on the side of caution. The stakes were high with Jen, and I couldn't afford to screw this up by scaring her off with an overly aggressive move. But I also had to be careful not to be too passive and end up in the dreaded "friend zone," which every guy knows is the emotional equivalent of getting stabbed in the pancreas with a samurai sword.

In college the best place to flirt and establish a physical relationship is on the dance floor, a place where a girl lowers her protocol bar and expects some physical contact. I wished I could've danced with Jen and potentially advanced our relationship, but it hadn't happened yet. It wasn't like I didn't get any opportunities; I spent several nights with her at The Hong Kong, Harvard Square's very flammable-looking Chinese restaurant that naturally had a dance club and full bar on the top floor. At the time, The Kong's bouncers were notorious for letting in anyone with a remotely passable fake ID (thirty-two-year-old Rodrigo Sanchez, right here), so it was a popular place for underclassmen to go for some drinks and dancing. Jen once tried to get me to go on the dance floor with her, but I declined and instead loitered on the side with the creepy local men who liked to spend their Saturday nights watching college girls get down to the Black Eyed Peas. It's not like I enjoyed hanging with these dudes who had beer guts and mustaches and dirty fingernails. I simply had no choice. I sucked at dancing.

This isn't your casual "Oh, ha ha, I suck at dancing," like most white guys say. This is not a joke to me. I SUCK at dancing. On a level you can't even comprehend. I'm so mind-bendingly bad at dancing I can literally ruin entire parties. My dance moves emit waves of second-hand embarrassment. A couple dancing passionately in the corner would lose their intensity, their eyes, previously fixated upon one another, suddenly unable to stop looking at that giant guy whose body is gyrating like a half-crushed insect.

And my reputation isn't the only thing in grave danger when I dance. I once caused physical harm to a girl on the dance floor when my left arm, in the middle of its own solo dance tour that remained secret from the rest of my body, smacked her in the face.

It's not that I move my body offbeat. I just dance to a beat from a song that hasn't been invented yet.

As the show went on, it became clear that Chorus Credit's dancing was far superior to mine, in that they weren't convulsing like malfunctioning robots. But their singing maintained the remarkable ability to conjure your worst childhood memories.

About midway through the show, people started to file out of the theater, probably to seek grief counseling. As the performance went on, and on, and on some more, hoards of people fled for the exits. It was starting to get awkward. Maybe I was jealous, but the mass exodus struck me as pretty rude. By the end of the show, the audience, which originally consisted of a couple of hundred people, was down to a few dozen brave souls.

Contrary to legend, the show did, in fact, come to an end, and afterward Jen and I met up with Debbie in the lobby. We put on our smiles and congratulated her on a truly unforgettable performance.

"Are you kidding? It was horrible!" Debbie moaned. "Everyone left in the middle. I've never been so embarrassed in my life!" A murky mascara tear streaked down her cheek. The girl looked so devastated—it was breaking my heart a little.

Jen handed Debbie a tissue from her purse. "Don't feel bad, Deb. The show was—I mean, I thought it was…don't let those kids…"

"Fuck the audience," I blurted. "Seriously, fuck 'em. Those losers left because it was past their bedtime."

I detected a small smile, so I continued.

"You guys were rocking up there. Your solo during that song from *Rent* was delivered with so much passion and excitement, I literally forgot you were singing about AIDS. And that 360-degree jump-spin you did mid-solo? Very impressive. I'd like to see Michael Jackson try to pull that off in high heels! Did you bedazzle those yourself?"

And that got real smiles, from both of them.

———◆———

The silent winter night was a welcome cleansing for Jen and I as we strolled back through Harvard Yard. Despite the bitter cold, we took our time and carefully shuffled across the icy paths, Jen's hand holding on to my forearm for stability.

"You were really great back there. I think you made Debbie feel a lot better. Thank you." She gave my arm a light squeeze.

I acknowledged the praise with a shrug. I felt like a hypocrite for telling Debbie to not care what other people thought of her, but I had to do *something* to cheer her up. It felt so wrong watching a bunch of Harvard kids display ineptitude like that.

I have to admit, though, it was also strangely satisfying. Not that I was delighting in their failure, but their deficiencies made me feel less alone at Harvard. You rarely saw public failure at the school, partly because the students were so damn talented, but also because hardly anyone wanted to expose themselves to the scrutiny of the student body. It was difficult to take risks at Harvard. Flopping could yield severe emotional trauma, so even if you really want to try something new and bold, you think twice about it. Harvard students are incredibly critical thinkers—it's one of the reasons they are so bright academically—but it also means they are more likely to rip apart another's unsatisfactory work, whether it be an article for the school paper, an art show, or an a cappella jam. If you are going to submit a product or performance to the community, it better be exceptional.

"You know, I've never been inside Lionel," Jen said as we approached her dorm. "Is it nice?"

"It's okay. I have my own bedroom, which is pretty sweet. I was supposed to rotate it with my other two roommates, but they've been too lazy to switch rooms."

"Let's check it out. It's too cold to go out tonight anyway."

Once inside Lionel, Jen and I wiped our shoes on my room's makeshift doormat, a stack of unread *Wall Street Journals* that Harvard Student Agencies delivered to our door each day ("Like free toilet paper!" Dermot noted). When we stepped into my suite, I was relieved to see that the common room was both clean and devoid of any malicious odors. To my surprise, I also saw that the room wasn't unoccupied. Dermot was on the floor performing a series of hamstring stretches.

"Hey Derm, this is Jen." I gave him a hard "don't fuck this up" stare.

"Ah, Jen. Grand to meet ya." Derm said as bent forward and reached for his toes. "Quick request: would ya mind hoofing on my hindpart? I would ask this sky pilot, but he's no streak of piss, if you know what I mean!" Dermot flipped around and laid flat on his stomach. Jen looked at me and raised her eyebrows.

"He just asked you to step on his back." I translated. "You don't—"

"Oh, it's no problem, my friends used to do this to me all the time," Jen said as she slipped off her shoes. "Everyone needs their back cracked once in a while."

After Jen's brief stint as an amateur chiropractor, I offered to give her the Grand Tour of our suite, which consisted of peeking into the bathroom and two bedrooms.

"Aww, it's so cozy!" Jen remarked when she looked into my shoebox bedroom.

Dermot's continued devotion to electrofunk had forced me to move my desk from the common room to my bedroom, so now there was hardly space for two standing adults. It didn't stop Jen from stepping inside, though, causing my pulse to jump into overdrive. I followed her in and quickly inspected my room for potentially embarrassing items. Thankfully, a large blue comforter was covering my Red Sox bedspread. But there were a few snot-filled tissues on my desk. Also iTunes was open on my computer, and I was thoroughly shamed by the play count number next to Avril Lavigne's name.

Jen took her time examining my room, like she was a health inspector.

"Is there a mirror behind here that I could use?" she asked.

I nodded, and Jen closed the door, revealing a full-length mirror on the other side. She looked at her reflection and smiled. God, she was cute.

"Was this mirror here when you moved in?" she asked.

"Yeah, but I don't really use it."

"I could've guessed." Jen giggled and turned to me. She patted down another tuft of my hair that had gone rogue. She then shuffled past me and plunked down on my bed. I took a seat at my desk chair and spun it around to face her.

"You're bed is so comfortable!" she declared, bouncing slightly.

"You like it? My mom got me a foam egg crate. That's the secret."

"It feels good."

"Do you want to watch a movie or something? I've got *Big Daddy* on DVD."

"I just saw that, actually…"

Jen glanced back at the door-mirror and adjusted her hair. She then reached into her pocket and pulled out her phone. "Oh my god, come here and check out this text I just got."

Jen slid over on the bed a bit, and I walked over and sat next to her. She showed me the text, which was from her friend Caitlin who was clearly wasted.

"aT the KONG aend VAL KILMER iss heare!!!1 omg he so short COME NOW!!!"

"That's pretty funny," I said. "Do you want to go?"

Jen shrugged. "I dunno…what do you want to do?"

"I don't care," I replied, and I reached a hand behind my back to scratch a nonexistent itch. "I want to do what you want to do."

Silence.

Jen put her phone back in her pocket and looked at me with those green eyes. Our legs were touching. "You decide."

Silence.

"Uh, well, Val Kilmer is a pretty big deal. *Tombstone* is one of my favorite movies."

"You should go check it out, then," Jen said as she got up

from the bed. "I'm not sure I have the energy for the Kong, so I'm going to head back and get some sleep."

I followed Jen into the common room. "Thanks for coming to the concert with me," she said as she buttoned up her coat. "I know it's not the most fun thing to do on a Saturday night…"

I told her not to worry—I had good company. She gave me a hug goodbye, then walked out the door.

I don't know how long I stood there in the common room, trying to digest what had just happened. I snapped out of my trance when I heard the whoosh of a toilet flush. Dermot emerged from the bathroom a moment later.

"Where'd your bird go?" he asked.

"Oh—uh, she just went back to her room."

"What the feck are you still doin' 'ere? Aren't ya going to walk her back?"

Shit! What the hell was I thinking?

I put on my shoes and rushed out the door, slipping on my puke-green coat as I ran. Once outside I quickly scanned the Yard for Jen. But all I could see was darkness.

Chapter Fourteen

YELLOW IS THE
NEW CRIMSON

Peeing on the John Harvard statue is a bit of a logistical nightmare.

First, you have to climb up the five-foot-high stone pedestal that serves as the base for Johnny Boy and his throne. The best mounting technique, I learned, is to get a running start and vault your torso above the base, then swing your hanging legs up on the platform. This maneuver is literally a leap of faith, as you risk landing in a foamy puddle of nastiness, courtesy of a student who had already paid his respects to Mr. Harvard earlier that night. Next comes a balancing act, as the statue occupies the majority of the pedestal and leaves precious few free inches on which to stand. Once you manage to twist your body into an acceptable stance for urinary libation, you'll notice that you are mere inches away from the bronze statue, making splash-back a very real possibility. (The many female students who engage in this ritual have it even worse; they must squat on John Harvard's lap, discharging their liquid waste like a leaky toddler sitting on Santa's knee). The threat of splash-back was of particular concern to me, as I couldn't afford to spatter my jeans or my Sperry Top-Siders, which I now wore all the time.

"Jaysus, will you quit arsing around up there? I'm freezing my clackers off out here!"

The holler came from Dermot, who was serving the triple role of lookout/photographer/complainer. He stood below with one arm in a sling (the consequence of sledding off the roof of Lamont Library on a plastic dining hall tray a couple of weeks back) and the other clutching my digital camera, which he would use to document my completion of the First Harvard Act. If Dermot were to spot a night watchman approaching the statue, he would tip me off with our code phrase: "I'm hungry, let's go to Felipe's for a burrito."

So far, the coast was clear. It was close to 1:00 a.m. and the Yard was eerily quiet, the dim flickers of outdoor lamps the only suppliers of life to this otherwise dead night in early April.

I unzipped my fly and aimed my ray gun straight at John Harvard's heart.

Time to die, asshole. Just understand that you brought this upon yourself with the way you've treated me. Any last words?

John Harvard just sat there and basked in his trademark stoicism, his unflinching expression showing no hint of remorse.

Alright, pal. You've asked for it…

But I couldn't pull the trigger.

Of course, this wasn't the first time my bladder had left my dick standing at the altar, but this particular hesitation had nothing to do with stage fright. This time it was my conscience that was blocking my path to glory. I tried sneaking around it by reminding myself of my end goal: eventual acceptance into a final club. From what I understood, final clubs were only impressed with three things: obscene wealth, exceptional athletic prowess, and bold acts of vulgarity! I lacked in the first two categories, but if my time at Harvard taught me anything, it was that I was damn

good at public indecency. I had arrived tonight mentally prepared to sacrifice virtue in the name of social relevance. But now,
as I stared at the dark bronze effigy of Harvard's founder, my
conscious was pierced by the gleam of the statue's most famous
feature. Right now the only thing saving John Harvard from a
golden shower was his golden toe.

◆ ◆ ◆

Harvard Yard is split into two distinct areas: the west side consists
almost entirely of classically bricked freshman dorms dating back
to the eighteenth century, while the east side contains relatively
newer structures, including the Widener, Lamont, and Pusey
libraries, Memorial Chapel, and a couple of the college's primary
classroom buildings. The west side is called the Old Yard, while
the east side is named Tercentenary Theater (because calling it
the New Yard would've made way too much sense).

The John Harvard statue resides in the Old Yard, directly in front
of University Hall. A prominent white granite building among its
red-bricked neighbors, University Hall was constructed in 1815
and once contained several classrooms, a small chapel, a library,
and a special room to store newfangled scientific apparatuses (these
devices—you know, your typical everyday science junk like oph-
thalmoscopes and planispheric astrolabes and an orrery wired by
Benjamin Franklin himself—are now kept in the basement of the
Science Center, like excess sweaters tossed into a dusty attic). The
U.S. government has declared University Hall a National Historic
Landmark, though now it's primarily used for mundane admin-
istrative tasks, like levying punishments when another Leader of
Tomorrow has been caught tinkling on the founder.

You can tell by his puffed chest and upright posture that

the John Harvard statue thinks he's hot shit, but I suppose you would too if you were the third-most photographed statue in the United States. During the daylight hours, camera-wielding tourists relentlessly bombard the effigy with flashes and clicks. Asian tourists typically comprise the majority of the horde, but visitors of all nationalities and demographics stop by to see the father of higher education, patiently waiting for their turn to rub the toe of the founder's shoe for good luck.

The crowds are a huge nuisance to Harvard students, since the primary footpath through the Yard crosses directly in front of the statue. At first I tried to avoid cutting in front of the statue while tourists were snapping pictures, but I soon learned the photographs were so incessant that, if you wanted to be on time for class, you had to ignore the sightseers altogether and continue on your way. I can't imagine how many mantels in China have a framed picture of a smiling family as they posed in their newly purchased Harvard sweatshirts (made in China) with an oblivious me passing through the background picking my nose.

To many of the tourists, the only better memento than a picture of the John Harvard statue is a snapshot of an authentic Harvard student. It's not uncommon for a tourist to sneak up to a student traversing the Yard and snap a photo, as if they were on a safari and we were the wildlife scampering across the plains.

Look, kids, there goes one now! According to my field guide, the Harvardian Pencilneck is easily startled, so move slowly and avoid eye contact! Get some photos! They're an endangered species, since the typical one mates zero times per year. Don't get too close, Stephen! It says here that the Pencilneck wards off its natural predator, the jock, by emitting a toxic gas called "body odor."

Most tourists were discreet with their photographs, making an effort not to disturb us in our natural habitat. Sometimes, when I could feel someone quietly stalking me through the Yard, I'd wait to hear a couple of rapid "clicks," then spin around to catch the culprit in the act. But all I'd see is a guy staring up at the clouds and whistling casually, no incriminating evidence other than the faint outline of a digital camera in his pocket or maybe a hulking tripod in his arms.

Occasionally the tourists would be far more aggressive, especially if you were doing something stereotypically "Harvard." One time I caused a tourist frenzy when I walked through the Yard holding a calculus book while wearing a Harvard T-shirt and eating a bag of Smartfood. I might as well have been Mickey Mouse strolling through Epcot Center. Visitors assaulted me with epileptic flashes, and one foreign sightseer even approached me with a flurry of hand gestures to request a posed photograph. (Either that or he wanted some of my Smartfood, and there was no fucking way he was getting that.) I should have told the crowd that I was in a hurry, that there were equations to be solved, cancers to be cured, Facebooks to be invented. But I just shrugged and acquiesced to the mob, agreeing to pose in a picture with the foreign man's two daughters. Somewhere out there is a photograph of me with my arms around two pigtailed Korean teenagers in short skirts and knee-highs.

I think most Harvard students enjoy the attention from outsiders. It's a nice little ego boost, a reminder that you are special. To me, though, it was only a reminder of what was at stake. Every time I walked by John Harvard and his throng of captivated visitors, I would remember that I wasn't going to college, I was going to *Harvard*. And I was wasting my opportunity. People would travel halfway around the world just to visit my school, yet here I was, barely motivated enough to travel the zero miles required to attend one of its renowned classes. Wasn't I supposed to be proud that I went to the "World's Greatest University"? I was just embarrassed. Embarrassed that people anointed me as "special," when my only accomplishments had come in high school, where I could tackle football players and fill out SAT bubbles better than the average student. Embarrassed that strangers wanted to take my picture as if I were somebody. Embarrassed that my fly was down in my photo with the jailbait Korean girls.

The John Harvard statue is undoubtedly the most iconic symbol of the university, and most visitors glamorize him like he's a demigod. Like a lot of superheroes, though, John Harvard takes on an alternate identity once the sun goes down. He's kind of like Bruce Wayne, only instead of turning into an invincible caped hero, John Harvard transforms into an oversized urinal. Come nightfall the throngs of enthusiastic tourists lining up at the statue would be replaced by Harvard students intending to shower John Harvard with a different type of attention.

Most of them claimed to be there to fulfill the first requirement of the Three Harvard Acts, though frequent return visits seemed to suggest that there was more to peeing on John Harvard than merely satisfying an ancient school tradition. There was just something irresistibly appealing to pissing on Harvard's immortal icon. It was a form of therapy for the students, who would take turns releasing all their stress and frustration on the statue—a metaphorical "Fuck you!" to the renowned university.

Throughout their lives, these students were used to being the best: the prodigy, the golden child, the high-school valedictorian. But Harvard would pull you down and rub your nose in your shortcomings until you realized you weren't as good as you had thought. Lifelong A-students became C-students, chief editors of high school newspapers would get flat out rejected by the *Crimson*, and former football captains were told they were weaker than a fart in an astronaut suit. Harvard would cut your legs out from under you, and just like that, you went from thinking you were hot shit to thinking you were a piece of shit.

It was frustrating for the students to feel belittled by their own university, especially when they saw the worldwide slobber-fest over Harvard, an imperfect institution with an invulnerable image. It didn't seem fair. Every day we saw the blind glorification of John Harvard, so naturally we felt compelled to climb up on his pedestal and take him down a notch. Show him how it feels.

The juxtaposition of external versus internal perceptions of the university was divided by a sunset: by day, tourists photographed the statue because it symbolized Harvard; by night, students pissed on the statue because it symbolized Harvard.

———◆◆———

"Fercrissakes, what's taking so flipping long?" Dermot moaned.

"It's not that easy!" I shouted back. "I'm worried about splash-back."

"Well I'm worried about ghosts!" Dermot believed in ghosts. "I swear to Saint Mary I've seen things tottin' around in the shadows."

"Relax, will ya? If a ghost comes after us, I'll protect you."

"With what? Your skinpipe? Ghosts are immune to urine. Believe me, I've tried."

"Just give me a sec, I need to find a better angle for this."

Splash-back was a lame excuse for my hesitation, but I needed

to buy some time for my conscience to fully process the significance of John Harvard's golden toe. Over the years, how many
visitors had rubbed that shoe for good luck? The tally was surely
in the hundreds of thousands, probably the millions. Regardless
of the actual number, enough hands had rubbed the toe to convert
its once dark chocolate bronze into a brightly burnished gold.

I think most students don't even consider the outside visitors
as they spray the school's main tourist attraction. Their irrev-
erent assault is more focused on Harvard itself. But my pesky
conscience couldn't stop thinking about all the people who
had naïvely rubbed that toe and made a wish: the harmless old
lady with her fanny pack, the gap-toothed ten-year-old on his
school fieldtrip, the traveling hippy with his giant backpack and
random carabineers. Thinking of these characters made me feel
sad, but there was one image in particular that wrenched my
heart. Buried deep somewhere in my parent's photo drawer is
a picture of seventeen-year-old me on my first Harvard tour. I
am standing next to John Harvard, a wide grin on my face as I
silently wished with all my heart to get accepted into this school.
My hand gripped his glossy shoe, trusting my hopes and dreams
on an entity that, beneath its perfectly shiny façade, was soaked
in urine.

Like the old lady, the kid, the hippy, and every other tourist
who's ever stood awestruck in the Yard, I had bought into the
hype. I had faith in Harvard, that it was a paragon of human
achievement, that it had the power to elevate people to extraordinary heights. I doubt most people believed the golden toe actually made wishes come true, but that didn't stop any of us from
rubbing it, just in case.

As I stood there now, my skinpipe locked and loaded on John

Harvard's chest, I was overcome with nostalgia for that photograph, for that period in my life when I still believed in Harvard, in a better future, in myself. It was a little over a year ago, but it felt so much further away than that. From the moment I stepped into the Yard in my Hulk underwear, a naked teenager among well-dressed students, my optimism had been choked out of me.

It was such a painfully sobering thought that I almost unleashed on John Harvard at that moment. But then my thoughts turned to tomorrow, when the sun would rise again and there would be new people lining up at John Harvard. There would be more seventeen-year-olds grabbing that shoe, holding on to aspirations of a brighter tomorrow. They had hope, life's most powerful gift. Who the hell was I to piss on their dreams?

Throughout the year, there had been dozens of times when I fantasized about desecrating John Harvard as I passed by the statue on those miserable treks from the weight room to calculus lecture. I would picture myself guzzling down some of my Diesel Venom supplement, then using my lightsaber pee to slice through the statue like he was Darth Vader and I was a freaking Jedi knight. How badass would that be? Okay, maybe not. But Vikas would have thought it was cool.

But this profane urge had lessened dramatically in the previous few weeks, probably because I was starting to hate Harvard slightly less. The elements of the school that bothered me were still there, of course. Adderall-popping students who took on their homework with the same focused efficiency as Jack Bauer defusing a bomb, girls who rolled their eyes at my unsophisticated outfits (like they had never accidentally worn their shirt inside-out before), guys who said "fairly certain" when "pretty sure" would've worked just fine. Recently, though, I had been making an effort to shift my concentration to the parts of the school I did enjoy. I had been focusing so much energy before despising the asshole minority of the student body that I wasn't paying enough attention to some of the truly phenomenal people around me. For all the hype of Harvard's eye-popping endowment, its true wealth was in its students. There was, after all, an abundance of really great people at Harvard, students who were talented and funny and good-hearted. One of them was with me right now, a guy who would ace any loyalty test in front of him. Shit, the kid was willing to face ghosts *and* freeze his clackers off for me—a double whammy, and quite a sacrifice just to help your friend pee on an old man.

Of course, my newfound appreciation of the student body was largely influenced by Jen, who, in my eyes, was the best part of Harvard. Following the awkward conclusion to our "date" a couple of weeks back, I was terrified my actions (or lack thereof) would permanently damage our relationship. That night in my room, I kind of had the sense Jen wanted me to make a move, but I couldn't get my mind past the conviction that girls like her didn't hook up with guys like me. No smokeshow has ever had a make-out session on a Red Sox bedspread—that's a fact.

Luckily, though, Jen didn't hold my timidity against me. And though we never talked about that night, we had been hanging out regularly since then. I was so relieved our relationship hadn't been damaged, mostly because I cared about her so damn much, but also because she strengthened some weaknesses in my emotional makeup. You may find this hard to believe, but I had some self-confidence issues. Jen helped me tremendously in this area, because she actually saw something in me. When I was with her I felt like I was on my own pedestal, with her holding an umbrella to protect me from Harvard's demoralizing yellow showers. She was making me feel better about myself and, consequently, our school. I just wished I could translate some of this new confidence into an actual kiss.

And deep down, I knew that was the real reason I came to John Harvard tonight. I was sick of being a pussy. I was tired of being so self-conscious. Peeing on the famous statue was bold, an act of blatant irreverence that I never thought I'd actually have the balls to do. It would be a "fuck you" to both Harvard and my insecure personality. If I wanted to be Jen's boyfriend, I needed a self-injected shot of confidence. She deserved a guy who had enough poise to accept her advances, regardless of which short celebrity was ripping shots at the Kong. She didn't want a passive guy who stands with his bat on his shoulder, too afraid to get to first base after she lobs a meatball right down the middle.

And that's when it hit me: there was really only one way to demonstrate my confidence, and it wasn't this roundabout attempt that was actually more cowardly than courageous. Peeing on a 367-year-old man cemented to his chair? Now *that* was pussy. What would I really be proving, anyway? It wasn't even a moving target. Girls are attracted to guys who are self-assured, not spineless chumps whose fantasies involve urine and Jedi knights. I had to see Jen and prove myself face-to-face. And I had to do it right now.

———— ◆ ————

Once I was finished contemplating the deepest thoughts ever had by a man holding his dick, I zipped up my fly and swiveled myself away from John Harvard. The hostage situation was over. Dermot looked annoyed that all this amounted to nothing, but he had to be relieved it was over, considering he had been waiting out in the cold for ten-and-a-half pages. I bent my knees into a crouch and prepared to jump down from the pedestal.

"STOP RIGHT THERE!" Still perched on the statue's base, I turned toward the voice. Hank, the old guy from the superintendent's office during my semi-nude adventure on the first day of school, stood ten yards away.

I was now squatting on the pedestal, looking like I was about to take the desecration of John Harvard to a completely new level. I froze in my crouch, my brain scrambling for a reasonable explanation for my current position. Fortunately, Dermot swooped in to save me.

"Oh! Um…I feel like a Felipe's, let's go to burrito!"

Thanks, Derm.

"I…I haven't done anything, I swear," I stuttered to Hank.

"Oh, right. I'm sure you were just having a heart-to-heart with John Harvard!"

"Kind of."

"Don't play me for a fool, kid. I know what you're doing. I saw your tallywacker!"

"My what?"

"Your tallywacker! You know, your pecker, your willy, your dipper in the zipper!"

"Your beef bayonet, your one-eyed trouser snake, your donut puncher, your Captain Winkie, your…"

"That's enough, Derm. I think I understood him."

Hank approached the statue with a flashlight as I jumped down to the pavement below. I thought about running, but that would imply guilt. And it's not like I could've ditched the accused assault weapon by tossing my tallywacker into the bushes or down a drain.

"I'm fed up with you ungrateful Harvard kids, running around like a bunch of spoiled hoodlums!" Hank looked like he couldn't decide whether to scream or cry. "Tonight I already caught a kid in Grays attempting to reprogram the vending machine to drop the Ho Ho's every time you type in '69.' Then some knucklehead in Matthews set off the fire alarm trying to weld a metal claw to his homemade robot. Now I've got you, treating the founder like he's a goddamn Porta-Potty—"

"G-G-GHOSTS!" The shout came from Dermot, who was now booking it across the Yard toward Lionel. I looked around the Yard to see what had caused my trusty watchman to transform into Scooby Doo.

It was like the apparitions materialized out of the darkness, roughly forty cloaked figures striding down the footpath, directly toward Hank, me, and John Harvard. The leader of the procession, his face veiled by a black hood, held a ten-foot pole with a clock attached to the end. His followers trailed behind, chanting a low, ominous mantra.

"Societas artis fabulae sumus…Societas artis fabulae sumus… Societas artis fabulae sumus."

Hank threw his hands in the air in defeat. "That's it, I'm done. I'm too old for this bullcrap." He clipped his flashlight to his belt, muttering expletives as he slogged away. "Kids in robes speaking in devil tongue, for Pete's sake…"

I probably should've followed Dermot and Hank's lead and gotten the hell out of there. But come on, I wasn't about to pass up the chance to see a parade of dementors. At the very least, there was a decent chance I was about to witness some sort of final club ritual, the sacrifice of a virgin to John Harvard, maybe.

But once the horde of veiled creatures drew close enough for me to see a little beneath their cloaks, I noticed a few elements that were completely incongruous with final club conventions: mismatched socks, a few calculator watches, cheap sneakers, a black guy. The cloaked figures came to a stop at John Harvard and formed a semicircle in front of the statue. I stood on the periphery of the group and watched as they passed around candles and began to light them one by one.

In most life scenarios, if you find yourself questioning why someone is lighting candles, it's probably time to leave. This seemed like unprecedented access to an exclusive ritual, though, and a rush of excitement and curiosity kept me locked in my observation stance, a look of gripping anticipation on my face, like I was Jane Goodall about to watch a gorilla gangbang.

The cloaked figures were completely ignoring me, as if I didn't exist. Just when I started to think these were final club members after all, the figure in front of me removed his hood, revealing a familiar tangle of orange curls. I knew this dude; we were friends for a couple of weeks in the first semester. And his presence explained exactly who these mysterious people were.

———— ◆ ————

Maximillian Finch despised his curly red hair. Which is weird considering he allowed it to grow into a massive 'fro, making his head look like an overgrown Chia Pet that had caught on fire. He also hated it when you called him anything other than "Maximillian." Who knows why; maybe it was a nice confidence boost for him to know he was a high score in Scrabble, but calling him "Max" would drive him fucking crazy. Anyway, Max was the roommate of my buddy Ryan, and he was also in my first-semester course on aliens. Max was obsessed with aliens, a firm believer that when it comes to extraterrestrials, only the first half of the term "science fiction" is applicable. He even had a special screensaver on his computer that relayed elaborate charts and frequencies from a satellite that supposedly searched for alien activity in outer space.

I often visited his suite to play games of *Madden* with Ryan, and one afternoon when Max wasn't around, we changed his screensaver to a flashing text that read "ALIENS FOUND." Max must've discovered it was me, because a few days later my computer had a new screensaver with a big picture of my face and the message "DOUCHEBAG FOUND." We didn't speak much after that.

Max was a devoted member of the Harvard-Radcliffe Science Fiction Association, or HRSFA for a short mouthful. It probably won't come as a surprise when I tell you that the Sci-Fi Club at Harvard College tended to be a tad dorky. The club participates in the kind of events you'd expect, with *Star Trek* marathons, *Magic: The Gathering* tournaments, video game sessions, and frequent "Milk & Cookies" meetings where members read aloud science fiction stories for literally three to four hours. Then there's the more quirky side of HRSFA.

Walk through the Yard on any given day, and you might see a few members handing out blank fliers, or tying a peanut to a string for some "squirrel fishing," or dancing with their arms stretched to the sky in an attempt to control the weather. Every year, on the Ides of March, they dress in togas and reenact the assassination of Julius Caesar on the steps of Widener Library. Another annual event is the "Wyld Hunt," where barely-clothed members cover themselves in blue paint and sprint through Harvard Square, whooping and hollering under a full moon as they relentlessly chase down a fleeing stag. (The "stag" being, of course, a fleet-footed freshman wearing antlers tied to his head.)

I'd say the members of HRSFA were easily the most eccentric students on campus. The most recognized member of HRSFA was Cape Boy, who wore a cape everywhere not because he thought it was funny, but because he believed it was awesome. While not quite on Zuckerberg's level, Cape Boy was certainly more famous on campus than Rivers Cuomo, the lead singer for Weezer. And when Cape Boy decided to retire his legendary outfit in December of my freshman year, Harvard students discovered the shocking news from an emotional tribute story in the *Crimson*. I'll always remember exactly where I was the day I flipped open the paper and saw the jolting headline, *CAPE BOY NO LONGER INTERESTED IN CAPES.*

It's scary that HRSFA isn't even the clear-cut winner for "Nerdiest Harvard Extracurricular." So Long, Princess, the student rock band that writes and performs all their songs with lyrics from *Star Wars*, has to be in the discussion, with bonus points awarded because their lead vocalist was a contestant on the hit reality TV show, *Beauty and the Geek* (he was not a Beauty). The Tiddlywinks Club shouldn't be counted out, either. Technically listed as an "intercollegiate" competitive group, the members of Harvard's team only played against each other, presumably because the tiddlywinks clubs of other colleges dissolved shortly after the invention of electricity. Still, that didn't stop our team from tiddlying the shit out of those winks. And then there's my personal favorite, the Harvard Quidditch team. A coed group that mounts brooms and dons capes for fierce Quidditch matches, this team turns the fictional *Harry Potter* sport into reality. It should be pointed out that they don't actually fly (I'd describe their movements across the field more as "waddling with a sense of urgency"). There are balls and goals and teamwork, though it's not the best display of athletic prowess out there. Let's face it: these kids have a hard enough time running *without* a broomstick shoved up their ass. There was no way I'm a big enough *Harry Potter*-loving loser to want to play intramural Quidditch. Plus, they don't even play by the correct rules—the quaffle should be thirty centimeters in diameter, if you want to get technical about it.

My senior year in high school, my parents asked me why I wanted to go to Harvard, other than the football. I couldn't tell them my real reason—that I thought Harvard guaranteed a life of success, riches, and bitches—so I told them I loved how the school had so many opportunities and activities. It was true: with over four hundred extracurricular clubs, Harvard had plenty to do. A few students groups were fun and silly, like HRSFA, but in typical Harvard fashion, many of them were over-the-top with their intensity. The student government, or the Undergraduate Council as we called it, was the primary offender.

In high school I ran for student government because I thought I could get different flavors of freezy pops in the cafeteria. At Harvard, students ran for president of the UC as a precursor to actually becoming president of the United States. Candidates took their campaigns very seriously and, prior to the elections, my room was blitzed by waves of UC hopefuls making door-to-door visits. Each candidate would give me their pitch as they pretended they cared about things other than their résumé, and I would nod my head as I pretended to care about their commitment to get more kosher options in the dining halls. Following the introduction, the candidate would try to impress me with a detailed list of all the clubs that supported him: "…and, as

I'm sure you've already heard, I'm officially endorsed by the Pro-Choice Club, the Right to Life Association, the Vegetarian Club, the Harvard Hunting Coalition, the Black Men's Forum, the Polo Club, and the Harvard Contrarian Club." Candidates would jockey for the endorsement of every last club, as if the support of the Chinese checkers team was a major key to victory. But when it came down to it, the winner would be whoever promised to extend the library hours the longest.

I didn't know who HRSFA endorsed in the UC elections, but I was now sure it was their members who lurked beneath the long, black cloaks that flapped in the early April breeze. When the last of the candles had been lit, the eerie Latin chanting ceased and was replaced with a more energetic and authoritative incantation:

"ALL HAIL CHRONOS! ALL HAIL CHRONOS!"

The guy carrying the long pole with a clock duct-taped to the top stepped in front of John Harvard and faced his followers. I tapped Max on the shoulder.

"Hey, Maxipad," I whispered. "What the hell is going on?"

"We are celebrating the 'Going of the Hour.'" Max kept his gaze locked straight ahead.

I assumed the "Going of the Hour" had something to do with the end of daylight savings, which happened tonight—in just a few minutes, actually.

"And who's Chronos?"

Max turned and looked at me like I was a fucking idiot. "You serious? Chronos? The benevolent God of Time?"

"And why are you holding a water pistol?"

Max now looked at me like I was an idiot whom he wanted to kill. "It's *not* a water pistol. It's a plasma chrono-cannon. Every member of the Temporal Police has one."

I decided to end my line of questioning there. You don't fuck around when plasma chrono-cannons are involved. And anyway, the leader was preparing to speak.

"Disciples, we are gathered here tonight, at the Going of the Hour, to give thanks for the wondrous gifts of the benevolent Chronos, the Sensational Sponsor of Seconds, the Mystical Minister of Minutes, the Honorary Overlord of the Hour!"

"ALL HAIL CHRONOS!"

"We shall begin with a reading from Maximillian, who's been working all year on a one-word poem, specifically scribed for this wondrous occasion!"

A polite applause percolated throughout the small crowd as Max slowly made his way to the front of the pack. His hands fumbled beneath his cloak for a moment before producing a piece of lined paper that was folded six times over. He unfolded it slowly before reading from the crinkled scroll.

"This is a poem entitled *All in Good Time: An Ode to the Prince of Perpetuality.*"

Max spoke meekly, the nervous waver of his voice matching the flutter of the paper held in his quivering hands. He cleared his throat and took a deep breath.

"Imminent."

A pause, a bow. "Thank you."

Max folded up the paper and triumphantly returned to the crowd to a boisterous applause and pats on the back all around.

The leader quieted the disciples with an outstretched arm. "Thank you, Maximillian. That was as subtle as it was mind-blowing."

He motioned toward a shorter cloakie standing to the left. He/she/it was holding a paper disc, about ten inches in diameter,

with a small right triangle protruding from the top. It was supposed to represent a sundial, I think, though it looked more like
an origami experiment gone horribly wrong. The carrier, escorted
by two high-ranking members of the Temporal Police, delivered
the paper sundial to the master of ceremonies. He put down his
clock-staff and now held the sundial above his head for all to see,
like it was the future Lion King of Pride Rock.

"Oh, benevolent Chronos, we present this sacrifice to you
on the night you take back the extra hour you so benevolently
bestowed on us in October. You are a generous, benevolent God,
and your gifts of temporal splendor have so enriched our lives.
Without your bestowals of time, we would not have the final
whistle of a football game, *Back to the Future*, instant coffee,
and—fingers crossed—extended library hours!"

"ALL HAIL CHRONOS!"

"And to you, disciples of the Benevolent Benefactor of
Boundlessness, remember to hold Him close to your hearts! At
times, it feels as though we are held captive by a community en-
slaved to its Past. At times, the maladies of our Present may hold
us prisoner. But fear not, Children of Chronos, for the Future is
always one second away! Break through these chains of tradition
and carve your own Future! Through Chronos, the Past matters
not. He always grants us new beginnings, new hope…a chance
at redemption!"

"ALL HAIL CHRONOS!" Even I joined in on this one.

The master lowered the paper sundial and held a small plastic
lighter directly beneath it. At that instant, the thunderous ringing
of bells atop Memorial Chapel signaled the new hour, as we shot
into the future, from 1:59 to 3:00 a.m.

"Benevolent Chronos, we salute you!"

The lighter didn't work. After several more failed attempts, one of the cloakies brought over the scented Yankee Candle he was holding (Banana Bread, from the smell of it), and used its flame to ignite the sundial. As the sundial burned and HRSFA cheered, I slipped out of the pack and made my way across the Yard, toward Jen's dorm.

The time was now.

------◆◆◆------

Outside of Hollis, I could see the light of her third-floor bedroom was still on. Jen was a night owl—reading magazines and chatting on the phone and brushing her hair and doing whatever else hot girls do late at night.

Before entering Hollis, I had made a quick pit stop at my dorm to grab a couple of packs of instant hot chocolate for us to share. The packets now sat snugly in my jeans pocket as I climbed the old Hollis stairway slowly, anxiously. I ran through the plan in my head. There would be no awkward pauses, no moments of hesitation. As soon as Jen opened the door, I would put my arms around her and give her the moment we had both been waiting for.

When I reached the third floor, my heartbeat was out of control. I tried to calm down by telling myself it was just a kiss. But I knew it was much more than that.

Standing outside her door, I could hear Jen's muffled voice from inside. I smiled when I heard her laugh. That contagious giggle that had rescued me from Harvard.

But now her muted laughs were joined by another sound. Something gut-wrenching: a distinct, revolting cackle. I stood there, unable to move, unable to breathe, as Jen's and Tripp's giggles snuck out from under her door and into my breaking heart.

As painful as these sounds were, they were only an imminent future away from something worse. For it was the seconds later, when I no longer heard any talking, that really killed me.

———————◆———————

I don't even remember leaving Hollis. Back in the Yard, my feet carried me to the now deserted statue. I climbed up, unzipped, and aimed specifically for John Harvard's golden toe.

Chapter Fifteen

MAC AND P.C.

On March 15, a pack of journalists prowled hungrily outside the Loeb Drama Center while 421 Harvard faculty members inside passed a vote of no-confidence on one of the smartest men in the world. Though it would be another year before he officially resigned, this marked the beginning of the end for Larry Summers's troubled presidency.

Meanwhile, Jen Wesker cast a less-publicized vote of no-confidence on me. It didn't make the CNN nightly report, but it was just as traumatizing, since the vote was Jen's tongue and the ballot box was Tripp's mouth.

Larry Summers might've been the one guy at Harvard having more "girl problems" than I was.

The trouble started at a Conference on Diversifying the Science & Engineering Workforce, where Larry sealed his fate with (surprise, surprise) a terribly mishandled speech. While speaking to an audience comprised of some of the top female scholars in the world, Larry fielded a question about why so few women are tenured in science and engineering at elite institutions like Harvard. A shrewder speaker would have responded to this question with the one answer that most of the audience was dying to hear: "Well, it's sexism, of course!" Instead, Larry decided it would be a good idea to take a different, slightly bolder approach by mooning the audience and declaring that all women are a bunch of brainless morons.

Okay…he didn't *exactly* do that. But he might as well have, given the outraged reaction of the audience (and worldwide media) when they heard Summers cite a study suggesting that in the fields of math and science, there may be an "intrinsic aptitude" difference between men and women. Following this provocative statement, several appalled attendees walked out in the middle of the lecture, including MIT biologist Nancy Hopkins, who later told the *Boston Globe* that if she hadn't left, "I would have blacked out or thrown up."

Like Larry, I too was on the fast track out of Harvard. Jen had been my primary motivation to continue enduring the school, and without her I didn't have much to get up for in the morning. So I didn't. I stopped going to my classes, switching off my alarm clock and telling myself that I would watch the lectures on my computer at a more convenient time.

Harvard professors videotape most of their lectures and upload them to an online archive for students to review additional times later, if they want (and trust me…they want). Students would rewatch the lectures on their laptops or listen to them on their iPods for some on-the-go mental stimulation. (If a Harvard guy is on the Internet past midnight with his door closed, there's a decent chance he's either: (a) spanking his monkey; (b) watching a lecture video; or (c) all of the above.) It wasn't unheard of for students to flip on their iPods for a quick hit of knowledge whenever their restless minds got bored, like when they were eating dinner, sitting on the toilet, or having a conversation with me.

A popular time-saving technique was to increase the speed of the playback to 2.5 times the normal pace, so you can inject your brain with three complete lectures in a little over an hour. I knew one guy who would listen to these super-speed lectures on his iPod as he drifted to sleep, similar to the way his parents played Mozart recordings when he slept as a child. I tried this approach when I got desperate with calculus in the first semester, but the sped-up lecture was like *Alvin and the Chipmunks Sing Antiderivatives* and was way too fast for me to keep up with. By the time I slowed down the playback to a pace I could follow, the lecture was crawling at half-normal speed and Professor Phlegm's slow, distorted voice sounded like the "Hooked On Phonics" recordings my parents played for me when I slept as a child.

I never ended up watching the videos of my missed lectures because there are literally fourteen billion more interesting things to do on the Internet than watching class. My bed became my permanent home and I only ventured outside for meals, once my industrial-sized case of animal crackers had been poached to extinction.

Dermot diagnosed me as being depressed, suggesting that, in his medical opinion, I should stop being so sad. I could tell it really bothered him to see me upset, and though he still refuses to take credit for it, I'm pretty sure he had something to do with the fish fillet "get well" present that appeared in my bedroom one afternoon. The fish was wrapped in butcher's paper with a small red bow on top, and it came with a note that read, *There's plenty of 'em in the sea....*

It was the nicest cut of halibut anyone had ever left on my pillow, but this still didn't cheer me up. Logically, I should have been able to get over Jen pretty easily, because who wants a girl who is attracted to an asshole like Tripp? But that's not how it works. I wanted her more than ever. I had less hope than ever. And the two feelings combined to make me more depressed than ever.

My next decision was to quit football. It had been my lifelong dream to play college football, but there was little reason for me to remain on the team. At Harvard I needed every brain cell I could get, so it made no sense to play a collision sport that turned the baked potato in my head into mashed. I was largely irrelevant on the team anyway, and the coaches didn't even bother yelling at me anymore, with the exception of Coach Mac. Plus, the time commitment (even in the offseason) was really getting in the way of my moping. So at noon on a mid-April weekday, I rolled out of bed and walked across the river to tell my coaches that I had worn the Crimson jersey for the last time.

———◆———

I emptied out my locker and deposited my remaining bottles of midnight thunder into my backpack. I no longer needed my Diesel Fuel supplement, but I decided against throwing it away (like batteries, old A/C units, and tube TVs, that shit needed to be disposed of by a hazardous waste professional).

I recall really wanting to keep a small piece of equipment as a memento, since no one would believe I once played Harvard football without some proof. The personalized crimson name-plate above my locker would have been perfect, except a few weeks earlier one of my teammates had stolen it as a joke (or maybe a prediction). My next choice was an old practice jersey, or even a pair of my football pants, but our equipment manager made me return everything so he could pass it along to future players. He let me keep my jock strap, at least, for he stopped recycling that type of equipment "since the outbreak of '97." The jockstrap had my name and number stitched in it, which was kind of cool, *and* it was a size large. But still, not the type of keepsake you show off to future houseguests.

I wasn't thrilled with my haul—I was expecting to get more out of my Harvard football experience than a bruised ego and a frayed ball pouch—but I tossed the jock into my backpack and headed for the weight room. Before going to speak with the head coach, I wanted to tell Coach Mac that I was quitting. I didn't know why I felt like I owed him an explanation, but I did.

Coach Mac had a small, windowless office attached to the weight room, and he was in there exactly six times a day, during his meals. This is where I found him, sitting in his tiny desk chair in concentrated silence as his incisors tore into a sandwich that had more animal meat on it than Noah's Ark. I wavered outside a moment, trying to summon the courage to step inside. Everyone knew that you didn't startle Mac during one of his feeding sessions, and I was in extra peril considering I had skipped our last two workouts. I muttered a quiet prayer, then stepped inside.

When Mac finally sensed my presence in the office, he lowered the sandwich from his mouth and set it down in his lap with supreme caution, like it was a baby. A thick, delicious baby.

He lowered one eyebrow and gave me a hard stare. "You're alive," he growled. Maybe I was paranoid, but I swear I heard him whisper under his breath, *"for now…"*

There was no other chair in the office, so I sat down on an unopened case of protein bars. "I, uh, just wanted to apologize for not coming to the workouts and for not telling you that I was not coming to the workouts." Under the circumstances, this was the best sentence I could formulate. Like patting your head while rubbing your stomach, it's difficult to simultaneously talk to Coach Mac while contracting your sphincter.

Mac didn't say a word. Instead, he picked up something round off his desk and took a big bite of it. I was having a hard time seeing straight; it was either a large plum or a human heart.

I continued. "I figured there was no reason to keep coming to our sessions, since I'm not going to be back at Harvard next year."

"You joining the army?"

"Well, no, not exactly. I just don't think Harvard is a good fit for me."

"Take a look at me." Coach Mac took another bite of his succulent orb, then placed it on top of the keyboard of his 1994 desktop computer. Red juice trickled down his sharp chin. "Do I look like I fit in here?"

"No."

Mac leaned back and his puny desk chair creaked under his massive frame. "And do I look like I give a fuck?"

I responded with a shake of my head, but I could tell by his suddenly detached gaze that Coach Mac's mind had vacated the building. He got like this whenever his thought-train careened off track and headed toward whatever enchanted world it was that was located deep within the inner recesses of his brain. It's a dangerous journey—you can only hope that he doesn't take you along with him.

"Kester, do you know anything about science?"

Outside of this office I would have definitely responded "no," but the answer is sort of relative to the company you're in.

"Yes."

"So then you know how weight lifting works. When you come in here and start crushing weights and pushing yourself to the max, you are physically breaking down the tiny fibers that make up your muscles. Only when your muscles are limp-dick and broken down can your body rebuild them bigger than before. That's how you get stronger. See what I'm getting at?"

I nodded.

"We focus on a total-body workout," Mac continued, "but at the end of the day, your strongest muscle has to be right here." Mac tapped the center of his chest with his index finger.

"Your heart…" I interjected softly.

"Fuck no! What is this, fucking Oprah? I'm talking about your pecs." Coach Mac reached for his man-wich and took a ferocious bite, probably to eliminate the lingering taste of my wussy comment. "Kester, you weigh two hundred and forty pounds, right? And what goal did I set for you on the bench press? How much did I want you repping?"

"Two hundred and forty pounds."

"That's right. You know why I chose that exact number? Because a man who can't bench-press his own weight isn't worth a damn."

I shifted uncomfortably on my Power Bar stool. I wasn't sure where Mac was going with this. I'm not sure he knew, either.

"I gotta be honest with you, Kester. When you showed up in the fall, you were so weak that calling you a pussy would have been an insult to pussies."

"But you *did* call me a pussy. A lot."

"Yeah, because I love insulting pussies! But then you worked your balls off, and your bench-press numbers started to go up."

"Only with the help of Diesel Fuel," I pointed out.

"The FDA shut down that shit for false advertising. Turns out Diesel Fuel doesn't cause muscle growth. Just UTIs."

"Umm…good to know."

"Anyway, the point is now you're benching two-forty, but you're still playing like a scared little bitch. It's like you're intimidated by everyone because they look better, and act more confident, and have accomplished more. Sure, they may talk a big game, but you'd be shocked how many talented people can't bench-press their own weight. So stop worrying about how you compare to everyone else. You have no way of knowing how strong they really are. All we know for sure is that you're strong enough to lift yourself, and that's pretty damn good."

Coach Mac jerked his head up slightly, then looked around, as if he was gaining his bearings. He spotted his sandwich on his desk, smiled, and then went back to work on it as I digested his words. In between chews, he asked why I wasn't saying anything.

I shrugged. "You gave me a lot to consider."

Mac released a short, dilapidated chortle. "Shit, I should be a teacher here."

Before leaving the weight room to head to the Yard, I assured Coach Mac I would wait a little longer before coming to a decision on football. I was still leaning toward quitting, but I didn't want to do it just then, since Mac seemed to care so much. Also, I had to factor in the likelihood that quitting the team would result in Mac tearing off my limbs and beating me to a pulp with my own arms, a possibility he made sure to suggest as I walked out of his office.

I decided to actually go to class that day. I was already out of bed, so why not?

Harvard Yard was packed with people that day, as usual. The lingering chills of winter had finally evaporated, leaves reunited with branches, and the tourist numbers were experiencing their typical spring spike. I hadn't been out much during the day the last couple of weeks, because I wanted to avoid seeing Jen or Tripp or the sun. Surveying the Yard now, it looked like business as usual. A grungy hobo sifted through a trashcan in front of University Hall and received glares of disgust from nearby tourists as they vigorously rubbed John Harvard's golden toe. A freshman guy argued emphatically with Hank about whether his Segway technically fell under the "no biking in the Yard" policy. The Tightrope Walking Club practiced their craft on a cord tied between two oak trees in front of Hollis. A contingent of news reporters and cameramen filmed interviews as they covered a boisterous student protest in front of Massachusetts Hall. This was the Harvard I had come to know.

I don't think I'm breaking any new ground when I say that college students *love* protesting. They protest more often than they do laundry. It's a natural occurrence, I suppose, since college kids are still young enough to hate authority, but just old enough to think they are right about everything. They are also at a stage in their lives when they have the time to think about stuff to complain about, and then actually do so in a semi-organized fashion. Adults don't have this opportunity because they have to spend their time worrying about their family and bills and healthcare and getting their kids into college. Meanwhile college students are freaking out because at this rate the Salt Creek tiger beetle will be extinct in three hundred years if we don't raise awareness *RIGHT FUCKING NOW!*

Protesting is taken to a whole new level at Harvard. It's what happens when a society takes six thousand college kids and labels them as the smartest students in the universe. Soon those kids are convinced that everything they say is important and noteworthy, an attitude that often leads to the writing of autobiographical books. It also results in a bunch of protests—and holy crap, do Harvard kids get into their protests. Almost every day at Harvard there was some form of protest, rally, or demonstration. It had gotten so out of hand that a group of students actually started an anti-protest club. (Their first order of business? Convene in the Yard to protest all the protests. I'm serious.)

Perhaps the most legendary Harvard student protest, one that made national headlines a couple of years before I entered the school, was the infamous "living-wage sit-in" at Massachusetts Hall. Unhappy that the university was paying its custodians a single-digit hourly wage, nearly fifty students stormed Massachusetts Hall (a surprisingly modest eighteenth-century-style brick building that housed the president's office in the Yard) and refused to leave until Harvard agreed to increase the wages of its staff. The administration wasn't sure what to make of it at first, and I can't say I blame them. Harvard students and janitors are not two demographics you imagine teaming up for social justice. The students were demanding that the custodians get a raise to $10 an hour (after graduation some of these same students would be *effing pissed* that Morgan Stanley was paying them "only" eighty grand a year to fill in spreadsheets).

How serious were these students in their support for people

they couldn't really relate to? The students were armed with sleeping bags and threatened to live in the hallways of Massachusetts Hall for as long as it took. But the administration refused to give in to their demands, figuring that this little slumber party would be over in a couple of days when the seductive thought of class would lure the nerds out of their entrenchment. The administration underestimated the freakish focusing capabilities of Harvard students, though, and soon "a couple of days" turned into "a couple of weeks," and the sit-in escalated into a national story with round-the-clock coverage. (A documentary of the protest was narrated by none other than Ben Affleck, who likes to remind everyone that he used to go to Harvard…to visit his buddy Matt Damon.)

The living-wage sit-in became a public-relations disaster for the multibillion dollar school. Finally, after a twenty-one-day student occupation of Massachusetts Hall, the administration agreed to raise the hourly wage of the custodial staff in exchange for a few minor cutbacks in university operations. The students were positively elated, until the following Monday, when they began protesting the dining service's sudden switch to off-brand cereal.

The subject of today's protest in the Yard, Larry Summers, had dominated recent debate on campus, though his "Women in Science" scandal was far from the only controversy at Harvard that year. One major protest occurred when a contingent of Harvard students decided to express their dissatisfaction with the U.S. government at a CIA career panel in a Science Center lecture hall. As high-ranking government officials attempted to entice the audience with a career in counter-terrorism, protestors rained down with spontaneous boos, shouts, and insults. One student, to show how sick the government made him, even stuck a finger down his throat and intentionally vomited in the middle of the lecture hall. (I wonder if this guy was also part of the sit-in on behalf of the custodial staff a couple of years earlier.) This occurred only a few weeks after the Summers vote of no-confidence, culminating a typically contentious year on the Harvard campus that left many demographics feeling angry and isolated. Some black students were still pissed about Larry's treatment of Cornel West, the popular (and now former) professor of African American Studies. Women were enraged because their president thought they should be setting the periodic table, not studying it. And white guys were devastated because Princeton had just defeated our nationally ranked water polo team.

I was running a little late for my social anthropology class, so I avoided the Larry Summers protest by cutting across the Yard's grass on my way to William James Hall, a towering building located behind Annenberg. I was making good time until I passed the Science Center and was slowed considerably by yet another demonstration, this one comprised of a mass of students lying motionless on the ground, pretending to be the victims of whichever international act of violence they were protesting that day. This was a very popular form of demonstration at Harvard, though no one could ever know *which* act of violence they were protesting, since everyone involved would just lie there, impersonating corpses.

I carefully weaved through the bodies, like a kid at a slumber party tiptoeing around sleeping friends on his way to the bathroom. I'm sure this demonstration was for a good cause, but it wasn't helping my nerves. Jen was in my anthropology class, and each step I took was bringing me closer to her. And now on top of that, I had to be careful not to leave a footprint on Timothy Wong's face.

The typical Harvard course meets for four hours a week. Three of those hours are devoted to lectures, where the professor is paid the big bucks for leading you through PowerPoint presentations with text copied straight from a book he or she authored fourteen years ago. The average lecture will have between one hundred and two hundred students, who then get divided into smaller classes, called "sections," where a dozen or so students meet in a classroom to discuss the course material. Sections are scheduled once a week for an hour, and are led by teaching fellows (TFs), who are enrolled in various Harvard graduate schools.

Asking me whether I liked sections at Harvard would be like asking someone if they enjoyed getting publicly cannibalized once a week. Because the formula for a section was: take a small classroom and add twelve self-appointed geniuses who estimate that they've been wrong, at most, a total of zero times in their lives. Now tell them to debate an academic topic, and that their performance will be judged and subsequently converted into a grade. There are no rules. Low blows are accepted, big words are encouraged, and any weapon of their intellect is in play. The result is an absolute bloodbath, the kind that leaves no victors, just a dozen losers.

Harvard might be the only place in the world where a discussion of Charles Dickens can drive one person to tears and another into therapy. The reason class discussion got so personal was that Harvard students realized that the key to success wasn't so much how *smart* you sounded, but how much *smarter* you sounded. In other words, your comments only had to sound intelligent compared to your competition. This could be achieved either by making a brilliant point yourself, or by making someone else sound like a goddamn buffoon. The latter was much easier to do.

So yeah, I was a popular target in sections.

My social-anthro section was on the ninth floor of William James Hall, which is one of the tallest buildings on campus. It seemed like an appropriate place for a Harvard class, way high up there like that. When I finally made it to William James I rushed through the lobby and into the elevator, swiped my Harvard ID, and rode it to the top.

I didn't realize how tightly I was gripping the strap of my back-pack until my hand started to cramp up. I noticed my breaths were short and my palms were damp, and I began to question why the hell I was even going to this class. It wasn't to satisfy my desire to learn, that was for sure, so clearly this had to do with Jen in some way.

She had texted me several times following the night I dis-covered she and Tripp were hooking up, asking me why I had suddenly gone MIA. One night she sent a message that said, "u alive? the rumors are starting to spread," and I typed out the response, "kinda like ur legs." I never sent it, instead taking the passive-aggressive route by not replying to Jen at all, my tacit way of telling her I knew about Captain Douchehole. Soon she stopped trying to contact me, and our relationship, or friend-ship, or whatever, was over.

My only support system at Harvard had caved in beneath me, and that's when I began to believe it was time to move on from her and, more importantly, from this school. Hibernating in my man-cave seemed to accomplish both of those goals, so why was I now going to a section with her in it? Maybe this was a last-ditch attempt to prove to myself that I was strong enough to handle Harvard by myself. Or maybe I was trying to prove that to Jen. Either way, I was nervous as hell.

Part of my apprehension about attending this particular class, though, had nothing to do with Jen. You see, when I signed up for *An Introduction to Social Anthropology*, I assumed the course would cover a range of cultural topics, including religion, politics, gender relations, law, and especially no calculus. I had no idea the class would be almost entirely about gender roles in society. And that I would be the *only male* in a section of twelve females. And that my TF would be a woman named Corky, known around campus as "The Lioness," because she had been arrested in six different women's rights demonstrations. Looking back, I wish the course catalog had mentioned that every single class would feel like a prolonged prostate examination.

Before stepping into the classroom, I peeked through the door-window to scope out the scene. The room was small and sparsely decorated—there was nothing especially "Harvard" about this place of learning, other than a dated world map that still believed in the Soviet Union. Twelve young women sat upright around a large oak table that had an ovular—sorry—*oval* shape. Some had already assumed their battle position, leaning forward in their chairs with their elbows planted on the table and their hands together just under the chin, their fingertips lightly touching to form a steeple. Others prepared for combat by meticulously positioning rainbows of writing implements in neat rows on the table, the way a surgeon might arrange scalpels before performing a circumcision.

Jen was sitting on the far side of the wooden table, opposite the door. I was frustrated to see she was wearing a tank top, because now her eyes weren't the only things I would have to purposely avoid looking at for the next hour. On the wall above Jen's right shoulder was the blackboard, where Corky would always write a detailed outline of what we were going to discuss in class that day. Today was unusual, as there was only one item listed on our agenda.

MEN.

Son of a bitch. Looks like me and my jockstrap chose the wrong day to come back to class.

Corky had already begun addressing the class, so I quietly slipped through the door and headed toward the one available seat.

"Ah, speak of the devil!" Corky said as I stepped inside. "Eric, I was just asking if anyone had seen you the last couple of weeks. We were worried you had abandoned us for one of those fancy math or science classes."

"I've been sick."

"Haven't we all?"

My rhetorical question filter apparently broken, I answered "yes," and plunked myself in the only available seat, directly across from Jen. I glanced up at her, then averted my eyes toward Corky, who filled out her tank top in a far less distracting manner.

Believe it or not, Corky and I actually had a fair amount in common—physically, I mean. Both of us sported short, brown hair that looked like we walked into a barber shop and said, "Prepubescent boy, please!" Both of us sacrificed style for comfort in our faded corduroy pants, and neither of us wore bras. Really the main difference between Corky and me was that my underarm hair was mere shrubbery compared to the thriving forest she cultivated in her armpits.

Corky paced around the table, arms crossed. "I thought today it would be fun to extend our discussion on gender roles by tying in the recent debacle surrounding Larry Dummers—er, Summers." I could sense the Lioness hovering behind my chair; her warm breath shot chilling tingles down the back of my neck. As a former victim, I instinctively ducked my head to avoid the pair of free-swinging wrecking balls that swayed dangerously overhead. "Specifically, how does his leadership, or lack thereof, reflect the ongoing travesty of male dominance at Harvard, and society at large?"

Like a quick-fire duel, eleven eager mouths opened a millisecond after the final word escaped Corky's lips. The girl directly to my left had the fastest draw.

"I'd like to answer your question with a question: what *is* 'dominance'? While Machiavelli defines it simply as 'the power to influence others,' I subscribe to the extended interpretation of sociologist Dr. Linda Bernfew, who hypothesized in our optional reading assignment that dominance is a self-fulfilling concept promulgated by insecure leaders to further the subjugation of their subordinates."

I had no idea what this girl was talking about—Harvard students often walk the line of saying everything while saying nothing. But Corky was picking up what this girl was putting down.

"That's an excellent, excellent point." The Lioness nodded pensively and plopped down in her chair, as if the pure genius of this comment had caused her limbs to go numb. "So if we accept the conventional wisdom that President Bummers is compensating for feelings of inferiority by demeaning women, is there a way to measure the cultural impact his so-called leadership has had on our community?"

Debbie, an African-American girl sitting next to Corky,

fielded this one. "Some argue that President Summers has in-stilled a culture of male elitism, but that ignores the fact that Harvard has *always* been this way."

Corky leaned forward in her seat. Her upper lip started to quiver with a barely contained grin. "Yes…go on…"

"It reminds me of this article by Dr. Pauline Gorman, which was referenced in a footnote of our optional reading assignment. She argues that the more established an organization is, the more likely its leaders will maintain dominance through the uncon-scious assertion of anachronistic ideals."

Debbie paused a moment to hydrate with a sip from her water bottle. I glanced at Corky. Her eyes were half-closed, her grin now full-bore, her face slightly twisted yet disturbingly relaxed. "Yessss…go on…"

"And Harvard is a perfect example of this problem. It estab-lished itself four centuries ago as a white-male school, and it was considered America's first and greatest university. That public perception hasn't changed in four hundred years, so the school has never felt the need to change its white-male mentality."

Corky placed both palms on the table, tilted her head back toward the ceiling, and let her jaw dangle slightly. She was shaking a little. "Yeeeessss!! Oh that is *good*."

Corky was thoroughly satisfied, but Debbie wanted to keep going until she was finished herself. "And this white-male men-tality isn't only reflected in its pervasive sexism, it shows up in all aspects of life at Harvard. Like, it's ridiculous that the head of each dorm here is called the housemaster. How do you think I feel calling someone 'master'? That term is degrading and brings me back two centuries to a time when my ancestors knew nothing about freedom, and everything about pain and suffering."

Corky snapped out of her rapture and adopted a look of grave concern. "I'm so sorry, Debbie. I know exactly how that feels, only worse. How do you think I feel being called a teaching *fellow*? It's a term that calls to mind *millennia* of unjust male supremacy."

We were about ten minutes into class at this point, so naturally all those who hadn't spoken yet were starting to panic. As Corky took a break from her mini-rant to release a dramatic sigh, Allison, a soft-spoken girl whose squeaky voice was so absurd it almost seemed like an act, interrupted with an observation of her own.

"We would be remiss if we discussed sexism at Harvard and pretended the administrators are the only offenders. The male students themselves can't be held blameless. Obviously, the snow penis immediately comes to mind."

My ears pricked up. I had mentally checked out somewhere around "promulgated," but I was back on board with "snow penis." The controversy Allison was referring to occurred the year before I came to Harvard, but its aftershocks could still be felt around campus to this day. The trouble started following a blizzard in the previous winter, when a few guys from the men's crew team decided to make a snowman. They rolled a couple of giant snowballs, then realized, "Hey, why create a snow*man* when we can create a snow *penis*!" Several hours of work later, a giant, nine-foot dong stood erect in the middle of Harvard Yard. Of course, when Harvard kids take on a project, they make sure to do it *right*, so the ice phallus was shockingly realistic, garnished with the type of horrifying details most girls don't discover until it's too late. Several female students were offended by the Yard's new monument to masculinity, and proceeded to destroy the ice statue in a hostile thrashing that would've done Lorena Bobbitt proud.

The power of the snow penis endured, however. Outraged campus feminists asserted that the sculpture was an implied threat to the women of Harvard, and it deserved to be destroyed. Others claimed that demolishing the snow penis was a violation of freedom of speech. Caustic arguments spilled into the front page of the *Crimson*, and soon the campus was divided by the giant wiener.

In an attempt to keep discourse civil, the university scheduled several open forums for students and professors to debate issues of women's rights, property rights, and the First Amendment, as they related to the snow penis. Counselors were made available for women who wanted an outlet to talk about how the ice penis made them feel. Professors contributed scholarly position papers on the topic. Anti-snow penis demonstrations were scheduled; Darfur genocide demonstrations were cancelled. The snow penis was all the rage at Harvard, and soon the mainstream media picked up on it. Only Harvard could find a way to create a story relevant (and absurd) enough to make its way into *Playboy*, *The Economist*, and "Weekend Update" on *Saturday Night Live*.

Corky was always game to talk (or more like scream) about the snow penis. "I'm glad you brought that up, Allison, because I've been thinking about the snow penis a lot lately, in light of the comments made by Harry Bummers," she said. "The snow penis was built by a group of guys who were clearly threatened by the strong, powerful women at this school. Now it's obvious that Fairly Dummers feels the same way, only he didn't have snow in the lecture hall that day, so he built a *figurative penis* with his words."

If you've gotten to know me at all, you'll know by now that I was not the type of person to speak in class. In fact, I had only spoken once in a class all year, back in the first week of the first semester. I made some comment, I can't remember about what, that prompted an animated rebuttal from another guy in the class. He said he respectfully disagreed, but there was nothing respectful about the way he threw out the term "asinine" so liberally while referring to my point. I never spoke in any of my classes after that, which was too bad, since 15 percent of your final grade in many Harvard courses is based on class participation. So right off the bat subtract 15 percent for never participating, then another 20 percent for "not knowing stuff," and you can see why I was on academic probation.

The thing is, I actually had something to say about the snow penis, a discussion topic that was finally on my intellectual wavelength. There was no way I was going to get involved, though. Not because I didn't have the balls, but because I *did*. Participating in this debate would be like taking off my pants and standing spread-eagle on the table while twelve angry women take turns swinging at the piñatas. Other dudes at Harvard would probably disagree, but in my mind, 15 percent wasn't worth it.

Another girl chimed in now. "As anthropologists, we must look at this cultural issue from every perspective. I think we do an excellent job at analyzing these subjects through an objective lens, but still there are certain biases we cannot escape. Personally, I would love to hear a male outlook on this topic."

The room became very still. For the first time ever, not a single one of the girls was jumping to speak, leaving the previous comment lingering in the air with the dim hum of fluorescent lights. I swallowed hard. My Adam's apple felt like a bowling ball.

The Lioness arose from her chair and stalked around the table, toward my seat. Remembering what the Nature Channel taught me, I made sure to avoid eye contact as she advanced. When she placed a hand on my shoulder I remained still, only slumping my posture slightly like I was dead. She didn't fall for the ruse.

"Eric, why don't you help us out here with a new perspective? What do you think was the motivation behind the ice phallus?"

I found myself instinctively looking at Jen, like she was going to jump in and save me. Her eyes dodged mine.

"I'm going to answer your question with a question," I said softly. "Can I go to the bathroom?"

Corky rejected my bathroom proposal, leaving me with only one more option in my "fight or flight" instinct. I was cornered and left with no choice but to defend myself and my gender.

"Honestly, I think these guys were just trying to have some silly, immature fun. It wasn't a statement about women or the First Amendment or whatever. It was just their way of bringing humor to a place that takes itself way too seriously, an attitude that was further proven by the community's insane backlash to a harmless snow sculpture."

A handful of girls began speaking at once, but the Lioness cut them off. "Hold your thoughts for a second. Whether he realizes it or not, Eric has actually brought up a central question in anthropology. How responsible should a community be for an individual's actions and beliefs? Let's try a little experiment on this matter."

Corky shuffled over to the blackboard and scrawled a sentence across the dusty slate: *A woman without her man is nothing.*

"Eric, will you come to the board and punctuate this sentence, please?"

"Eric, will you unzip your fly and approach this toaster?" is what I heard. I walked slowly to the blackboard and hesitated before inserting two commas: *A woman, without her man, is nothing.*

Corky gave a wry smile as she erased my commas. "Now Allison, will you punctuate this same sentence?"

Allison practically sprinted to the blackboard. A couple of swipes of chalk and the sentence transformed yet again: *A woman: without her, man is nothing.*

"I didn't know colons were in play," I muttered nervously.

"Colons are *always* in play," Corky glared at me, then spoke to the entire class. "One set of words, two people, two opposite interpretations. Now, do we condemn Eric for being sexist, or do we sympathize with him because he's just a product of a society that has ingrained this gender bias within him? Same goes for the boys who made the snow penis. Who's at fault: the environment or the agent?"

See, this is why I hated participating in class at Harvard. One minute you're slouched in your chair spacing out, doing your best to stay awake and not stare at boobs, then the next you're on trial for human rights violations. I had a rock-solid defense, considering I didn't even write the sentence to begin with and Allison's interpretation was equally as sexist as mine. But this was a battle I could never win. Somehow, I had to get this room full of women to stop thinking about snow penises and figurative penises and colons. Luckily I had a tangential point I felt strongly about.

"I'd like to connect the idea of 'environment versus agent' back to Larry Summers," I said, surprising everyone in the room. "Personally, I think this whole fiasco was largely the community's fault. Obviously what Larry said was stupid. But he pointed out that he was merely citing a study to stimulate debate, and he's apologized for his poor choice of words. Yet people at Harvard will never let this go. It's like you're not allowed to screw up here.

Everyone expects perfection at this university, and when they get a little awkwardness instead, they can't handle it. You're tossed to the curb and replaced by someone else."

"Don't you think blaming Harvard for one's failure is kind of a cop-out?" Every head turned from me to Jen, who had broken her silence with the authoritative statement. "Sure it's intense here, but that doesn't mean you can just use that as an excuse. It's ultimately up to each individual to realize their own potential and make something of the opportunity in front of them."

"But he never got a full chance," I responded, a bit louder than I meant to. "He had the potential to be great, but he never got a chance to develop it and show what he's capable of. Everyone at Harvard expects excellence right away, but he needed more time."

"He had plenty of time. He had his chance," she said, looking directly at me. "But his behavior…it's like he was never fully committed, for whatever reason. That's his own fault, not Harvard's."

I flailed my arms in exasperation. "You're implying that Harvard has no impact on one's behavior," I retorted. "I think everyone in this room would agree this community is a virtual pressure-cooker. When you have to live up to standards that can't be reached, it's impossible not to be negatively affected in some way. If anything, people here deserve more leeway and more patience as they try to survive this hyper-intense atmosphere."

Jen folded her arms and took a moment to collect her thoughts. Finally she looked up and said, "I'm not denying that Harvard can be an incredibly difficult environment to cope with. Everyone struggles with it in some way. But I don't think it's okay when individuals start using difficult circumstances as a way to justify their actions."

I couldn't come up with a decent response to Jen's last point.

Neither could the rest of the class, apparently, as their faces oscillated between Jen and me with looks of dumbfounded shock.

"I don't even know why we're still talking about Larry Summers," I finally said in frustration, defeated. "He's going to be gone by next year, anyway. And he'll probably be better for it."

Jen's emerald eyes cut right through me, but this time I couldn't look away. "I'm just saying it's dangerous when individuals or entire communities start blaming external factors for all of their internal issues," Jen explained. "That's how great things get ruined. Even in the most difficult conditions, you have to stop making excuses and take responsibility for your actions. Persevere in the face of adversity. That's an attitude people find attractive in a leader. You can't waste your potential just because of tough surroundings. Sometimes you have to suck it up and be…"

"…a man."

Chapter Sixteen

RASH DECISIONS

L eave it to a Harvard girl to write the most grammatically correct sex solicitation in Craigslist history:

So here's the deal. I'm a Harvard freshman, and of the three obligatory Harvard acts—Primal Scream, pissing on the John Harvard [statue], and sex in Widener Library—I have so far completed two. I think it would be really novel to manage all three while still in my first year here. But having sex in Widener requires not only a great deal more coordination and planning than the other two, but also a willing other party. I don't have a boyfriend and don't currently want one. So therein lies my dilemma: how do I find someone who'd be willing to give it a try?

I won't lie: though I like to think I'm not an eyesore, I'm hardly the hottest chick around. In fact I'm not even particularly good in bed: my sexual experience consists largely of a bunch of one-time, clumsy drunken hookups. And given the limitations of doing it in a library— the need to be fast and discreet, for instance—it would probably be fairly mediocre sex. But I'm banking on the idea that even bad sex is better than no sex, and I'm looking for someone who finds the idea novel enough to give it a try for the bragging rights alone.

*You don't have to be a stud: so long as you're a Harvard student
(i.e., no sketchy old men) and you're generally okay-looking, I'm
not all that picky…*

The Craigslist "Personals" section—the back alley of the
Internet—sees a fair amount of sex requests, but this message in
particular generated quite the buzz since the author wasn't your
typical mustached Internet creeper, but someone who properly
employed the word "therein." You have to give the girl credit for
her idea—the second Harvard Act is by far the most difficult one
to pull off, especially when you refuse the generous assistance of
"sketchy old men." And she showed impressive (if not alarming)
initiative to solve her quandary.

The personal ad seemed right up my alley, since I think I met
her rigorous requirement of being "generally okay-looking." But
I didn't have the audacity to pursue it. My goal to complete the
Three Harvard Acts in order to attain some social renown, and
hopefully prove myself in the eyes of final clubs, was no longer
very important to me. It was mid-April, the school year was
winding down, and I had begun accepting that Harvard had
defeated me and I would not return next year. (I hadn't told my
parents yet, choosing to wait until it was a little warmer out, when
it would be easier for them to cope with the five stages of grief.)

Since I wasn't coming back, the Harvard Acts seemed like
more trouble than they were worth. At the end of the semester there would be one more opportunity to run naked in the
infamous Primal Scream (the first chance, which I missed, was
the night before fall semester exams). Primal Scream, though
potentially scarring, wasn't a logistical problem. But hooking up
in Widener Library, as our anonymous Craigslister so eloquently

puts it, "requires a great deal more coordination." I wasn't neces-sarily opposed to partaking in it, though the opportunity would have to magically fall into my lap. And the chances of that, I thought, were miniscule.

———◆———

I know this goes against everything I stand for, but bear with me a moment as I drop some knowledge on you in the form of a fancy mathematical proof. You should probably pay close atten-tion, because I don't know if you've heard, but I went to Harvard.

> Given *the conventional wisdom that:*
> *(College) = (The happiest time of your life)*
> *And* given *that:*
> *(Harvard) = (A College)*
> Then, *by the principle of transitive relations:*
> *(Harvard) = (The happiest time of your life)*

Only it wasn't. In March of my freshman year, the *Boston Globe* published a survey of undergraduates at thirty elite col-leges who were asked to rate, on a scale of one to five, their sat-isfaction with various aspects of campus life. The study showed that Harvard students were, on average, the least happy among their peers at other schools. Compared to other schools Harvard averaged notably lower scores in several categories, with only a 2.62 for "campus social life" and a sparse 2.53 for "sense of com-munity." Yet I guarantee Harvard students averaged a 5.00 when asked by their family and friends how they were enjoying the World's Greatest University.

While it was mildly comforting to know I wasn't the only

one miserable at Harvard, it was far from reassuring. Once in a while, usually around exam periods, I'd open the *Crimson* and read a short blurb about a Harvard student who had tragically passed away the previous day. These articles were left intentionally vague, though whenever the paper reported that a student had "died suddenly," the entire campus would understand the gut-wrenching implication. It was a devastating reminder of the type of pressure and hopelessness some students could feel at Harvard, and a demoralizing cloud of despair would linger over the already tense community. For some students there was a lot more at stake than a Harvard degree, and you would have to take a moment to reassure yourself that you would never fall into such a devastating mind-set.

To their credit, Harvard administration made a sincere effort to boost campus morale. Unfortunately, their attempts were like an out-of-touch parent desperately trying to be "cool" in order to win over their troubled teenager. They organized parties and free concerts in the Yard, dropping some serious cash to bring in hardcore rap groups like Wu-Tang Clan (because obviously Harvard kids were the perfect group for singing along to such classic hits as "Bring Da Ruckus," "Assed Out," and "Let My Niggas Live").

They also fed us copious amounts of liquor. Seriously, the quantity of free alcohol I received from Harvard was staggering (literally), and almost made up for my ungodly tuition.

A longstanding Harvard tradition is for each upperclassman dorm to host a "Stein Club" for their residents, which are university-funded social events held biweekly in the houses' lavish common rooms. Stein Club is always on a weeknight, with the idea that stressed-out students would benefit from a little study break where they could set aside their homework for an hour and help themselves to some chips, pretzels, carrot sticks, and 80 proof vodka. Freshmen were encouraged to come to the Stein Clubs, which was odd considering that almost all of them were underage. (A sign had to be posted somewhere in the room reading "Must be 21 to drink," and you can imagine how effective that was.) It seemed to me that Harvard didn't really care about underage drinking—as long as it was done outside the freshman dorms, which are located in the sanctified Yard.

Many freshmen would jump at this opportunity, as they would come for the booze and stay for the company. (I came for the booze and stayed for the Doritos.) Harvard would also roll in kegs at Stein Club and set up beer-pong tables for us to play on. *"Have fun, kids, just don't spill on our Turkish rug!"* Apparently using *Animal House* as their empirical research, Harvard concluded that drunk students equaled happy students, and happy students don't go crying to the *Boston Globe*. They even established a special fund where any student could fill out a simple form for a "party grant" and the school would happily fork over a wad of cash to pay for your weekend's alcoholic adventures— *"but only if you promise to share some with your pals!"*

But let's be honest: students don't go to Harvard because they want fun oozing out their ears; they choose it because they want a Harvard degree and the future opportunity to land a job they may not deserve. There clearly was a disconnect between what the student body found fun and what the administration thought would be fun (at Stein Club, the orange soda would usually run out before the booze).

The administration must've been pissed about the *Boston Globe* study, though, because Harvard never finishes last in anything that doesn't involve a ball. So the college went out and hired a young alumnus to be the college's official "Fun Czar." He immediately reached hero status among the students by organizing a dodgeball tournament.

It would have been embarrassing enough to attend a college that needed a Fun President. But a Fun *Czar*? Damn. When word of this new position got picked up by the media, they had a field day. People reacted to the report with almost a cruel delight—*Look, Harvard kids don't even know how to have fun!* It was like discovering that the most successful guy in school was actually a virgin. On his Fox News show, Bill O'Reilly labeled Harvard's Fun Czar as "The Most Ridiculous Item of the Day," a harsh declaration that was particularly hurtful coming from a guy who knows a thing or two about fun.

The public didn't know that, despite our need for a Fun Czar, Harvard students did like to party on occasion. Now, I know what you're thinking: *I bet they had some seriously dorky parties, like a special day of celebration for Charles Darwin's birthday*. But please, give me a break—we didn't have Darwin Day. We had Darwin *Week*. Birthday cakes honoring the great naturalist were served in all the dining halls, science-themed rock bands performed, and students in gorilla suits danced in the halls. It was a joyous celebration that Darwin himself would have approved of, had we not shown that humanity had actually devolved since his lifetime.

So Harvard students did have parties—they were just different. While a typical college may celebrate homecoming with an entire day of drinking and revelry, Harvard would celebrate John Milton's birthday with a ten-hour marathon reading of some the poet's lesser-known works. Those are different styles of parties, sure, but both are well-attended social opportunities which, if you played your cards right, could end with a one-night stand.

Harvard students do want to be happy and are always seeking ways to cure the blues. It's no coincidence that Positive Psych, a course that taught the psychology of happiness, was by far the college's most popular class. And some people did find contentment at Harvard. To my amazement, there were students who even loved the college and were genuinely happy there.

Take Dermot, for instance. Night after night I would watch him with envy as he smiled and worked on his homework while sitting on the giant bouncy ball he used as a desk chair. He would bounce up and down happily in rhythm to the jackhammer beat of "Freak-o-holic" or whatever electrofunk song he was listening to. I recall wanting nothing more than to have that carefree mind-set or, failing that, a BB gun to pop a hole in his inflatable bubble. Why was he so happy? He was thousands of miles from home, didn't have a girlfriend, sucked at *Halo*, and his favorite football team was a soccer team. He had settled into this new environment and was getting better grades this semester, good grades even. But he didn't give a shit about them. On nights before a midterm, he'd stop studying around 10:00 p.m., head to the dining hall to snack on a couple of Splenda packets, then return to his bedroom and sleep like a baby.

"Are you really done studying already?" I asked in frustration one night. "Aren't you nervous you haven't prepared enough? What happens if you fail?"

Dermot looked confused, and shrugged his shoulders casually. "Then I guess I fail."

Sometimes I think Dermot was the smartest kid at Harvard.

I avoided all Harvard dances because, as I've previously discussed, I suck at dancing, which I figured would be the primary activity at a dance. But Dermot was adamant that I come along with him to the infamous Mather Lather, because there would be music and bubbles, his two favorite things in the world.

Dermot loved these all-school social events, and he was happy at Harvard, so I figured maybe he was on to something. I only had a few more weeks to figure out how to be happy at a place I didn't belong, so it made sense to follow a kid who had already figured out the secret. Plus, Mather Lather was the one place I was guaranteed *not* to see Tripp and Jen. The final club social scene is entirely separate from all-school dances and events. Final club guys and their girlfriends almost always prefer to spend a Saturday night drinking in their luxurious clubhouse than fraternizing with the rest of Harvard's "lame" student body at a public dance.

"This looks disgusting," I complained, flicking a soapy puff of foam off my shoulder.

"Sharing a cock-manger with you and Josh is disgusting," Dermot replied. "This," he gestured to the crowded yet unimpressive party unfolding in front of us, "looks bloody impressive."

Mather House is one of the least desirable dorms at Harvard. When the results of the Housing Lottery are announced each spring, groans echo throughout the campus from any freshman assigned to live the next three years in the dreaded Mather Tower. According to Harvard history books, Mather was built in 1971 and designed in the refined postmodern architectural style known as "ugly." While most Harvard dorms fit in seamlessly with the old-school Georgian red brick and white pillar style of the campus, the immense Mather high-rise erupts skyward like a cement middle finger flipping off its gentlemanly, nineteenth-century neighbors. The ocular nightmare is tucked away in the southeastern corner of the campus, and its location is the primary complaint of residents. It's settled about a half-mile from Harvard Square, which may not sound bad, but if you're a college student and the closest pizza place is a ten-minute walk, your dorm might as well be in Siberia.

Mather's isolation, however, yields above-average camaraderie among its residents, which is a source of great pride for them. Devout Matherites are also quick to point out the dorm's sweet-ass woodshop and pottery studio, which are great if you're into things like carpentry and clay and not getting laid. There's also their most famous alumni, Conan O'Brien, who lived in Mather (though he was only placed there because he needed a nineteen-story building to fit his hair). Of course, none of those things even compare to the dorm's primary claim to fame: their annual and much-hyped foam party, known as "Mather Lather."

Dermot and I stood at the entrance of the Mather dining hall, which had all of its tables and chairs scooped out and replaced with a massive foam pit. A DJ was perched on a tall wooden platform in the middle of the pit, spinning ear-splitting hip-hop jams as flickering strobe lights and disco globes assaulted my brain.

I squinted my eyes as I tried to look into the pit, and in between flashes of darkness and light, I saw nothing but bubbles and masses of slippery flesh dancing and grinding and spanking and slapping in a primal behavior rarely seen outside of nature shows. I could only get quick glimpses inside the pit, but those were enough to catch sight of some things I can never unsee. There was Ji Min, the freshman guy rumored to have discovered his own solution to Fermat's Last Theorem, with two girls in bikinis dancing all up on him, slithering up and down his soapy body like he was a waterslide. A couple of feet from him was Maximillian, my HRSFA half-friend, doing the robot by himself in nothing but a microscopic Speedo that belonged on sale at a Baby Gap.

The room kind of smelled like the stale cardio area of a poorly ventilated gym, mixed with the scent of chlorine and desperation. But that didn't stop the horde of scantily clad students from grinding their asses off. It had to be the most awkward foam experience I'd ever seen, and this is coming from a guy who spent a good part of his childhood taking bubble baths with his sisters.

Dermot began stripping down to his bathing suit, and suddenly I felt an overwhelming desire to get the hell out of there. Before leaving Lionel I had taken some shots of whiskey and even put on my cleanest pair of jeans, but I still wasn't feeling confident enough to take the plunge into that massive dance pit of questionable fluids. I was about to tell Dermot that I was leaving when we were approached by Hannah, a freshman girl who had just emerged from the pit.

"Dermot! Eric! I'm so happy you guys are here!"

Hannah was part of Dermot's circle of friends, and was also in my anthropology course (though not in my section). She hung out in our common room fairly often. She was a really nice girl and always made an effort to include me in group conversations, even when I was super-focused on a wicked hard level in *Halo*. After Jen, she was probably the girl I had spoken to the most at Harvard, which isn't saying much. But still, I liked her. Not in a romantic way, I should point out. She wasn't unattractive by any means, but whenever I looked at her, all I could ever see before was not-Jen.

But for some reason, Hannah looked different tonight. She wasn't wearing her glasses, an obvious difference. But there was still something else about her that seemed new. Her shoulder-length brown hair had started to curl in the humidity of the room's hot and sticky atmosphere, and suds of white foam clung loosely to her clothes. She was wearing a black tank-top over her bathing suit—maybe because she was self-conscious of her not-Jen body, but she shouldn't have been. Pulses of strobe-light illuminated the small cluster of freckles peppering Hannah's cheeks, and her amber eyes seemed to light up with the energy of the room.

"Hannah! Enjoying the party so far, I see." I brushed some foam off the side of her arm.

"Ahrmmm, arah hmrhrrmm marhmma." This isn't what she actually said, presumably, but it was all I could hear over a deafening hip-hop song that was now blasting over the loudspeakers.

"What?!"

"Ahrmmm, arah hmrhrrmm marhmma!"

"What?!!!"

Hannah repeated herself once more, but I was still totally lost. Unfortunately, I had used up my quota of acceptable "what's," so I was left with no choice but to roll with it and pretend I could hear her now.

We continued a one-sided conversation for a few minutes, and I nodded randomly and enthusiastically, throwing in the occasional "yeah!" and "oh, nice!" while hoping she wasn't talking about a terminally ill grandfather or something. Finally the current song ended, yielding to a softer, more conversation-friendly ballad about bitches and ho's.

"So it's settled!" I heard Hannah say. "I'll see you at the library tomorrow morning. We'll beat the rush!"

For fuck's sake! Apparently, I just agreed to join a morning study group. Getting up early on a Sunday morning was one of the last things in the world I wanted to do, behind dancing, of course.

"Come on, let's dance!" Hannah grabbed me by the wrist and started toward the foam pit.

I resisted. "I—I can't! I didn't bring my bathing suit." This was a lie; my suit was on under my jeans. But I had no problem sinning in order to avoid dancing. I just hoped it wouldn't get to murder.

"You don't need your suit," Hannah said. "Look, there are plenty of people in there with clothes on."

"Okay, well I need to use the bathroom first. I'll meet you in there." I paused. "In the pit I mean, not in the bathroom, obviously." I laughed like an idiot. Hannah smiled and disappeared into the pit. I made a dash for the exit.

"Hey dickbrain, where ya shlunking off to?" Dermot caught me just before I reached the door. I explained to him that I had the scutters, and had to find a cock-manger, STAT.

"That's a horse's hoof, if I've ever heard one. You're just scared because you want to snog Hannah! I saw the way you were staring at her just now. That was intense!"

"I was trying to read her lips!"

"Whatever you say. Just know you're not doing yourself any favors sittin' on the sideline, scratchin' your arse like some sort of arse-scratchin' sideline-sitter. My grandfather always used to say to me, 'Dermot, you can't plow a girl by turning her over in your mind.'"

"Your grandfather never said that."

"Okay, he may have said 'field' instead of 'girl,' but the principle is the same! Get out of your mind and start plowing that field!"

I looked at Hannah in the pit, dancing and jumping and smiling. "Fine, I'll go in for one song—but I'm keeping my clothes on."

The best part about the excessive foam, I found out, was that it made it difficult for others to see my horrid dance moves. The worst part was when the foam got in my eyes—it stung like a bitch and felt surprisingly dirty, considering it was soap.

I began to rub my eyes excessively with closed fists. Hannah, after realizing that this was not another one of my ill-conceived dance maneuvers, offered a solution. She removed a pair of goggles from around her neck and handed them to me.

"I'm *not* wearing goggles!" I shouted over the music.

"They're not goggles," Hannah yelled back. "They're prescription recreational eyewear!"

Rec-Specs. You gotta be kidding me. I tried them on for a second and felt ridiculous, so I handed them back to Hannah. "Thanks, but I can't take myself seriously in these."

Hannah grabbed the goggles, then immediately placed them back on my face. "That's why you need to wear them!"

The song soon came to an end. But I kind of liked the next track, so I stayed in the pit for one more. Then another, and another. I have no idea how long I ended up staying in the pit, jamming with Hannah, Dermot, and whoever else got sucked into my vortex of dance disaster. The songs began to blend together and my adult beverages started to catch up with me, and I lost track of time. Everything was blurry from Hannah's prescription goggles, and my dancing didn't impress anyone. But I didn't really care.

To my surprise, no one else seemed to care either. No judgmental glares, no competitive one-upping—everyone was absorbed only in the music. As large puffs of foam floated through the air, blanketing the room and completely whiting out the floor, the walls, and the crimson Harvard flag hanging from the ceiling above, nothing else seemed to matter.

———————◆◆———————

The headline in the *Crimson* would later read: "LATHER SUDS RUB PARTIERS WRONG WAY: Many complain of itching, burning after Saturday night party."

The article went on to provide details of the massive outbreak of rashes that many students experienced following Mather Lather. There were several anonymous sources quoted in the article, but one in particular seemed to sum up the story (and my personal feelings) perfectly:

> *"Afterward, my nipples really hurt," said a male sophomore in Mather House who asked not to be named. "I loved Mather Lather, but this is kind of weird."*

My rash didn't seem as graphic as some described in the *Crimson*, but I was still relieved to know I wasn't the only person who woke up with a case of the itchies. Someone even created a Facebook group and opened it up for anyone suffering from the Mather Lather rash. I didn't join the group, because I thought the texture of my nipples was nobody's business but my own, but I couldn't have agreed more with the group name: "I Got a Nasty Rash, but Mather Lather Was Fun."

It was hard to tell if Dermot also got a rash because, well, he was always scratching himself anyway. I was too embarrassed to itch myself constantly, so I found relief by discreetly rubbing my body against pieces of furniture, the way a bear would with a tree trunk. I latched myself onto just about any solid object and went to town on it, and I didn't stop until Josh asked me why I was making sweet love to our mini-fridge. Then I thought of Hannah, and I wondered about the condition of her skin as I made the slow, hungover walk to meet her at the library for the study session I still couldn't believe I had agreed to attend. A marathon study session with a surely hyper-competitive group was the last thing I wanted to do the morning after a rash-inducing bash.

———◆———

You probably don't realize this, but when the *Titanic* sunk in 1912, Leonardo DiCaprio wasn't the only passenger who died. There were 1,517 other less-handsome victims, including a young Harvard graduate who tragically went down with the ship on that fateful night. The young Harvard man from Philadelphia, described by friends as an avid bibliophile (the term "nerd" hadn't been invented yet), reportedly left his lifeboat and returned to his cabin in order to save a rare book from his precious collection. Harry Widener never made it back to the lifeboat.

The Harry Widener Memorial Library was erected at Harvard shortly following the tragedy on the *Titanic*. A gift from Eleanor Widener in memory of her son, Widener Library is the leviathan of Harvard Yard, and it looms over the students as a powerful reminder that this is Harvard, the pinnacle of academia, and you better be willing to fucking die for your books.

Enormous marble stairs lead up to its impressive entrance, which is protected by intimidating white columns that lend the building a Parthenon-esque visage. The columns and foundation of Widener Library are made from a deposit of 330-million-year-old limestone, and fossils of primordial shells and unicellular organisms are literally embedded in the walls. The sheer size of the library is staggering, housing over three million books, and you can run the equivalent of two marathons and still not cover the fifty-seven miles of bookshelves that fold into the stacks of Widener. I know all this sounds far-fetched, but if you've come this far and still don't realize how ridiculous Harvard can be, then you haven't been paying attention.

Some students loved Widener Library because as far as they were concerned, three million books is the equivalent of three million boners. Personally, I detested everything about Widener. I hated that I was slightly winded every time I climbed up the marble stairs to its entrance; I hated that once inside I felt as insignificant as those microscopic, unicellular organisms; and most of all I hated the presence of the letter "D" in "Harry Widener," ruining what could have been the most epic library name since the Pusey.

I reluctantly entered the palace and proceeded up the grand staircase closest to the main entrance. Widener Library owns a pristine edition of the legendary Gutenberg Bible, the world's first printed book, and I met Hannah and my new study-buddies in front of its display case. There are only a few surviving copies of the Gutenberg Bible in the entire world, and I felt a little anxious standing near it. If there was anyone capable of accidently destroying Harvard's most prized possession, it was definitely me, and such an offense would incite a mob of livid bibliophiles to turn me into a target for necrophiles.

I stood off to the side as the group discussed the attack plan for our study-fest. Spring's final exams were approaching, so it

was time for us to put together an extensive study guide for anthropology. The group was divided into pairs, with each couple
responsible for writing an overview of a past reading assignment.
Hannah volunteered to be my partner, since no one else seemed
too keen in pairing up with that sheepish guy standing over
there, quietly scratching his nipples.

Hannah and I were responsible for an optional reading assignment in a book about Sri Lankan transvestites ("the defini-
tive study on gender roles in twentieth-century South Asia," as
Corky described it). Surprisingly, neither one of us owned this
must-have page-turner. Fortunately, we were standing in the one
building in the world that not only had a book on Sri Lankan
transvestites, but an entire section on it. So we looked up the
book's call number, filled our backpacks with a reasonable supply
of food and water, and began our long descent into the terrifying
stacks of Widener.

After a while, it gets difficult to gauge how many floors underground you are at Widener. Your body gets a general sense
of your depth, based on the diminishing supply of breathable
air, but your exact location is difficult to judge. Endless floors
of endless rows of identical bookshelves guarantee that you'll
get hopelessly lost, even if you know exactly where you're going,
which of course we didn't. On top of that, recognizing that the
majority of the underground levels are typically barren of people,
the university conserves energy by keeping the stacks in complete darkness. There are lights down there, obviously, but they
are connected to motion sensors and only turn on when they
detect somebody's presence directly beneath them. It's creepy
and desolate in the maze, and chances are you won't run into
another life form on your journey.

Hannah and I weaved through the perpetual rows of books, slowly following the narrow path of lights that magically flicked on with every step we took. It was eerily quiet. I swear I wasn't scared or anything, but I thought it would be nice to distract ourselves with light conversation—you know, in case Hannah was freaked out by the shadows and ancient books that smelled like my grandma's haunted basement.

"Did you have fun last night?" I asked.

"So much fun. You're quite the dance partner."

I chuckled in disbelief. "You're certainly the first girl who's ever thought that."

"Really?"

"Yeah, I think most girls find my dance moves embarrassing and silly."

"Well, I know girls who like it when guys act silly like that," Hannah replied. "Especially here—we need more guys to loosen up like that."

"It was kind of fun letting loose," I admitted. "And it definitely helped that I was dancing with such a loose girl." I heard the last sentence echo through the stacks, and immediately backtracked. "I mean, loose in your attitude, not in your, uhh—"

Hannah giggled and put her hand on my back. "It's okay, I know what you meant."

We came to the end of another row and faced a wall with a small floor map and a YOU ARE HERE arrow. It might as well have said YOU ARE IN NORTH AMERICA for the sense it made to me, but Hannah took a moment to try and decipher our place in the universe. She was wearing her glasses today, small brown borders around her eyes, like picture frames for a pair of aesthetic paintings. They rested casually on a small, perky nose, and I was taken aback at how cute she looked when she bit her lower lip and stared intently at the map. How had I not noticed this about Hannah before? Had something about her changed, or was it me?

We thought the map told us we were on the wrong level, so we found the closest stairway and headed down yet another floor. More books. More darkness. Less air.

"If we died down here, how long would it take to find our bodies?" I asked, wondering how my parents would react when they found out their son had perished looking for a book on South Asian he/shes.

"Someone would come down this far eventually," Hannah answered. "Probably a couple looking to complete the second Harvard Act."

I laughed. "I used to think the second Harvard Act would be almost impossible to do. But now that I've seen how desolate it is down here, it doesn't seem so bad. Peeing on John Harvard is much riskier, since it's out in the open."

"Did you know the John Harvard statue isn't even real?"

I stopped in my tracks. "What do you mean?"

"I mean that isn't even John Harvard sitting in the chair. I learned about this in my tour-guide training. It was just a random model the sculptor used, but they call him John Harvard." Hannah stopped a moment, waiting for me to say something, but I was still digesting the information. "Not only that," she continued, "but the real John Harvard didn't even found Harvard. He was just an early contributor to the school."

This information stunned me. The most iconic image of Harvard wasn't even real. Suddenly, I felt like an enormous idiot.

"It's funny," Hannah added. "Some people take the John Harvard statue so seriously. When really it's all just a big mirage."

I forced out a fake laugh. "Yeah, some people get way too caught up in the whole Harvard thing."

"The statue fits in perfectly with Harvard: a guy pretending to be someone he's not." Hannah laughed softly. We began walking again, and reached the end of another row of books. We took a left, hoping for better luck.

"You seem to have put a lot of thought into the Harvard Acts," Hannah said. "Are you trying to complete them or something?"

I'm not sure why, but I came right out and admitted it. "I was told that if I did them, I'd have a better shot at getting into a final club. It's a way for me to show that I can stand out and be like the members."

"So you want to stand out so you can fit in?" Hannah said. "I didn't think you were the final club type."

I shrugged. I felt comfortable with Hannah, so I told her the truth. "I want to join a final club so I can have an identity here. So I can be special. So I can get…"

"A girl like Jen Wesker."

I stopped. I didn't know what to say to this. I'd be lying if I said I didn't miss Jen and hadn't spent every day figuring out a way I might be able to get her back from Tripp. "What makes you say that?" I asked.

"Come on, Eric, you've been her shadow this semester. You like her. She likes final clubs. So you like final clubs."

We walked in silence for a moment. I was surprised Hannah had even noticed that Jen and I used to hang out a lot. "I don't blame you or anything," Hannah explained quietly. "She's beautiful. She's perfect. But final clubs? Is that who you are?"

Hannah's candor wasn't easy for me to hear, but I was grateful for it. Why did she care about all this? Why did I care that she cared?

We came to a new row of books, and inspected the call numbers. Still not even close to what we were looking for. Hannah threw her hands in the air in frustration. "Ugh, this is hopeless," she groaned.

I looked to our right and saw a glowing red EXIT sign. On the lowest levels of the Widener stacks, there are underground passages to the Yard's other libraries. Hannah saw this too, and read my mind. "Do you want to go in the Pusey Tunnel?"

I cracked up. Hannah seemed confused at first, then she cracked up too. She pushed me playfully. "You, Eric Kester, are a goofball."

"Alright, we should get out of here while we can. But before we go, can we try a quick experiment?"

I had heard about this game that some students played in the stacks of Widener. Apparently, there were a couple of spots on each floor that were not covered by motion detectors, called Widener Triangles. They're hard to find, but if you stand in the exact right location, you can blackout the entire floor. It was kind of silly, so of course Hannah was on board.

Standing side by side, necks craned at the ceiling for a view of the lights' positions, we crept and twisted through the stacks like secret agent ninjas. We had been searching for the mythical Widener Triangle for five pointless minutes when, suddenly, there was a fleeting burst of darkness.

"Shit, so close!" Hannah grumbled.

"I think, I'm standing right on the spot," I said excitedly.

Hannah slowly shuffled closer toward me. Then a little closer. Then closer still. Our faces were inches apart when the lights went off.

Neither of us said a word. I suddenly felt very hot, and it

wasn't because we were a quarter mile from the earth's core. Hannah's chest was pressed against mine, and I was slightly mortified that my initial thought was to wiggle around and use her body as a scratching post. Fortunately this was quickly overcome by another, less creepy instinct. I knew what I wanted, but I wasn't sure what was appropriate. I had known Hannah for a few months, but thanks to my Jen-blinders, I didn't actually get to know her until last night. Clearly, though, she knew me—maybe even better than I knew me.

As I hesitated, Hannah broke the silence and whispered in my ear. "You can tell the clubs that we hooked up down here, if you want." Her breath shot a wave of tingles from my ear down through my spine. "But just know that you don't have to stand out in order to be special." Hannah kissed me softly on the cheek, then slowly drew herself away.

I took a step forward, and that's when the light came on.

Chapter Seventeen

THE FINAL
HARVARD ACT

There's a difference between someone laughing *with* you and someone laughing *at* you. Hannah was definitely laughing at me.

We had spent the final weeks of school getting to know each other better, catching up and sharing some of our more interesting experiences from freshman year. I bravely told her most of my embarrassing stories, and in each case I would honor my lost dignity with a grim tone of voice suitable for eulogies. Hannah would try her hardest to respect the gravity of my anecdotes, but eventually her lip would begin to quiver, the corners of her mouth would peel upward, and she'd burst out laughing.

To be honest, at first Hannah's giggling at my horror stories would really piss me off. Involuntary bladder contraction is a serious affliction that affects men worldwide. But the more this happened, the more I started to see things from her perspective. I also discovered a little trick: if she laughed *at* me, all I needed to do was join her, and just like that, she'd now be laughing *with* me. It felt uncomfortable at first, targeting myself like that, but it made my memories easier to deal with, and it was way better than being miserable.

Compared to the fall semester, I entered the spring final exams in a much healthier state of mind. Which is to say I wasn't wetting myself at the mere thought of the tests. I wasn't magically smarter or anything, but I had managed to discover a realm of academics that I didn't utterly suck at.

This revelation was due to Harvard's curriculum, which adheres to the liberal arts vision of making every student intellectually well-rounded through a broad and diverse course load. For instance, Harvard requires every freshman to take a semester of Expository Writing, an intensive essay course where professors teach students how to write ten-page papers (and students teach themselves how to make significant yet imperceptible changes to margin width). Basically Harvard wants to ensure that all their graduates can express themselves well, but I suspect Expository Writing is also especially designed for the math and economic freaks, so when they graduate and run a big bank with sketchy practices that eventually spark a national recession, they won't embarrass the university with a poorly written public apology.

Most freshmen hated Expository Writing, but I really enjoyed it, mainly because it was a class that didn't intellectually rape me. My essays were far from perfect—my professor said that my writing style is "too colloquial," which is fucking bullshit—but she must've thought I had some talent because I actually got good grades in that class. Even Corky was giving me decent marks on my anthropology papers, which I think was her way of paying me under the table for being a good soldier and taking the psychological beatings during sections. Technically, I guess, that meant I was whoring myself out to twelve women in exchange for good grades, but I was fine with that.

In fact, I was suddenly fine with a lot of things about Harvard academics. I made tentative plans to major in archaeology, because it was a field that fused my two favorite pastimes: writing and playing in the dirt. I wouldn't have to decide on a major until my sophomore year, though, and I realized that this was the first time all semester that I had actually envisioned myself back at Harvard next year.

Unbelievably, I was finally beginning to find my academic identity. My social identity, however, was still murky at best. But I could now see the light there too. And so I thought to myself that if I wanted to find true happiness at Harvard, I needed to do the obvious thing. I needed to figure out a way to win back Jen.

———◆———

Students have been streaking through Harvard Yard for centuries. In fact, the university boasts the first ever recorded act of streaking on a college campus. I learned this from Hannah, whose part-time gig as a campus tour guide provided her with an endless supply of random Harvard trivia and factoids. She was like a more mobile, better-looking version of Wikipedia.

"Did you know that in 1785, Charles Adams, son of President John Adams and brother of President Quincy Adams, was severely disciplined for getting drunk and streaking through the Yard his freshman year?"

"Wow," I said, "that makes me feel better about my half-naked jaunt across the Yard on my first day here. If the son of a president did something similar, maybe I still have the chance to make something of myself."

"He drank himself to death at the age of thirty."

"I see."

Primal Scream, one of Harvard's most popular and infamous

traditions, didn't always involve streaking. Originally, Primal Scream was modeled (and named) after a popular psychotherapy technique in the 1960s where patients were encouraged to scream their brains out. The primal scream was supposed to cure neurosis, so naturally this was an appealing activity for Harvard students during exam period. Each semester when the clock struck midnight on the first day of final exams, students would open their dorm windows around the Yard and release their mounting stress by screaming like maniacs. Apparently though, this custom only made the students more crazy, because gradually the semi-annual ritual replaced the screaming with nudity, morphing Primal Scream into what it is today: a massive, naked nerd herd.

Primal Scream sounds like the title of a Stephen King book, though I assure you the image of hundreds of floppy Harvard kids running ass-naked through the Yard is way more terrifying than any horror novel. The Final Harvard Act is a semi-annual tradition, occurring each semester the night before final exams. I didn't participate in the December Primal Scream, but I certainly attended, because anytime an awkward nineteen-year-old has a chance to see some real live boobs without the help of Google, he has to do it. That night I briefly considered running the naked lap around the Yard, but it was negative 197 degrees outside, and my confidence wasn't the only thing that shrunk. Instead, I joined a crowd of other shameless spectators on the sideline, waited for Dermot to disrobe and start running, and then stole his clothes.

I wasn't planning on running in the Spring Primal Scream, but Dermot insisted that I try it. It was an exhilarating rush, he said, and I took his recommendation seriously because I had been blindly following his advice for the past couple of weeks, for reasons I still don't quite understand. Dermot's lifestyle suggestions ranged from minor ("to instantly make your dirty underwear clean, just wear them inside-out") to straight up *insane* ("deactivate your Facebook account"). While I didn't know whether these tips were helping me, I did know that I was feeling a little happier. So I tentatively agreed to run in Primal Scream with Dermot. Though I knew that if I saw Jen out there, or even Hannah for that matter, I would immediately abort the mission.

Dermot had a brilliant idea for Primal Scream: we would leave our dorm in nothing but a towel, so when the time came to run, we'd simply drop the towel and start sprinting with the rest of the stampede. That way we wouldn't waste time taking off our clothes, and we wouldn't risk getting our feet tangled up in our trousers and falling pecker-first into another chap. Because boy, would that be embarrassing.

It was ten minutes to midnight, and I paced around nervously in our common room. My towel was wrapped around my waist and securely tucked in, but my fingers still gripped it tightly, like I was hanging from a cliff.

"You seem nervous," Josh observed. He wasn't streaking with us tonight, but was coming along to Primal Scream anyway (*somebody* had to steal Dermot's towel).

"He's excited, is what he is!" Dermot shouted as he loosened up with some vigorous trunk-twists.

"A little of both, I think. The last time I walked into Harvard Yard with no shirt on, I thoroughly embarrassed myself."

Their blank looks made me realize that, in all this time, my roommates still hadn't heard the story of my fiasco on move-in day. So I recounted it as Dermot finished up his calisthenics.

"Jesus," Josh said once I finished the story, "I'm surprised you had the balls to go out in public in just your underwear."

"I was locked out—I didn't have a choice. I just sucked in my stomach, put my head down, and stepped outside, instantly lowering the community's pants-to-people ratio." The three of us shared a laugh at my idiocy, and I stowed that joke in my memory bank, in case I ever had a need for it again. It may not have been the same as getting an A or scoring a touchdown, but making people laugh felt immensely satisfying. Maybe this was my contribution to Harvard.

"Alright," I said, feeling much calmer now, "let's do this."

— ◆ — ◆ —

On the night of Primal Scream, Harvard Yard turns into a complete shitshow. Just before midnight, hundreds of students descend to the Yard, and that doesn't even count the crazy homeless men who stop by to watch others do the exposing for a change. On this particular evening, the Harvard Marching Band provided jolly fanfare for the event, performing a creative remix of the school fight song "Ten Thousand Men of Harvard" and Madonna's "Like a Virgin."

The Old Yard is shaped in a long, narrow rectangle of lawn, and a concrete path wraps around its perimeter and serves as the track for Primal Scream. Eager spectators lined the track, jockeying for the best positions to watch the ensuing natural disaster. The ideal vantage point, of course, was for the people who squeezed on top of the stone base of the John Harvard statue.

I no longer looked at John Harvard in the same way. I suppose it was only natural that after you unzip your fly and hold someone hostage with your wang, it's tough to look them straight in the eye anymore. But my view of the famous landmark had changed even more when I learned that it was essentially a mirage. I was embarrassed that I held John Harvard up on a pedestal, when in reality it was a different person entirely.

Part of me began to wonder if I had done the same thing with Jen. She was perfect, I had been sure of it. But would a perfect girl really lower herself to a guy like Tripp? I never got an explanation for what she saw in him, though it almost certainly had to do with the aura of power and prestige that he carried. I thought Jen was above that. But then again, once you have a taste of the elite social culture at Harvard, it's difficult not to get sucked in. I couldn't really blame her if she was social climbing, because I had been trying the exact same thing. She was a good person, I was positive of that. But was she really everything I had built up in my head? If I were ever lucky enough to get with her, would I discover that like John Harvard, beneath a veil of perfection, she was actually a dude named Sherman? It was a scary thought, but my heart still ached for her, and I had to find out for myself.

A huge crowd of students mingled in front of Hollis, the unofficial starting line of Primal Scream. We still had a few minutes before midnight, so I looked around the Yard and took in the spectacle, noticing that far more students came to Primal Scream than to our football games. My eyes darted from face to face, trying to see if either Jen or Hannah were around. I was relieved that neither were in the vicinity.

But surprisingly, given how much I had worried about them being there in the days leading up to the Primal Scream, now that I was here they weren't even my primary concern. How could they be, given the troubling news I learned earlier that day?

It wasn't unusual for Vikas to call me early in the morning. Sometimes he would have crazy dreams about flying and mythical animals and bazookas and the like, and he would be eager to tell me about his latest adventure. I noticed his calls and texts were becoming less frequent as the year rolled on, and this was clearly correlated with his assimilation into his new school. I was okay with our diminished relationship—he was making new friends and was happy at a place where he belonged. Boarding school, it turned out, was exactly what Vikas needed because it finally allowed him to be with kids his own age. Plus, it got him away from his parents and from Harvard, sources of academic intensity that no adolescent should be exposed to. His new school injected some much-needed balance into his life. He attended school dances, started a robotics club, and even joined the JV baseball team, where he was both the second baseman and team statistician.

Vikas did find time to check in every now and then, though, and the Inspector Gadget ringtone awoke me on the morning of Primal Scream.

"Vikas, what's going on buddy?"

"Not too much. Just chillin' like a villain and folding some laundry."

"School going well?" I asked.

"It's been freaking amazing! You know that girl I was telling you about earlier this year?"

"The one who likes puzzles? Yeah."

"I'm tapping that."

"Seriously? Nice work, dude!"

"Well, I mean we haven't gone all the way yet, but we've been watching a lot of *Battlestar Galactica* together."

"Well, sounds like you're halfway there."

"How's Harvard? Isn't Primal Scream tonight?" Vikas tried to throw out this question casually, but his interest in Primal Scream couldn't be contained. He didn't go to the first one, but of course I gave him a detailed account of its awesomeness.

"Yeah, it's tonight. Not sure if I'm running in it yet."

"Remember the last one, when you *walked* the entire lap, so you could better show off your wares?"

"Uh, yeah, how could I forget?"

"I wouldn't do that again, if I were you. The rumor mill is saying that Tripp may be planning something sketchy. I've heard he registered the domain name for *CrimsonFlesh.com* or something."

What Vikas said confused me. This was not a kid hooked into a rumor mill, or any mill, for that matter. Outside of making it up, there was really only one way he could have gotten this info.

"Vikas, did you hack into Tripp's email account?"

"No, I heard it through the rumor mill." Clearly Vikas was sticking to his story.

"That's a little disconcerting," I said. "Maybe Tripp is planning on taking some pictures and hoping to catch a future president naked. Or even better, the next Natalie Portman?"

"Or even better, the next Leda Cosmides!"

"Who's that?"

"Only the world's foremost evolutionary psychologist. Stop embarrassing yourself."

We chatted for a while, before Vikas had to get back to his laundry. But for the rest of the day, I couldn't get what he had said about Tripp out of my mind.

There was no sign of Tripp yet at Primal Scream. I had no idea if Vikas's information was even accurate, but it wouldn't surprise me at all if Tripp had concocted some sort of scheme to photograph naked Harvard students and then post them on the Internet. Or maybe hold onto them for blackmail purposes. Taking advantage of people for his own personal gain was a compulsion of his, and Primal Scream would be a perfect venue for him to strike.

The clock ticked closer to midnight, and more students poured into the Yard. There were easily over a thousand people there. Some were in towels like me, others in robes, and others were dressed in silly costumes (with the crotch cut out, of course). I spotted a group of girls carrying a pile of large poster boards with the numbers one through ten written on them. They positioned themselves on the edge of the concrete track and prepared to judge the male runners (because of course Harvard couldn't make it through even one event without grades). Generally, though, Primal Scream was an occasion marked by camaraderie and lightheartedness, not competition. Exam period was tough on everyone (the school in general was tough on everyone), and this was one of the rare occasions when we could come together as a unified student body and do something that was the opposite of serious.

I looked around at the army of my peers, a collection of the smartest and most accomplished people I had ever met, ready to strip bare. All of us had worked so hard to get accepted into Harvard, then even harder to get accepted *at* Harvard. Primal Scream was finally a night when we could accept ourselves. We needed this.

At that moment I began to feel a deep anger begin to boil for Tripp. More specifically, I was frustrated with what he represented. Not all legacies were douchebags (many were good people who deserved their place at Harvard), but there is a suffocating element of "Old Harvard" that the university cannot seem to escape. There was a fresh, exciting side of Harvard—the side that was on display tonight here at Primal Scream. That was overshadowed by a dominating presence of "traditional" Harvard culture.

The university has a reputation as being stuffy and pretentious for a reason. There are wealthy alumni who are pricks, and the school has current students who carry on that tradition. I'm not sure the administration even wants this elitist culture to endure at Harvard, but in many ways, they don't have a choice. The school has to hold onto this past because its history is so powerful, impressive, and wealthy. Yet sometimes it feels like Harvard's unparalleled pedigree prevents it from moving forward to an even better future.

Still, there has been a notable shift in the identity of the student body, and it was fascinating to watch "Old Harvard" and "New Harvard" pull the school in two different directions. The school has now brought in so many diverse, fresh thinkers that they are starting to overwhelm the traditional stereotypes of Harvard University. People like Dermot and Vikas never had a place in Old Harvard, but now those types of students fill the school's classrooms with much-needed energy and fresh perspectives. That's the real reason Harvard is still one of the best schools around—it's not because it has the world's oldest book, or a gazillion dollars sitting in a vault, or a bunch of dudes named Winston. It's been a difficult burden for a student body to pull a four-hundred-year-old school in a new direction, all while trying to live up to an unattainable reputation of excellence. And when it comes down to it, that's why my feelings of isolation at Harvard couldn't have been more misplaced. Sure, we were all trying to survive Harvard. But in many ways, Harvard was trying to survive itself.

———◆•◆———

The energy pulsing through the air minutes before midnight was palpable. The people wearing exotic costumes were definitely the most animated participants, and I got to fulfill a childhood dream of high-fiving Spiderman. (He looked just like I had imagined when I was kid, though I must admit his mystique was slightly devalued by his exposed genitals.)

Then I heard something that brought me crashing back down to reality. The shout was faint over the excited buzz of the crowd, but the voice was distinct.

"Good luck, Eric!"

My stomach wrenched when I looked ahead and saw Hannah amidst a crowd of spectators on the right side of the concrete path. I forced a smile and gave a short wave with my left hand as my right choked the life out of the towel wrapped around my waist. I was really hoping to not see Hannah here tonight. Or more accurately, for her to not see me.

I diverted my eyes further up the line of spectators, only to settle upon an even more unwelcome sight: a blond-haired guy wearing a green North Face fleece, khaki slacks, and a pair of loafers. And he was clutching a small silver object.

I squinted and confirmed that Tripp was indeed holding a digital camera. A lot of spectators bring cameras to Primal Scream, which still seems a little weird, but their pictures are usually zoomed out landscape shots to capture the spirit of the naked herd, no one person specifically. I doubted Tripp had such harmless intentions.

It was clear to me that someone had to confront Tripp. I instinctively looked at Spiderman, like he was about to leap into action, but he was too busy dishing out awkward high-fives to the congregation at the starting line. It looked like this would be up to me, and I was fine with that. In fact, I found that I actually *wanted* this opportunity. I had no idea what I was going to do or say, but I had enough of Tripp's shit. This was about much more than just tonight and whether he planned to take incriminating photos. His reign of terror over Harvard students—people like Vikas and, yes, me specifically—had to end.

My eyes were locked on Tripp as I approached him, and it took me an extra moment to notice Jen standing to his right. My pounding heart became even more rattled. No words came out when I opened my mouth. I stood there for a moment before Tripp broke the silence.

"Kester, surprised to see you here," he flashed his white grin, then pointed at my bare chest. "You gonna take that sweater off before you go streaking?" He laughed and looked at Jen, who didn't reciprocate.

"What are you doing with that camera?" The question seemed to materialize out of thin air, and I was surprised by the hostility of my tone.

Tripp opened his mouth, but his response was drowned out by the heavy toll of bells echoing from Memorial Church. Everyone in the Yard erupted in a simultaneous cheer, and articles of clothing went flying into the air like confetti.

The clock had struck midnight; Primal Scream had begun.

The ground seemed to shake as a stampede of naked bodies

rushed in our direction, a blur of body parts flopping and bouncing around like dozens of rolled up socks tumbling around a drier. Tripp clicked on his digital camera and pulled it up to his face.

"Is that for your new website?" I asked angrily.

Tripp lowered the camera. "What the hell are you talking about?" His eyes challenged mine.

"You're going to take pictures of people and then fuck everyone over. Just like you always do."

Jen looked confused. "What's going on?"

I felt a rush of air as the pack of streakers began to pass behind me. Tripp took a step closer to me, and for a moment I thought he was going to shove me into the stampede. "I'm taking pictures of the scene, not of people," he snarled. "Now get out of my way."

I didn't move. "You're not taking any pictures."

"I'm not blackmailing anyone, and even if I were, why the hell would you care? No one would give a fuck about a picture of you. There are way more important people out there." He took another step toward me. "Nobody takes you seriously here. You're a joke."

"You're right. But I'd rather be a joke than a fucking asshole."

Tripp's right hand shot forward, and with one swipe, ripped my towel from my waist. He laughed his terrible laugh as it flew through the air and landed five feet away. I looked at Jen, who was looking at the ground and shaking her head—at which of us, I didn't know.

To my surprise, my first move wasn't to retrieve my towel. A dense mob of my naked classmates continued to jog past me, and for the first time all year, I fit in perfectly with them. I left the towel there on the ground, and instead went for the camera. In one smooth movement I grabbed it out of Tripp's hand, raised it to the sky, and then spiked it as hard as I could into the pavement.

The camera bounced a couple of times on the concrete, then settled a few feet away, completely unharmed. I guess I should have taken more of that Diesel Fuel supplement.

A small crowd had begun to gather near what they perceived to be an almost-fight. Everyone stood in an awkward silence, staring at the pristine camera that had just severely humbled me.

Tripp looked stunned; the first time I had ever seen him speechless. "Come on," he finally said to Jen. "Let's get out of here."

He left his camera on the ground and headed toward Dexter gate, the same entrance to the Yard I had walked through on my first day at Harvard.

This wasn't the last time I'd see Tripp, but it was the final time we ever spoke. He cruised through his next year at Harvard, graduating with honors, and his father hooked him up with a very lucrative job (and a huge number of stock shares) at Lehman Brothers. I don't know exactly what he did there (my guess is neither did he), but it had something to do with structuring "collateralized mortgage obligations," or some fancy shit like that. Everyone said that Lehman thought Tripp was made of the right stuff for that sort of work.

That night, though, Tripp could only skulk back to his dorm. He stuffed his hands in his pockets as he proceeded to old Dexter Gate, and I recalled the inscription on the exterior that I had read on my first day at Harvard: ENTER TO GROW IN WISDOM. I doubted that Tripp had ever stopped to consider that message as he entered the Yard, and I'm sure he never read the gate's interior inscription on his way out of the Yard: DEPART TO SERVE BETTER THY COUNTRY AND THY KIND.

Tripp had walked only twenty feet toward the gate when he realized he was missing something.

"You coming?" he asked, turning around.

Jen hadn't moved. She looked at me, and the pandemonium of the Yard was muted as our eyes held. Her mouth was half-open, as if she wanted to say something to me, but it just hung there. Then she turned away and walked toward Tripp. They held hands as they walked out of the Yard.

I glanced down at the pavement. There was the camera, good as new. I looked back at Tripp and Jen, walking away from me, now arm in arm. Then I did something I realized I should've been doing all year. I laughed.

Tripp must have thought I was laughing at him and Jen, though neither of them were the target of my humor. Without turning around, Tripp held his fist in the air and extended a middle finger.

Suddenly, I felt an arm brush against mine. I looked over to see Hannah, who had apparently been by my side the entire time.

"What a dick," she said.

And I was the happiest naked man alive.

ACKNOWLEDGMENTS

I'd like to thank my editor, Peter Lynch of Sourcebooks, for his diligence and sense of humor throughout this project. I would also like to thank my agent, Helen Zimmermann, for her tireless enthusiasm in guiding a first-time author through this process. I am also tremendously grateful for Peter Olson, whose mentorship and encouragement have been invaluable.

Words cannot express my appreciation for my parents, who provided nothing but love and support when their 23-year-old son moved back home to write a book about stuff they'd probably rather not hear. To my sisters, Kelsey and Kirsten, Grammie, the Spielers, Evan, and Ian: thank you for all your love and encouragement.

I owe a debt of gratitude to all those who have helped make this book a reality: Liz Kelsch and the rest of the Sourcebooks team; the Warringtons; my friends and mentors at the Middlesex School; my editors at *The Crimson*; my football teammates and coaches; and the Delamarters.

Finally, I'd like to extend special thanks to all my college roommates (for helping me survive Harvard with a smile) and to Leigh (for being my inspiration).

ABOUT THE AUTHOR

Eric Kester graduated from Harvard in 2008, where he wrote a popular column for the undergraduate newspaper, the *Crimson*. Now a featured writer for CollegeHumor.com, Eric has also contributed to the *Boston Globe*, some Ecards.com, and Dorkly.com. His writing has been described as a perfect blend of Twain, Salinger, and Sedaris from critics such as his mom. He currently lives in Boston with his two sons, Xbox and PlayStation.